'I WAS TRANSFORMED'

Frontispiece of *Narrative of the Life of Frederick Douglass, an American Slave.*

'| WAS TRANSFORMED'

FREDERICK DOUGLASS: AN AMERICAN
SLAVE IN VICTORIAN BRITAIN

LAURENCE FENTON

AMBERLEY

For Katherine

First published 2018

Amberley Publishing
The Hill, Stroud
Gloucestershire, GL5 4EP

www.amberley-books.com

Copyright © Laurence Fenton, 2018

The right of Laurence Fenton to be identified
as the Author of this work has been asserted in
accordance with the Copyrights, Designs and
Patents Act 1988.

ISBN 978 1 4456 7019 5 (hardback)
ISBN 978 1 4456 7020 1 (ebook)

British Library Cataloguing in Publication Data.
A catalogue record for this book is available
from the British Library.

Typesetting and Origination by Amberley
Publishing.
Printed in the UK.

CONTENTS

INTRODUCTION

'THE TRAFFIC OF MEN-BODY'

Tall, strong and – most importantly – black, Frederick Douglass, the twenty-seven-year-old runaway slave recently catapulted to fame by the publication of his incendiary autobiography stood out among the crowd of passengers pressed against the railings of the *Cambria* on the afternoon of Saturday, 16 August 1845. He was sailing from Boston to Liverpool, having been advised to leave the country until the furore over his book, *Narrative of the Life of Frederick Douglass, an American Slave*, died down, the large number of supporters gathered to see him off singing and cheering until the sound of the ship's bell rang out loud across the harbour, the good spirits giving way to tears and a final frantic clasping of hands. Douglass waved his hat and was gone, the two great wheels of the almost 220-foot-long wooden paddle steamer turning powerfully to churn up the water and carry him out of the harbour, black plumes of smoke rising high from the Cunard ship's distinctive red funnel.[1]

Douglass was following a well-worn path for American abolitionists, the anti-slavery communities on both sides of the Atlantic having long drawn succour from each other's lecture tours and travels. Britain, indeed, held a special place in the minds of American abolitionists, having long led the way in the movement to abolish the international slave trade, one of the first great milestones of which was the passage of legislation banning British vessels from the trade in 1807, the result of a decades-long campaign headed by storied figures like William Wilberforce and Thomas Clarkson. Britain had then assumed the role of the world's policeman, negotiating anti-slave trade treaties with numerous countries and dispatching Royal Navy squadrons along the West African coast to intercept slave ships. In what was seen as another mighty moral gesture – one that placed the iniquity of America's continued slaveholding in ever-starker relief – it had also abolished slavery in the British West Indies in 1833, a move that freed more than 800,000 slaves. A few years later, hundreds of thousands of British and Irish women had petitioned the newly crowned Queen Victoria as part of a successful campaign to end the euphemistically termed 'apprenticeship' system – which compelled former slaves to work for free for their old masters for significant periods – that had come into place after emancipation, slavery in the West Indies finally coming to a proper end on 1 August 1838, just a few weeks before Douglass's own successful bid for freedom from the American South.

'As early as I can remember, I have thought of England in connection with freedom,' Douglass would tell an audience in London in the summer of 1846.[2] The sentiment would have been appreciated, Britain enjoying its position on the moral high ground of international affairs – especially in relation to its increasingly powerful former colony, the United States. What Douglass failed to mention, however, was the incredible extent to which slavery and the slave trade had permeated every facet of British life for more than two centuries: from the royal imprimatur Queen Elizabeth I afforded Britain's first real slave trader, Sir John Hawkins, to the investments the famous diarist Samuel Pepys made in the slave-trading Royal Adventurers into Africa Company; from Birmingham gun manufacturers like John Whately dumping excess supplies on African chieftains to the Church of England's missionary arm, the Society for the Propagation of the Bible in Foreign Parts, burning the word 'SOCIETY' into the chests of its Jamaican slaves; from the labourers processing slave-grown sugar at refineries like Lewin's Mead in Bristol to the locals purchasing it in nearby shops to sweeten their tea; from the ten-year-old 'Negroe Boy from Affrica' advertised for sale in Lichfield in 1771 to the proprietor of the east Midlands newspaper profiting from the advertisement; from the workers at Charles Roe's mines and smelters in Macclesfield producing many of the copper and brass goods that would go on to be traded for slaves; to artists like Thomas Gainsborough commissioned to paint portraits of wealthy slave-owning families; from the stevedores in Cowes on the Isle of Wight unloading shiploads of South Carolina rice before it was processed and sent on to Europe to the wealthy aristocrats reposing in vast country mansions built on the proceeds of slavery; from the savagely beaten young black slave Jonathan Strong wandering dazed through the streets of London in the winter of 1765 to the thirty-year-old civil servant Granville Sharp, who helped him recover before going on to become one of the founding fathers of the anti-slave trade campaign; and from Dido Belle, the illegitimate mixed-race daughter of an English sea captain and a female slave who became a fixture of the Georgian social scene to her uncle Lord Mansfield, the Lord Chief Justice whose ruling that slavery had no basis in common law in the famous Somerset Case in 1772 has long been seen as bringing an official end to slavery in England.[3]

Nor was the mark of slavery hard to locate in the early years of Victoria's long reign, despite the near-collective sense of amnesia that had quickly taken hold regarding the country's deep involvement in the slave system. It was in the names of streets all over the land, from Glassford Street in Glasgow (named after one of the city's pre-eminent 'tobacco lords') to Cunliffe Street in Liverpool (named after Foster Cunliffe, a slave trader and three-time mayor of the city), and on the walls of the finest galleries, *The Infant Samuel* (c. 1776) by Sir Joshua Reynolds, for example, bequeathed to the National Gallery by the slave-owning Lord Farnborough in 1828. Somewhat more subtly, it was also present in many of the great infrastructure projects of the age, a significant portion of the £20 million compensation package awarded to slave-owners following abolition in the West Indies reinvested in new coal mines, brass works, iron works and railway companies across Britain and Ireland, leading, indeed, to the construction of many railway lines Douglass himself would end up travelling on.[4]

While refraining from any overly damning survey of Britain's long involvement in slavery and the slave trade, Douglass was less circumspect in holding it to account for its role in introducing slavery to America, an English-owned corsair or pirate ship named the *White Lyon*, the first slave ship to land in North America, trading its cargo of '20 and odd Negroes' for food with the governor of the recently established English colony of Virginia in late August 1619. 'Americans, when they would wrap themselves up in their carnal security and use excuses for slavery, say "England entailed this evil upon us,"' Douglass would tell an audience in Taunton in Somerset. 'Although there is not absolute truth in the statement, there is just enough truth in it to save it from being an absolute falsehood,' he continued, urging the country 'to undo that which you have done ... and rid a country from the curse inflicted upon it by your fathers'.[5]

'Haynos and Crying Sinn'

Captured during fighting in the Portuguese colony of Angola on the west coast of Africa, the story of the *White Lyon* slaves is emblematic of horrors inflicted upon the millions of Africans forcibly transported across the Atlantic. They had originally been part of a larger group of 350 slaves loaded in leg irons and neck chains onto a Portuguese slaver, the *San Juan Bautista*, in the Angolan capital, Luanda. Their destination had been Veracruz in Mexico, the trade in African slaves to the European, primarily Spanish and Portuguese, colonies of the Caribbean and Central and South America having taken root more than a century before, not long after Christopher Columbus's epochal voyage. These first African slaves were used to complement the newly conquered indigenous workforces in, for example, the gold mines of Hispaniola and the sugar fields of Cuba and Brazil. However, it was not long before war, European diseases and overwork eviscerated the native populations. Demand for the more robust African slaves grew exponentially, turning the transatlantic slave trade into a devastatingly major enterprise.

Crossing the Atlantic, many of the slaves crammed into the dark and dirty hold of the *San Juan Bautista* died of disease. Then, nearing Veracruz, the ship was attacked by the *White Lyon* and another English-owned corsair, the *Treasurer*. The pirate ships opened fire on the poorly defended slaver, forcing it to heave to and allow their captains on board. A large number of the slaves were dragged from one ship to another, mid-ocean. The two corsairs then made their way up the Florida Strait to Virginia. The *White Lyon* was the first to reach land, depositing its traumatised cargo on a strange and frightening new shore.[6]

The trade in slaves, although slow at first, gradually insinuated itself into the fabric of American – especially southern – society. African slaves were a vital source of cheap labour for the white settlers, especially when the numbers of indentured white labourers from Europe fell away in the last third of the seventeenth century. Initially, the distinction between slavery and servitude was somewhat 'fuzzy'.[7] The racial divide hardened, however, as the number of slaves started to soar. The white settlers felt threatened and put in place laws – the notorious slave codes – that made clear the subservient status of black slaves. Slave-owners were also given virtually a free hand in how they disciplined slaves. Whipping was routine, but slaves could also be mutilated or even burned to death quite legally for minor infractions of the slave codes.

By the time of the American Revolution there were about half a million slaves in the thirteen colonies soon to form the United States. This was out of a total population of just under 2.5 million. In every colony from Maryland southwards at least one third of the population was enslaved, significantly more in South Carolina and Georgia. These slaves, second-class citizens in the eyes of the law and subhuman in the eyes of many masters, worked as domestic servants, carpenters, blacksmiths and butchers in northern cities like New York, cleared forests and picked tobacco in Virginia and Maryland, and cultivated rice in the vast plantations of the Deep South. The slave system seemed strong despite periodic slave revolts – an immutable feature of the American landscape. And yet there were fractures in the edifice, with Thomas Jefferson, a slave-owner himself, denouncing the slave trade in his first draft of the Declaration of Independence. It was an 'execrable commerce', the future President wrote, one that violated the 'most sacred rights of life and liberty in the persons of a distant people [Africans] ... captivating and carrying them into slavery in another hemisphere'.[8] This strong statement did not make it into the final draft of the Declaration, removed for the sake of unity between the states. However, the fact that it was written at all was a sign that dissenting voices had started to push anti-slavery onto the political agenda.

As early as 1646 Puritan magistrates in Massachusetts had condemned the 'haynos and crying sinn of man stealing', ordering the return of two captured Africans to their native land.[9] In February 1688, four German-born Quakers from Pennsylvania (the then recently established Quaker colony founded by the Englishman William Penn) drafted a set of resolutions against slavery, or what they called 'the traffic of men-body'.[10] They had been shocked at the inconsistency of Quakers, refugees from Europe's religious intolerance, buying and selling people against their will. Quakers, however, would go on to play a disproportionately large role in the anti-slavery movement, the London Yearly Meeting, to which many American Quakers still looked for guidance, issuing a series of anti-slavery epistles throughout the 1700s. It was also Quaker campaigners like Anthony Benezet and John Woolman who brought anti-slavery to the fore of public debate in America in the 1760s and 1770s. Indeed, after many years of equivocation, the Pennsylvania Yearly Meeting of 1776 finally banned Quakers in America from owning slaves. Benezet had already made contact with British anti-slavery activists like Granville Sharp by this time, Britain having taken over from Spain, Portugal and the Netherlands as the dominant force in the slave trade, carrying, indeed, as many slaves across the Atlantic as all the other European nations combined in the eighteenth century. Parliament was petitioned, politicians lobbied, books and pamphlets published in profusion as anti-slavery become a truly transatlantic crusade. The outbreak of the American Revolution, however, 'dramatically subordinated the question of slavery to other priorities'.[11]

The immediate aftermath of the American Revolution saw several states in the North, such as Vermont, New Hampshire and Pennsylvania, move to ban or partially abolish slavery. Others like New York and New Jersey followed more reluctantly. The Revolution, however, was far from a watershed moment for slaves. Action in the North, which accounted for just 6 per cent of the enslaved population, was one matter, but what of the South? For every state making a move against slavery, there seemed to be another slave state waiting to join the Union, like Kentucky in 1792 and Tennessee in 1796. The Louisiana Purchase of 1803 – where a vast area of land stretching from the Mississippi River to the Rocky Mountains was bought from France – also brought thousands more slaves under American jurisdiction. The cotton boom, too, gave a fresh impetus to slavery. Even the passage of legislation prohibiting the slave trade in 1807 – the same year that a similar law was passed in Britain – was not a cause of celebration. Slaves could still be imported, albeit illegally, through Spanish Florida quite easily. Furthermore, unlike the sugar islands of the Caribbean, where slaves were worked so hard and died in such numbers they needed constant replenishing from Africa, American slave-owners were actually more reliant on natural increase among the slave population than on the slave trade, some states in the Upper South becoming known as slave-breeding states. There was also the not inconsequential fact that while in Britain the abolition of the slave trade was seen as the triumphant end to a long moral crusade, in America a lot of support for the act came from a belief that the country already had enough people of colour. Racism rather than morality got the law passed.

'*I Will Be Heard*'

By the time Douglass was born, America was increasingly delimited into zones of free and slave states, the Ohio River providing a rough boundary between the two. There were 1.5 million slaves (about 20 per cent of the total population) in the still-expanding United States, and although the question of slavery had been the source of discord and weak compromise among politicians, as an institution it seemed secure. The anti-slavery campaign was also in the midst of a long period of abeyance. This all changed with the arrival of the remarkable William Lloyd Garrison onto the anti-slavery scene in the late 1820s.

Born in Massachusetts in late December 1805 to a deeply religious Baptist mother and a sailor father who walked out on the family, Garrison had been a campaigning journalist from his early twenties. Determined to raise 'the moral tone of the country', he had put his energies into the burgeoning temperance movement at first.[12] Then, in 1829, about the same time that the young Douglass was playing on the docks in the same city, he started work on the Baltimore-based *Genius of Universal Emancipation*, edited by the forty-year-old Quaker Benjamin Lundy. Inspired by Lundy, a thin, wispy man who had travelled on foot across much of America, quietly convincing many slaveholders to manumit (from the Latin *manumittere*, meaning to release or 'send forth from the hand') their slaves, Garrison took the fateful decision to make anti-slavery his life's work. More specifically, he made abolition his cause: the immediate – not gradual – emancipation of all slaves, without compensation for slave-owners and without deportation of the freed people to Haiti or Africa, as proposed by other anti-slavery activists.

Garrison quickly made a name for himself, printing graphic accounts of the murders of slaves and attacking other Baltimore papers for accepting advertisements for local slave auctions. He was convicted of libel for an article denouncing a wealthy merchant's participation in the slave trade. Garrison refused to pay the fine of $50 (about three months' pay) and was jailed for forty-nine days. 'A few white victims must be sacrificed to open the eyes of this nation, and to show the tyranny of our laws,' he declared, happily assuming the mantle of a martyr. 'I am willing to be persecuted, imprisoned and bound for advocating African rights, and I should deserve to be a slave myself, if I shrunk from that duty or danger.'[13]

Still in his mid-twenties, the awkwardly angular and already balding Garrison moved to Boston, launching the *Liberator* on 1 January 1831. 'I am aware that many object to the severity of my language, but is there not cause for severity?' he asked in the paper's first editorial, continuing:

I *will be* as harsh as truth and as uncompromising as justice. On this subject, I do not wish to think or speak or write with moderation. No! No! Tell a man whose house is on fire to give a moderate alarm; tell him to moderately rescue his wife from the hands of the ravisher; tell the mother to gradually extricate her babe from the fire into which it has fallen – but urge me not to use moderation in a cause like the present. I am in earnest – I will not equivocate – I will not excuse – I will not retreat a single inch – AND I WILL BE HEARD.

A few years later, Garrison, a lifelong advocate of non-violent moral force, was one of the main figures behind the formation of the American Anti-Slavery Society. Where previously many Americans had looked upon slavery as a distasteful relic from colonial times, a problem for future generations to resolve, increasing numbers now got involved in the cause, establishing a network of anti-slavery associations across the North. 'With a Biblical prophet's power and a propagandist's skill,' Garrison (in the words of his biographer Henry Mayer) 'forced the nation to confront the most crucial moral issue in its history'.[14] Keen to maintain links – financial, moral and organisational – with anti-slavery activists in Britain, he also crossed the Atlantic in the aftermath of the abolition of slavery in the West Indies, returning again for a World Anti-Slavery Convention held in London in the summer of 1840.

Douglass's own journey across the Atlantic would turn into a near two-year tour the escaped slave called one of the most transformative periods of his life, fundamentally altering his political outlook, social conscience and sense of self. Revelling in the freedom of movement and mind afforded by being away from the oppressive climate of the United States – where in even the 'free' northern states he was a victim of beatings and racial abuse – but bristling at the attempts of white British abolitionists to manage and control him, Douglass would travel through all the major cities of the British Isles, including London, Liverpool, Birmingham, Edinburgh, Dublin and Belfast. He was feted by the elite and brought crowds of thousands to their feet with devastating denunciations of slavery, often brandishing a pair of bloody manacles before his astonished audiences as part of the spectacle. He also gained his freedom – paid for by British friends – before returning to America in the spring of 1847 a celebrity and icon of international standing.

I

'THE FUGITIVE'S SONG'

Built in Scotland in 1844, the *Cambria* was the latest addition to the Cunard Line's Boston–Liverpool transatlantic mail route, able to complete in less than two weeks a crossing that a short time previously had taken more than a month. It had room for about 120 people, but with a focus on the delivery of the mail and most of the space allocated to engines and coal, passengers and their comforts were something of an afterthought. Charles Dickens, the great English novelist, had discovered as much travelling on another Cunard ship, the *Britannia*, a few years earlier, likening the experience of settling down on the cramped and narrow bed in his cabin to sleeping in a coffin in *American Notes*, the book that would come out of this transatlantic journey, one chapter of which was devoted to the 'deformity' of slavery.[1]

There were about 110 passengers on board Douglass's sailing, the rich tapestry of American life – its revolutionary past and still-tempestuous present – written in the lives of his fellow travellers, with J. Sturgis Nye, for example, a thirty-three-year-old dry goods merchant from Boston whose grandfather had fought at the Battle of Bunker Hill during the American War of Independence, able to trace his lineage back to the earliest days of the American colonies. Another passenger, Edward Hutchinson Robbins, a doctor from Boston, was well known to the family of John Adams, the second President of the United States and one of the fabled Founding Fathers of the young republic, while the recently married Revd Henry Hotham, a Protestant minister in Quebec travelling with his new wife, was the nephew of Sir Henry Hotham, a British admiral who had fought against America in the War of 1812. Edmund A. Grattan, the young British vice-consul at Boston, was a link to more recent Anglo-American tensions. His father, the Irish-born author and diplomat Thomas Colley Grattan, was heavily involved in the negotiations that led to the Webster-Ashburton Treaty, which had just settled a long-running border dispute between Britain and America, one focused on the line between the American state of Maine and the Canadian province of New Brunswick, then still under British dominion, militias from both regions coming close to armed clashes. The almost fifty-year-old Revd François Norbert Blanchet, meanwhile, was the recently appointed Catholic Bishop of Oregon, the vast area of land in the Pacific Northwest that was at the heart of yet another tense territorial dispute between the two powers. America's frontiers were still in the process of delineation and 'manifest destiny', the rallying cry of leading politicians, including the new President, the boldly expansionist Democrat James K. Polk.[2]

With what would prove to be dramatic consequences before the end of the trip, both sides of the slavery debate then tearing through the country were also present on board the *Cambria*, several slave-owners and supporters of slavery, including J. C. Burnham, a successful Havana-based businessman who may have been travelling to London to arrange loans with Barings Bank, brushing up against not only Douglass and James Buffum, the white abolitionist neighbour from Lynn, Massachusetts, who was travelling with him, but also the Hutchinson Family Singers, a famous musical group with a strong activist streak.[3] The group – Jesse (manager and songwriter), Judson, John, Asa and Abby, four strong-shouldered brothers raised on a New Hampshire farm together with their lithe sixteen-year-old sister – had actually shared the stage with Douglass on a number of occasions in the past, working up the crowds with fervent anti-slavery songs like 'Get Off The Track' before he launched into his talks. In fact, it was only after meeting Douglass at an anti-slavery rally a few days earlier that they had decided to travel, bidding farewell to America with a poignant rendition of 'Home Sweet Home', one of the most popular songs of the era, from the deck of the *Cambria*, their joy at fulfilling a long-held desire to tour the British Isles tempered by thoughts of their aging parents and the siblings they were leaving behind. Douglass, too, was leaving family behind, a wife (Anna) and four very young children. However, it is hard to believe he felt the same emotional pull at leaving America – the land of his birth but also the land that enslaved him.

Other passengers on board the *Cambria* included Jacob Dunnell, a Rhode Islander who ran one of the country's largest calico printing works; Baron Gottlieb Heinrich von Schröter, a forty-three-year-old German artist; the Spanish diplomat Antonio G. Viega; and an American circus owner named 'General' Rufus Welch.[4] There were also a number of British soldiers on board, officers returning from service in Canada, including two, Sir James E. Alexander and Captain George Warburton, who moonlighted as travel writers. We know their names because they paid the $70 required for first-class tickets and were consequently listed – as was the custom of the day – in the pages of the *Boston Daily Atlas*; those travelling in steerage, the part of ship reserved for the poorest travellers, were not worthy of such notice. Douglass and the thirty-eight-year-old Buffum were an anomaly, listed in the paper but not travelling first-class. Money had not been the problem; Douglass was forced into steerage solely on account of his colour, the British-owned Cunard Line bowing before the pro-slavery sentiment of the American South, while Buffum went with him in solidarity.[5]

'American prejudice against colour triumphed over British liberality and civilisation, and erected a colour test and condition for crossing the sea in the cabin of a British vessel,' wrote Douglass of the Cunard Line's stance. 'The insult was keenly felt by my white friends,' he added, 'but to me, it was common, expected, and therefore, a thing of no great consequence, whether I went in the cabin or in the steerage.'[6] Douglass had not always been so calm and equitable in the face of prejudice, almost getting beaten up when he refused to move to the 'Negro car' of a train on the Eastern Railroad, which ran from Boston to Portland, Maine, a few years earlier, holding onto his chair in the first-class section so tightly it had to be lifted up and thrown out onto the platform with him.[7] On this occasion, however, he was willing to take the insult, eager to leave America as quickly as possible having disclosed not just his own real name – Frederick Bailey – but that of his owner – Thomas Auld – in his famous autobiography, opening up the possibility of recapture by slave-catchers. Douglass had been aware of this danger but, as one of the most prominent black speakers in the country, had felt compelled to act, believing any failure to confront the suspicions that had arisen surrounding his past would prove fatal to his work in the anti-slavery cause.

Published in the early summer of 1845, Douglass's autobiography had been an immediate sensation. While far from the first slave narrative to have been printed, it was the best written and most precise in detail, a work of art as well as a powerful anti-slavery tract. Mixing scenes of great emotional warmth with brutal outrages that shocked readers, it had begun with the stark admission that Douglass was not even sure of his age, a majority of masters keeping such precious, deeply personal information away from their slaves. Douglass's best guess was February 1817. He was out by a year – the real date falling somewhere in February 1818. His sense of place was far more secure: born in Talbot County, Maryland, the latest in a long-established line of Talbot County slaves, one that stretched back to the early years of the colony.[8]

Douglass's childhood was spent in a cabin by a creek on the rural Eastern Shore of the Chesapeake Bay. He lived with his grandparents, Isaac and Betsey Bailey, and an ever-changing collection of siblings and cousins. It was a cramped and basic shelter, with windowless log walls and some planks thrown over the rafters to act as beds. Douglass's clothes were few and the food, despite his grandmother's best efforts, was often of the coarsest kind, cornmeal mush picked off a wooden tray with an oyster shell. And yet his memories of this time were positively bucolic, the many hardships leavened by the thrill of being a child in the warm countryside, running wild through the trees, rolling in the dust and plunging headfirst into the muddy waters of the Tuckahoe Creek.[9]

Douglass's father was a white man, most likely his owner, Aaron Anthony, a farmer in his fifties who was also estate manager at the nearby plantation, Wye House. His skin colour, certainly, was of a far lighter hue than the rest of his family. Douglass's mother, Harriet Bailey, worked on one of Anthony's farms a few miles away. (Anthony owned about thirty slaves, spread over a couple of farms). He saw her rarely, for although the distance between them was not great, it was extremely difficult for field hands to leave their place of work. Harriet died quite young, when Douglass was six or seven years old. 'I was not allowed to be present during her illness, at her death, or burial,' he wrote bitterly in his *Narrative*, the pain of never really knowing her a source of lifelong grief. 'She was gone long before I knew anything about it.'[10]

Cut off from his mother, the greatest influence on Douglass's early years was his grandmother Betsey, to whom he was extraordinarily close. It appears that Betsey, about forty-four years old when Douglass was born, was left to look after the children so that the mothers – her daughters – could be put back to work in the fields as soon as possible after giving birth. She was illiterate, like most slaves, but extremely resourceful when it came to providing food for her extended family, no matter how trying the circumstances. A 'capital hand' at making large seine nets for catching shad and herring, the striking image of her wading waist-deep in the water for hours at a time during their annual spring runs to spawn in the upper reaches of the Tuckahoe never strayed far from her adoring grandson's mind.[11]

Douglass's time in Betsey's care came to an end in the late summer of 1824, when he was six years old and ready to begin work running errands for his owner. Betsey did not tell him this as they set off on the long, hot 12-mile trek to Aaron Anthony's cottage on the grounds of Wye House, the vast 10,000-acre estate of Col Edward Lloyd V, an influential politician and scion of one of the oldest and wealthiest families in the state of Maryland. They walked west, towards the bay, winding their way down dusty roads, across great fields and through heavy woods, the now fifty-year-old Betsey carrying the boy for long stretches over her shoulders. They arrived in the sweltering heat of mid-afternoon, and after gulping down some much-needed water, Douglass was sent out to play with his older brother and sisters, Perry, Sarah and Eliza, siblings he hardly knew, siblings who had made the same journey some years before. Betsey slipped away without saying goodbye, thinking it easiest for the child. 'Fed, Fed! Grandmammy gone! Grandmammy gone!' called one of the children after a while, Douglass running into the kitchen and falling to his knees in despair when he saw it was true.[12]

It was not long before Douglass got his first real taste of slavery, waking up one night to the sight of Aaron Anthony pulling the clothes off his fifteen-year-old Aunt Hester's back. Having earlier refused her owner's predatory advances, she had been caught out at night with one of the Lloyd slaves – they had about 500 – a boy her own age named Ned Roberts. An enraged Anthony tied her hands to a hook in the kitchen ceiling, rolled up his sleeves and whipped her naked back until blood dripped down to the floor:

> No words, no tears, no prayers from his gory victim seemed to move his iron heart from its bloody purpose. The louder she screamed, the harder he whipped; and where the blood ran fastest, there he whipped longest. He would whip her to make her scream, and whip her to make her hush; and not until overcome by fatigue would he cease to swing the blood-clotted cowskin.[13]

The years that followed would be filled with similarly gruesome scenes, Douglass's memoirs replete with the beatings and killings of slaves by the cruel and callous overseers at Wye House.

A more positive experience at Wye House was the friendship Douglass forged with Aaron Anthony's married daughter, Lucretia Auld, who was about twenty years old and sometimes gave him extra pieces of bread when he sang for her. 'Miss Lucretia', as Douglass always referred to her, lived in the same simple stone cottage as her father and new husband, Thomas Auld, the captain of the *Sally Lloyd*, the luxurious private sloop on which Col Lloyd ferried guests from the state capital, Annapolis, to lavish parties at Wye House. Her two elder brothers, Andrew and Richard, also stayed occasionally, Douglass and the other slaves sleeping in closets or on the floor under the kitchen table.

We can never know what sign of precocity, what quirk the young lady saw in Douglass. Perhaps she was just starved of company, with the great house out of bounds, a father who was cold, stern and uncommunicative, a husband often away on Col Lloyd's business, and brothers – Andrew especially – who were heavy drinkers. She may also have heard the whispers concerning Douglass's birth – that he was her half-brother. Whatever the cause, it was a connection that would soon shape his life indelibly, 'Miss Lucretia' arranging for him to be sent to Baltimore, the great shipbuilding city across the Chesapeake Bay, where her husband's brother, Hugh Auld, and his wife wanted a black boy to serve as a companion to their young son, as was common practice at the time. A delighted Douglass, who at eight years old was just about to reach the age at which he could be put to work in the fields, spent the best part of three days washing the 'plantation scurf' off his body, 'Miss Lucretia' having promised him a pair of trousers if he got clean.[14]

There was no sense of loss at the prospect of leaving his family and the Eastern Shore.

'Miss Sopha'

Striking out from Boston Harbour on board the *Cambria*, it would have been natural for Douglass's mind to wander back to his first journey on a ship, the *Sally Lloyd*, carrying him from the wide open spaces of Wye House to the maze of narrow cobblestone streets that made up the busy shipbuilding district of Fells Point in Baltimore. He was still a slave, the property of Aaron Anthony, but not treated as one, with his new master Hugh Auld, a carpenter trying to set up his own shipbuilding business, generally too busy to pay much heed to the new arrival, and his new mistress welcoming him into the house on Aliceanna Street with a warm smile. Coming from a simple country family that had never owned slaves, Sophia Auld treated Douglass as well as she did her own son Tommy, and he soon came to regard her as something more like a mother than a slaveholding mistress.

A pious Methodist, 'Miss Sopha' also taught the young slave to read some passages from the Bible, before the lessons were ended by her husband who, although not a slaveholder, still held the prejudices of the age. 'Learning would *spoil* the best nigger in the world,' he declared coldly, warning her off future lessons.[15] Nevertheless, a door had been opened in Douglass's mind, never to be closed. He read in secret from the Bible, newspapers and Tommy's old school books. He also asked the white playmates he met on the streets while out running errands to act as teachers – skin colour no impediment to the forging of friendships at that young age. Later, Douglass would teach himself to write, drawing inspiration from the way shipbuilders made marks on the different pieces of timber – 'S.' for starboard, 'L.' for larboard (or port), 'L.A.' for larboard aft, and so on. He would copy these marks onto the pavement with chalk, again asking his young white friends for help.

By this stage ownership of the young slave had changed hands, the death of Aaron Anthony seeing his property – including his slaves, essentially the extended Bailey clan – divided up between his two sons and Thomas Auld. The prospect of ending up the slave of the cruel and drunken Andrew Anthony was very real. This, Douglass makes clear, was seen as a certain prelude to being sold south to new slave states like Alabama and Mississippi and put to work on vast plantations of cotton and rice that matched the infamous sugar islands of the Caribbean in their severity. Douglass's fears were heightened by the fact that his protector, 'Miss Lucretia', had also died by this time, possibly after giving birth to a daughter, Amanda.

As prophesied, some of the slaves given to the dissolute Andrew Anthony, including Douglass's sister Sarah, were soon sold south. Douglass, however, escaped this most fearful of fates, assigned instead to Lucretia's widower, Thomas Auld. Perhaps in respect of his deceased wife's wishes for the bright slave boy, Auld allowed Douglass to remain in Baltimore where he continued his clandestine studies, buying a copy of *The Columbian Orator* – a compendium of heroic speeches boys learned at school or for public speaking competitions – from a bookshop in Fells Point with fifty cents he had surreptitiously earned shining shoes. With contributions ranging from the Greek philosopher Socrates and the Roman politician Cato to the soldier-statesmen George Washington and Napoleon Bonaparte, the *Orator* was one of a handful of essential texts found in nineteenth-century American homes, alongside the Bible, a spelling book and a farmer's almanac. Douglass, who enjoyed a remarkable degree of freedom for a slave under the generally lax watch of the Aulds, read it for hours at a time (just like the young Abraham Lincoln), checking the many words he did not know with a dictionary, making notes in the margins and re-reading passages again and again until he grasped their full meaning. His vocabulary grew immeasurably and he also gained important lessons for the future in the art of public speaking from the wide-ranging introduction. Most importantly, however, the constant invocation of words like liberty, freedom and equality made a deep impression on his rapidly developing young mind.[16]

Douglass was also learning more and more, albeit often obliquely, about slavery. He read of attempts to close down slave markets in nearby Washington, DC, and may have heard fragments of talk about Nat Turner's bloodily suppressed slave rebellion in neighbouring Virginia. He certainly heard the clank of chains as slaves were led out at night from their slave pens in the city to the harbour prior to sailing south. Words like 'abolition' began to filter into his consciousness, through overheard conversations or newspaper articles:

> Of *who* or *what* these [abolitionists] were, I was totally ignorant. I found, however, that whatever they might be, they were ... hated and ... abused by slaveholders ... If a slave, for instance, had made good his escape from slavery, it was generally alleged, that he had been persuaded and assisted by the abolitionists.[17]

Douglass's trusty second-hand copy of *The Columbian Orator*, hidden from Hugh Auld's view in the loft of the house, also had a memorable piece on slavery, an imagined dialogue between a master and a slave that concluded with the slave gaining his freedom. Douglass memorised this section – slipped in among the worthy, patriotic speeches by the book's compiler, the anti-slavery Massachusetts educator Caleb Bingham – and began to read it aloud to the boys – black and white – with whom he played and worked on the docks, the powerfully built and increasingly strong-willed youth already stepping into the role of orator and leader. The thought of being a slave for life weighed ever more heavily on his heart, and dreams of escape began to enter his mind. Then, suddenly, in the spring of 1833, Douglass's Baltimore world was torn apart, an argument between the brothers sending him back across the Chesapeake to the town of St Michaels, where his newly remarried owner Thomas Auld now ran a store and post office.

Douglass, like every slave, was still not in control of his own destiny.

'Beaten With Many Stripes'

Following a north-easterly course and enjoying mainly good weather, the *Cambria* reached Halifax, Nova Scotia – a strategically important town filled with soldiers following a series of failed uprisings against British rule in Canada in the late 1830s – early in the morning of Monday, 18 August 1845. It dropped anchor for a few hours for the delivery of mail before continuing on past Cape Race – the southernmost tip of Newfoundland – and out into the choppier waters of the North Atlantic. Water, no matter how rough, had always symbolised freedom for Douglass – that trip back across the Chesapeake in late March 1833 a distressing exception, presaging what would prove to be by far the worst period of his life.

Douglass was fifteen years old when he landed on the wharf of St Michaels, a rundown town far removed from the bustle of Baltimore. Life with Thomas Auld and his new wife, Rowena, was fractious from the beginning, any lingering regard for the now thirty-eight-year-old Auld, a man who had previously facilitated his path out of the Eastern Shore, dispelled when Douglass saw him whip his disabled cousin Henny while quoting verses from the Bible (Luke 12:47) – 'He who knoweth his master's will, and doeth not, shall be beaten with many stripes.' Rowena, meanwhile, who came from an old slaveholding family, despised all the 'worthless niggers' in the house – Douglass, his sister Eliza, their Aunt Priscilla and cousin Henny. She treated them coldly and let them go hungry. They, in turn, were constantly 'forgetting' to carry out chores, one of the age-old means of slave resistance. Douglass, who chafed under the new restrictions after years of relative freedom in Baltimore, also became involved in a short-lived Sunday school for blacks, earning the reputation of a 'bad nigger' around the bigoted town.[18]

Within a year, the increasingly rebellious Douglass was sent to work as a field hand for Edward Covey, a few miles outside St Michaels. Covey, a poor but hardworking tenant farmer in his late twenties, whipped Douglass – who had little understanding of farm animals or implements – almost as soon as he arrived, tearing off the slave's clothes and lashing him until 'he had worn out his switches'.[19] This was the first real whipping of Douglass's life. Covey, revelling in his reputation as a 'nigger-breaker' among blacks in the area, would go on to whip him every week for more than six months, cutting his back severely and leaving large welts on his flesh. The hard work and constant beatings wore the slave down:

> I was broken in body, soul and spirit. My natural elasticity was crushed, my intellect languished, the disposition to read departed, the cheerful spark that lingered about my eye died; the dark night of slavery closed in upon me; and behold a man transformed into a brute.[20]

Douglass's suffering reached its apogee one day in the late summer of 1834, after he collapsed from sunstroke while threshing wheat. Dragging himself painfully to some shade, he was repeatedly kicked in the side and beaten over the head by Covey, who shouted at him to get back to work. Bloodied and bruised, barefoot and faint, Douglass got up and half ran, half fell 7 miles through fields and woods to Auld's home in St Michaels, where he begged to be sent to work on another farm. Auld, however, seemingly unmoved by the wretched, blood-covered figure trembling before him, insisted that he return to Covey. The vicious farmer was on the attack again within days. This time, however, Douglass fought back:

> I found my strong fingers firmly attached to the throat of my cowardly tormentor ... I flung him on the ground several times, when he meant to have hurled me there. I held him so firmly by the throat, that his blood followed my nails.

They wrestled and grappled with each other for a long time, to the point of exhaustion: 'He held me, and I held him.' Douglass could have been whipped or even hung for his resistance. Instead, the fight proved a turning point in his life. 'It rekindled in my breast the smouldering embers of liberty; it brought up my Baltimore dreams, and revived a sense of my own manhood. I was a changed being after that fight. I was *nothing* before; I WAS A MAN NOW.'[21]

Douglass stayed at Covey's farm a few months longer, but was not struck or whipped again. The only explanation he could come up with – one he admitted was not entirely satisfactory – was that Covey, the famed 'nigger-breaker', was ashamed to have it known that he had been 'mastered' by a teen.[22] There may, however, have been other forces at work, with some intimations that Thomas Auld, despite his cold rebuff that desperate night in St Michaels, interjected on his slave's behalf and ordered Covey to ease off.[23]

Either way, Douglass was hired out to William Freeland, an older farmer on the Eastern Shore, at the beginning of the next year. The work was just as hard but it was a much fairer environment, with warm clothes, good sleeping quarters and no beatings. Douglass stayed with Freeland for more than a year and began to take some pride in his work, even if it was just spreading manure over the worn-out wheat fields. He also forged perhaps the deepest friendships of his life, with John and Henry Harris, brothers owned by Freeland, and some other slaves in the area. 'I never loved, esteemed, or confided in men, more than I did in these. They were as true as steel, and no band of brothers could have been more loving.'[24]

Douglass worked hard, played games and drank with these young men. He also helped a number of them learn to read and write, his literacy giving him a special status among the slaves. At one point he had more than twenty students at the secret Sunday school held under an oak tree in the summer, his much-thumbed copy of *The Columbian Orator* put to good use again. Dreams of freedom, too, returned to Douglass's mind as he looked out across the broad waters of the Chesapeake Bay and watched steamers head north toward the newly built Chesapeake and Delaware Canal and through to Philadelphia, in the free state of Pennsylvania. On New Year's Day 1836, he resolved to put these dreams into action.

With escape by land from the long peninsula that was the Eastern Shore deemed next to impossible, Douglass started to disclose to his friends a bold plan to steal a log canoe from a neighbouring farm, paddle furiously to the head of the bay – a distance of some 70 miles – and slip into Pennsylvania. The time chosen was early April, just before Easter, when restrictions on slaves were usually relaxed. There would be difficult waters to contend with and slave-catchers prowling the border areas to avoid. What awaited them in the North was also somewhat vague. Nevertheless, the band of brothers continued to prepare, anxious and excited at the prospect before them. Their plan, however, was discovered – Douglass never found out how – the five would-be escapees rounded up as they started work on the day that was to have been their last in slavery.

Tied together behind two horses, Douglass and his friends were marched barefooted the 15 miles from Freeland's farm to the county jail in Easton, jeered along the way by small crowds of white people. 'The ever dreaded slave life in Georgia, Louisiana and Alabama – from which escape is next to impossible – now ... stared me in the face,' Douglass recalled, the jail in Easton soon swarming with excited slave traders.[25] But there was no trial, no hanging, no sold south. The young men stuck together, denied everything. No escape attempt had actually been made; nothing could be proved. Within a few days, the four other slaves were taken home by their respective masters. They went back to work unharmed. Thomas Auld, however, left the by-now eighteen-year-old Douglass to languish in his cell a little longer. Everyone knew he was the ringleader and custom dictated that he should be punished as a warning to other slaves. Auld, however, far from the stingy, feeble villain of Douglass's later writings, clearly struggled with the idea of sending him south. Their lives had been too long entwined, the curly headed little boy singing songs for Auld's first wife, Lucretia, at the stone cottage at Wye House. Perhaps promises had been made to look after her favourite? There have also been suggestions that it was in fact Auld, not old Aaron Anthony, who was Douglass's father, the then captain of the *Sally Lloyd* happening upon the attractive Harriet Bailey on an errand to Wye House.[26]

Whatever the reason, the far-from-affluent Auld turned his back on the substantial sum of money a slave of Douglass's age and strength was sure to fetch. He talked loudly of selling him to a friend in Alabama, but this was only for public consumption. Instead, he sent Douglass back to Baltimore to live with his brother Hugh again and learn a trade. There was even the vague promise of manumission when he reached the age of twenty-five.

'Darkey, Blast Your Eyes'

The *Cambria* was not long past Newfoundland when its passengers were woken early by a steward calling them out to see a large group of icebergs float past. 'I counted from 10 to 15 which appeared to be of prodigious magnitude and towering height, as our gallant steamship ploughed between them,' wrote Asa Hutchinson, wrapped up in his great coat and cloak to stave off the chill the icebergs brought with them, the ship's thermometer dropping 8 degrees in their vicinity, such sudden sharp falls in temperature one of the key signs of danger ship captains kept a look out for on transatlantic crossings of this time, especially at night.[27] Another passenger, the clearly awestruck Warburton, one of the soldier-writers on board, was moved to muse on the 'dismal' fate of these 'cold and lonely wanderers of the deep', breaking loose 'by some great effort of nature, from the shores and rivers of the unknown regions of the north, where, for centuries perhaps, they have been accumulating' before commencing 'their dreary voyage, which has no end but in annihilation'.[28] The icebergs, one of which Warburton likened in size and shape to St Paul's Cathedral in New York, were certainly an impressive sight, by far the most noteworthy event of the journey until the coast of Ireland came into view five days later.

'I shall never forget the thrill of pleasure and excitement, the eager rush of passengers from cabin to deck, when … it was announced by some keen-eyed mariner that the shores of Ireland were in sight,' wrote Douglass of the evening of 26 August. 'Our voyage had been a pleasant one and the ocean had been more than kind and gentle to us; but whatever may be the character of a voyage, rough or smooth, long or short, the sight of land, after three thousand miles of sea, ship and sky, is unspeakably grateful to the eye and heart of the voyager.' The 'Emerald Isle', as Douglass called it, was even clearer the next morning, the ragged coastlines of Kerry, Cork and Waterford all coming clearly into view. 'Oh, the dear spot where I was born!' exclaimed one passenger from Philadelphia.[29]

Douglass had worked with a number of Irish in Baltimore – one of the major gateways into America for European immigrants – including two dockers with whom he shared a revelatory encounter at the age of just twelve or thirteen. They had been unloading stones from a scow, a small vessel used for transporting cargo to and from ships lying in harbour. It was heavy work, but Douglass, a powerful youth clearly familiar with the world of the docks, had been quick to help. When they finished, one of the men asked him if he was a slave:

> I told him I was. He asked, 'Are ye a slave for life?' I told him that I was. The good Irishman seemed to be deeply affected by the statement. He said to the other that it was a pity so fine a little fellow as myself should be a slave for life. He said it was a shame to hold me.

The Irishmen told Douglass to escape to the North. Douglass feigned ignorance, wary that their encouragement could be just a trap to catch him and claim reward. Nevertheless, he remembered the advice, pinpointing this meeting in his *Narrative* as the moment from which he resolved to run away.[30]

Douglass was back on the docks a few years later, sent to work as an apprentice caulker at one of the big shipyards after his return from the Eastern Shore. Douglass, however, learned little of caulking, the back-breaking method of making wooden boats watertight by driving fibrous material into the wedge-shaped seams between boards. Instead, he was treated as general factotum about the yard, called a dozen ways every minute of the day. 'Fred, come carry this timber yonder … Fred, go get a fresh can of water … Fred, go quick and get the crowbar … Halloo, nigger! Come turn this grindstone … I say, darkey, blast your eyes, why don't you heat up some pitch?'[31] He was also attacked by some of the white apprentices about eight months into the job, racial tensions on the rise as the ever-increasing numbers of white immigrants, free blacks and hired-out slaves in Baltimore competed desperately with each other for the same menial jobs. Douglass fought back but the blows across the head and body with bricks, handspikes and fists burst his eyeball and left him badly bloodied and scarred.

Things improved for Douglass after this brush with death – he never saw it as anything less. He went to work at another shipyard where Hugh Auld was foreman (Auld's own shipbuilding business had closed down). He learned to caulk and within a year was earning the comparatively substantial sum of $9 a week during busy periods, all of which, of course, was collected by Auld. By the summer of 1838, however, Douglass was allowed to hire himself out. This was an increasingly common practice in Baltimore. For slaves, it meant a degree of autonomy over their lives; for masters, a guaranteed fee and less expense incurred in bread and board. In Douglass's case, he would be allowed to find his own work and collect his own wages provided he paid Auld $3 a week – irrespective of whether or not he had worked – and supplied his own bed, board and tools.

The twenty-year-old Douglass embraced this newfound piece of freedom. He took lodgings in Fells Point and, although a slave, got involved in Baltimore's vibrant and expanding free black world, Baltimore being long regarded as America's Black Capital. He joined clubs, forged friendships with other articulate young blacks and even got engaged to a free black woman, Anna Murray, a quietly determined domestic servant five years his senior. He also started to learn about the Underground Railroad, the surreptitious network of safe houses for fugitives along well-established routes, helping some runaways plan their escapes.[32] When an argument with Hugh Auld brought Douglass's partial freedom to an end, the never-distant thoughts of his own escape rushed back to the fore. And so it was that after several weeks of careful planning he boarded a train of the Baltimore & Ohio Railroad (B&O) on 3 September 1838, jumping on just as it set off.

This new line of the B&O went north from Baltimore to Wilmington, in the slave state of Delaware, before steamboat and rail connections brought passengers on to Philadelphia and New York. There were many obstacles to cross, with the B&O extremely conscious of runaway slaves trying to use their trains and determined to protect slave-owners' property. Consequently, black people were only allowed to travel by day, and always in possession of their 'free papers', a passport-like document that detailed their appearance and certified their free status. Douglass obtained a sailor's protection pass (an equivalent to free papers) from a contact in the Underground Railroad. He also bought a set of sailor's clothes – a red shirt, black cravat and tarpaulin hat – with some of the ever-resourceful Anna's savings. Douglass did not really look like the man described in the papers, which had an image of an American eagle on their front cover. Nevertheless, his years on the docks helped him play the part of a seaman. 'I knew a ship from stem to stern, and from keelson to cross-trees, and could talk sailor like an "old salt".'[33]

The train was halfway to Delaware before the conductor entered the dusty, dirty carriage reserved for blacks. 'You have something to show that you are a free man, have you not?' the conductor asked. 'Yes sir,' Douglass answered. 'I have a paper with the American eagle on it that will carry me around the world.'[34] Assuaged by the nonchalant response or simply eager to get to the end of the crowded black carriage, the conductor glanced at the pass, took the fare and moved on. There were several more dangerous moments, but Douglass survived them all, arriving in New York City early the next morning and making his way to the home of David Ruggles, a black journalist who headed the New

York Underground Railroad, Anna joining him a few days later. They were married at Ruggles's home, Douglass having carried a new wedding suit alongside his copy of *The Columbian Orator* and a few other possessions in his sailor's satchel.

With slave-catchers scouring the streets of New York, Douglass and Anna moved on quickly to the safer environment of New Bedford, Massachusetts, a prosperous whaling town with a well-established black population and grand houses overlooking the harbour that would provide the setting, some years later, for the opening passages of Herman Melville's *Moby Dick*. They spent their first few weeks with Nathan Johnson, a black Quaker, and his family. After finding them a small house to rent, Johnson helped the young fugitive slave decide on a new name, a vital accoutrement for any runaway, suggesting 'Douglas' after a swashbuckling character in a book he had just finished reading, *The Lady of the Lake*, the long narrative poem that had brought the great Scottish writer Sir Walter Scott to international attention when it was first released some thirty years earlier.

With the extra 's' added by mistake, Frederick Bailey gave way to Frederick Douglass.

'Cut Out For a Hero'

Although there were a few stormy days en route and a number of passengers – including Douglass's travelling companion Buffum – fell seasick, the *Cambria*'s journey across the Atlantic was generally quite calm, the first-class passengers whiling away the hours with books, card games, checkers and prodigious dinners washed down with brandy and wine. Mealtimes, indeed, were the focal point of the day, often concluding with speeches from one (usually intoxicated) passenger or another, the Scottish-born soldier, traveller and author James E. Alexander recalling an American passenger declaring one night how he was 'as happy as a clam … sailing as we are on the boundless ocean, in a most splendid vessel, commanded by a most gallant Captain, and with the noble representatives of people from all parts of the world on board'.[35]

There was also music aplenty, with the Hutchinson's giving impromptu little concerts on deck most evenings, Captain Judkins, the commander of the *Cambria*, and other passengers, including the Irish-born Warburton, joining them occasionally with their own party pieces. 'The ladies gave much encouragement in regard to our singing in England,' wrote Asa Hutchinson, singling out a Mrs Widder, with whose three children he sang one morning, in particular. The Hutchinson's may even have performed 'The Fugitive's Song', a new composition of Jesse's that had been inspired by Douglass and carried the defiant refrain 'I'll be free, I'll be free'.[36]

Although Douglass's escape was not as dramatic as the sheet music cover for 'The Fugitive's Song' imagined, depicting the slave fleeing barefoot from a pair of gun-toting pursuers and a pack of slavering dogs, there had certainly been a fevered edge to his final few months in Baltimore. This faded away as he settled into life in New Bedford, Douglass working hard – be it sawing wood, digging cellars, sweeping chimneys or labouring at the docks – reading voraciously and getting involved in the local black community. He and Anna also started a family (a daughter, Rosetta, was born in June 1839), played the violin together – the more talented Anna teaching her husband – and enjoyed dinners with new friends. A relatively safe, comfortable existence was within reach.

Douglass, however, could not switch off his slave past, his dreams plagued by the 'dead, heavy footsteps' and 'piteous cries' of the chained gangs of slaves he had heard marching to the docks in Baltimore at night prior to sailing south.[37] He began to speak at local anti-slavery groups, his words picked up by the *Liberator*, the radical abolitionist newspaper edited by William Lloyd Garrison. It was not long before Douglass saw the tall, gaunt, passionate and improbably charismatic figure of Garrison speak in person in New Bedford. A short time later, Douglass was thrust even deeper into the Garrisonian world, delivering his first major public speech to a meeting of the Massachusetts Anti-Slavery Society in Nantucket in late August 1841.

'My speech on this occasion is about the only one I ever made, of which I do not remember a single connected sentence,' Douglass recalled. He was twenty-three years old, a fugitive slave, addressing a room full of anti-slavery luminaries. His hands shook as he spoke and his legs felt like they were about to give way. Douglass worked through the initial nervousness to deliver an emotional speech that had the predominantly white middle-class audience straining forward to make out the features of the tall, attractive and remarkably articulate young black man. 'Have we been listening to a thing, a piece of property or to a man?' Garrison demanded of the audience when Douglass finished. 'A man! A man!' came the united response, with Douglass approached that very evening to become a paid agent of the Massachusetts Anti-Slavery Society. He would go on the road and tell of his experience of slavery – albeit without such sensitive details as his real name or the names of his masters, for although the chances of recapture were far less in Massachusetts than New York City, they still had to be borne in mind.[38]

'Young, ardent and hopeful, I entered upon this new life in the full gush of unsuspecting enthusiasm,' Douglass wrote, moving his burgeoning family – a son, Lewis Henry, born in October 1840 – nearer to Boston, then the centre of the anti-slavery world. He was soon criss-crossing the northern states, making up to 100 speeches a year. The venues ranged from street corners, parks, Town Halls and chapels to Boston's famous Faneuil Hall; the audiences anywhere from single figures to several hundred. 'I was a "graduate from the peculiar institution," Mr [John A.] Collins [secretary of the Massachusetts Anti-Slavery Society] used to say, when introducing me, *"with my diploma written on my back!"*'[39]

An imposing figure and increasingly impressive speaker, Douglass quickly became the biggest draw on the anti-slavery circuit, which up to this point had been dominated by whites like Garrison or free blacks like the Massachusetts-born Charles Lenox Remond. The fact that Douglass was a fugitive slave, a 'chattel', a 'thing', with the mark of the whip still fresh on his back, set him on a different plane. It was also an unmistakable boon to the American Anti-Slavery Society at a time of deep division in anti-slavery circles, Garrison's radicalism, including his insistence on the immediate (rather than gradual) emancipation of all slaves, his virulent dismissal of not just the two main parties (Whigs and

Democrats) but the whole system of government itself as corrupt, his denunciation of the Constitution as a 'covenant with death and an agreement with hell' and his support for women's rights, splitting the movement in early 1840s and leading to the formation of both the Liberty Party – which believed in putting candidates forward for elections – and the American and Foreign Anti-Slavery Society – a much more moderate organisation whose members saw slavery as a 'grotesque anomaly' in an otherwise 'wholesome' American society.[40]

'The fugitive Douglass was up when we entered,' wrote the noted abolitionist Nathaniel Rogers of the *Herald of Freedom* after one meeting, continuing:

> This is an extraordinary man. He was cut out for a hero ... As a speaker he has few equals. It is not declamation – but oratory, power of debate. He has wit, arguments, sarcasm, pathos – all that first rate men show in their master efforts. His voice is highly melodious and rich, and his enunciation quite elegant, and yet he has been but two or three years out of the house of bondage.

Even writers far from friendly to the cause were impressed, a correspondent from the conservative *Boston Courier* stating: 'We have seldom heard a better speech before a popular assembly.' The lessons from *The Columbian Orator* had clearly been well learned.[41]

Despite the acclaim, Douglass's new life as an anti-slavery speaker was not without its troubles, with Town Halls and church doors often closed to black speakers, the northern states free from slavery but not from prejudice. Even Quaker meeting houses were regularly out of bounds, such instances pertinent reminders that while many Quakers had strong activist streaks a much more conservative majority looked askance at public agitation, these tensions coming to a head with a divisive split in the Indiana Yearly Meeting in 1843, a split caused in large part by the refusal of anti-slavery Quakers to heed the warnings of the Yearly Meeting to stop breaking the law by aiding slaves on the Underground Railroad.[42] A subtler form of racism, meanwhile, was apparent in the snobbery and condescension of the white abolitionist grandees in Boston, with Douglass, for instance, paid less than white lecturers even though he was immeasurably more important to the cause. As his biographer William S. McFeely has written, Douglass and other black anti-slavery speakers were always treated as 'visiting artists in a production of which the white Bostonians never dreamed of losing the direction'.[43]

Abolitionist meetings were also often broken up by racist crowds across the North, a mob of about thirty men attacking Douglass and two other anti-slavery speakers at an outdoor meeting in Pendleton, Indiana, in late 1843. Douglass, who was used to fistfights from his days at the shipyards in Baltimore, found himself in the middle of the crowd, brandishing a stick in direct violation of Garrison's insistence on non-violence. 'Kill the nigger, kill the damn nigger,' screamed the mob, the swing of a club breaking Douglass's right hand. It was an injury that would plague him all his life, including, it can be presumed, during the long hours he put into writing his famous autobiography.[44]

Written during the early months of 1845, Douglass's *Narrative* was a response to the increased questioning of the authenticity of his story. 'People doubted if I had ever been a slave. They said I did not talk like a slave, look like a slave, nor act like a slave, and they believed I had never been south of Mason and Dixon's line.' An avid reader by now of Byron, Burns, Shakespeare, Milton and Emerson, he did not conform to the common view of an escaped slave. How could a man who claimed to have never had a day's schooling speak so powerfully and eloquently? Even abolitionists had suggested he keep 'a *little* of the plantation' in his stage manner. Douglass, however, would not play the role of the plantation stooge, dressing formally and refusing to disguise the rich voice that even Covey had admired, forcing Douglass to lead the singing at prayer time.[45]

Narrative received great praise in the northern press. It was 'unspeakably affecting' and an 'excellent piece of writing' (*New*

York Tribune), an 'extraordinary performance' (*Boston Transcript*), the 'most thrilling work which the American press ever issued – *and the most important* (*Lynn Pioneer*). 'Frederick is a strong man, and will not fail to arouse the sympathies of his readers on behalf of the oppressed,' wrote the *Practical Christian*. 'May he live long with his burning eloquence, to pour truth on the naked conscience of this wicked nation.' The reaction in the South, however, was one of outrage, the whole book denounced as a 'catalogue of lies' in the *Delaware Republican*.[46]

Anticipating the furore, Garrison and his fellow Boston abolitionists had decided to send Douglass on a year-long lecture tour of Britain and Ireland. He would stop in Dublin first, where Garrison arranged to have an Irish edition of *Narrative* published by his friend Richard D. Webb, the Quaker printer who had hosted Remond during a similar tour a few years earlier, even bringing him on holiday to the west coast of County Clare, where the soberly dressed Quaker and dark-skinned stranger walking along the cliffs were a source of amusement for the Gaelic-speaking locals, especially the children.[47]

Webb and his family were at the heart of a small but well-connected anti-slavery lobby in Ireland. Garrison had met them at the World Anti-Slavery Convention in the summer of 1840, the friendship sealed when Webb and the other Dublin delegates (mainly his relatives) joined Garrison in protesting against the exclusion of women from the main body of the conference hall, the convention's organisers, the British and Foreign Anti-Slavery Society, not quite as advanced when it came to women's rights as slavery. Garrison spent three days at Webb's home soon afterwards. 'That visit to Dublin!' he exulted to Webb's wife, Hannah, several years later. 'To be so cordially entertained by strangers, being a "foreigner" [myself] – to be welcomed to their firesides and their hearts ... my heart has ever since ... been welling over with the crystal waters of gratitude.'[48]

According to Webb's son, Alfred, Webb was 'the best friend and most active worker the anti-slavery cause had on this side of the Atlantic'. He wrote articles for the anti-slavery papers in America, organised their distribution among subscribers in Ireland

and opened up his home to an array of visiting abolitionists. Webb was also central to the gathering together of donations from Britain and Ireland for the annual Boston Bazaar, the important American Anti-Slavery Society fundraiser held each Christmas, the house in Dublin filling up with box-loads of handmade purses, bags, pincushions, scarves, gloves, clothing, ornaments and toys each November. Even the children were involved, Webb's young daughter Deborah knitting little woollen bags to be shipped across the Atlantic, the overseas items always fetching the highest prices at the Bazaar.[49]

Genuinely afraid of being 'spirited away' by slave-catchers, Douglass was happy to go along with Garrison's plan, if anxious about leaving his growing family for so long – two more sons, Frederick Jr and Charles Lenox, born in 1842 and 1844 respectively, the latter's name a clear indication of the close bond Douglass and Remond had formed on their lecture tours together.[50] Douglass, an ardent Anglophile in his literary tastes, had actually been thinking about just such a trip for several months, exhausted in body and mind by the relentless lecturing across New England and the Midwest, but also excited at the prospect of speaking before an international audience.

The tour would surpass all his expectations – though there would be some difficulties along the way.

'That's a Lie'

Determined the make the most of the voyage, Douglass and Buffum paid little heed to the conditions in steerage. Instead, Douglass recalled fondly how the Hutchinsons often came down 'to my rude forecastle deck, and sung their sweetest songs, enlivening the place with eloquent music, as well as spirited conversation'. The Hutchinsons, who became friendly with the ship's captain, a 'bluff old sterling Englishman' named Charles Judkins, also ensured that Douglass was allowed onto the promenade deck each morning, which despite his stoicism must have been a welcome break from life amidships. He could take the sea breeze and marvel at the wide array of passengers on board, ranging from diplomats, doctors, businessmen, soldiers and sailors to

Catholic bishops, Protestant ministers and Quakers – not to mention the 'large, surly, New-York lion-tamer', as Douglass referred to the circus owner Rufus Welch. He also talked about slavery to anyone who would listen as the ship made its way across the Atlantic, selling copies of his *Narrative* in full view of disgruntled pro-slavery Americans.[51]

Although Douglass's presence was a source of intense displeasure to a number of passengers, many others were intrigued by the famous escaped slave and eager to hear him speak. A deputation headed by the Hutchinsons approached Judkins on the matter and the captain, well-known to generations of transatlantic travellers and normally brusquely dismissive of passengers' requests, acquiesced, his mood softened, perhaps, by late-night talks and sing-songs with the musical family. The date arranged was Monday 25 August. The sea was rough, however, and Judkins deferred the lecture until they were in the smoother waters of the Irish Sea. And so it was that at half past six on the evening of Wednesday 27 August, just as the light started to go down on the final full day of the 3,000-mile journey across the Atlantic, the ship's bell was sounded and a large number of passengers gathered around to hear the fugitive slave.

Standing beneath an awning on the saloon deck, Judkins made a few introductory remarks before slipping away to his cabin to sleep off the champagne he had been sharing with the first-class passengers at the traditional captain's dinner on the last night of a voyage. The Hutchinsons then launched into 'A Song for Freedom', which, sung to the air of popular minstrel song 'Dandy Jim O' Caroline', went in part: 'There is a country far away/Friend Hopper says tis Canaday/And if we reach Victoria's shore/He tells us we are slaves no more/Then haste all bondsmen let us go/And leave this Christian country, Oh!/Haste to the land of the British Queen/Where whips for Negroes ne'er are seen.' Finally, Douglass stepped forward to speak, giving thanks for the safe voyage and hailing Britain's example in having freed its slaves before beginning his lecture with a reference to the notorious slave codes of the American South.

'That's a lie,' called one of the American passengers almost as soon as Douglass had begun. The escaped slave tried again, listing some of the punishments set down in law for slaves in the southern states:

If more than seven slaves are found together in any road, without a white person, twenty lashes a piece; for visiting a plantation without a written pass, ten lashes; for letting loose a boat from where it is made fast, thirty-nine lashes for the first offence, and for the second, shall have cut from off his head one ear ... for having any article for sale without a ticket from his master, ten lashes; for travelling in any other than the most usual and accustomed roads, when going alone to any place, forty lashes ... for riding or going abroad in the night, or riding horses in the day time, without leave, a slave may be whipped, cropped, or branded on the cheek with the letter R, or otherwise punished, not extending to life, or so as to render him unfit for labour.

The hecklers, however, led by a 'scheming Connecticut wooden clock-maker' named Hazzard, continued to interrupt him at every opportunity, swearing and threatening violence. 'Down with the nigger,' one shouted. 'He shan't speak,' yelled another. 'Oh, I wish I had you in Cuba,' said a third, possibly J. C. Burnham, the Havana-based businessman who had just lived through the 'Year of the Lash', the name given to the vicious crackdown on thousands of slaves in Cuba in 1844 in response to rumours of a slave revolt. Other listeners, however, including an Irish-born soldier, Captain Thomas Gough, encouraged Douglass to continue and it was not long before the whole scene verged on riot, with passengers who half an hour previously had been drinking each other's health now shouting furiously into each other's faces and clenching their fists.

The pro-slavery Americans, Douglass claimed, were ashamed to have their laws read in public. 'These laws were not intended for British eyes – they were not intended to be known but by slaves – nor to see the light, for to be abhorred, they need only be seen.' He also portrayed the disturbance as one in which the British passengers on board supported him wholly while Americans tried to shout him down. Judson Hutchinson concurred, writing how the 'Yankee Baptist [Hazzard] was backed up by the slave-mongers, while Douglass was sustained by the Englishmen'. But the split was not quite so clear-cut, the accounts of Warburton and Alexander decidedly unfavourable to Douglass, with Warburton describing how the slave, the 'demon of discord', eventually gave up on the talk, disappearing back down into steerage. The arguing, however, went on without him, one passenger, perhaps a man named John Phillippe from New Orleans, threatening to throw 'the damned nigger overboard', to which the 'gigantic' six-foot-plus Gough replied 'that two might possibly play at that game – and that two might possibly be thrown overboard'.

By this stage, Captain Judkins, woken by an aide, had returned to the deck, pushing aside one of the pro-slavery Americans who seemed ready to punch him. 'Gentlemen,' he called out, 'since I left the wharf at Boston, I have done all in my power to make the voyage a pleasant one. We have had every kind of amusement ... I have tried to manage so as to please all my passengers. Many of them came to me and asked me to give Mr Douglass an opportunity to speak, as they were anxious to hear him ... I introduced him to you ... You have acted derogatory to the character of men, of gentlemen, and of Christians.' His words, however, had little impact upon the disturbance and it was only when he ordered his boatswain to get the ship's irons that the pro-slavery agitators began to slip away, reliving the events in the safety of their rooms for the rest of the evening. Judkins then told those who remained how he had once owned 200 slaves in the West Indies. 'If I had them now, I should not be obliged to follow the sea. But they were liberated, and it was right,' he said, his actions ensuring he would be presented as the hero of the piece in Douglass's writings about the voyage, the fugitive slave seemingly unaware that the captain had been at the centre of some controversy a year earlier for refusing to allow a black passenger who had paid the full fare to enter the dining room of another Cunard ship, the *Acadia*, in an incident that saw a number of the ship's passengers write a letter of complaint to the company's directors.[52]

With the chief protagonists of the fracas having repaired to their rooms, the Hutchinson's brought the evening's unexpectedly volatile entertainment to a close with renditions of 'God Save the Queen', 'Yankee Doodle', 'America' and 'A Life on the Ocean Wave', the *Cambria* continuing up through the Irish Sea before docking in Liverpool the next morning – Thursday 28 August – eleven-and-a-half days after setting sail from Boston. Together with their friends Douglass and Buffum, the musical family took rooms at a local hotel and began to explore a city so synonymous with the slave trade that it was said every brick of its buildings was 'cemented by the blood of a negro'. A number of the pro-slavery passengers, meanwhile, took to the press to denounce the 'ignorant calumniator' Douglass for heaping the 'most outrageous abuse' on America, one even suggesting that 'if there had been a southerner on board, his carcass no doubt would have been food for sharks'.

Their attacks were counterproductive, serving merely to bring greater attention to Douglass's arrival on British shores. 'Men, in their senses, do not take bowie-knives to kill mosquitoes, nor pistols to shoot flies; and the American passengers who thought proper to get up a mob to silence me, on board the *Cambria*, took the most effective method of telling the British public that I had something to say,' the escaped slave noted. The British public, however, would have to wait, Douglass and Buffum leaving Liverpool within a couple of days to commence their tour in Ireland.[53]

2

'A TOTAL ABSENCE OF PREJUDICE'

'Our success here is even greater than I had anticipated,' a delighted Frederick Douglass wrote to William Lloyd Garrison from Dublin in mid-September 1845. 'We have held four glorious anti-slavery meetings ... all crowded to overflowing.' Douglass's greatest pleasure, however, came not from the success of his lectures, but rather the manner in which he was treated on the street:

> One of the most pleasing features of my visit ... has been a total absence of ... prejudice against me on account of my colour. The change of circumstances, in this, is particularly striking. I go on stage coaches, omnibuses, steamboats, into the first cabins, and in the first public houses, without seeing the slightest manifestation of that hateful and vulgar feeling against me. I find myself not treated as a colour, but as a man – not as a thing, but as a child of the common Father of us all.[1]

Dubliners were used to the sight of black men and women on the streets, be they servants, sailors or singers. The numbers were small, no more than a few hundred at any one time, but this was still enough to give Dublin a larger black population than almost any European city outside of London. The black presence in Ireland spread further still, to other port cities like Cork and Belfast and even – in rare cases – rural counties such as Longford, Mayo and Donegal. Occasionally, a newspaper article might describe a crowd of white people staring strangely at a black mother and child. For the most part, however, their presence was unremarkable. They certainly do not appear to have been subjected to any widespread racist abuse; accounts of mixed-race marriages or parties where black men danced with white women containing no hint of reproach. This would not have been the case in Douglass's homeland of the American South.[2]

Nevertheless, Ireland's relationship with slavery and the slave trade was far from unblemished, for although slavery as an institution had largely disappeared from the British Isles by the late 1500s, small numbers of slaves were still being held up to the mid-1700s. They may not have been subjected to anything like the terrible conditions of slaves in America, Brazil or the Caribbean but they were still denied the same rights as their white owners – still referred to and seen as property. 'A Negro Boy and Slave, called Brazill, the property of William Nicholson, Esq., has been missing since Thursday evening last,' ran one notice in a Dublin paper in 1756. 'Run away from the service of Mrs Fullerton of Carrickfergus, on Sunday last, a Negro slave boy,' read another a few years later.[3]

Prominent Irish families also owned large slave estates in the West Indies and Antoine Walsh from Kilkenny was just one example of an Irishman amassing a fortune in the French slave trade. Even the great Irish leader Daniel O'Connell's famous claim that no slave ship ever left Ireland's shores was mistaken. They may have been illegal and in the distant past, but they certainly existed, the last recorded Irish slave ship, the *Prosperity* from Limerick, sailing into Barbados on 31 July 1718 with ninety-six slaves aboard. It was also legislation rather than moral scruples that kept the Irish from getting more involved in the slave trade, a series of Navigation Acts passed during the seventeenth and eighteenth centuries prioritising British ports and vessels over their Irish counterparts and denying Irish merchants the right to trade directly with the West Indies in goods such as sugar or slaves.

Despite the limitations on what they could trade, many Irish merchants became rich supplying the British, French and Dutch islands of the Caribbean with provisions – the islands themselves focused solely on the production of their cash crops (sugar, cotton, indigo and coffee). The port of Cork, in particular, owed much of its success in the eighteenth century to this trade, devising special techniques to ensure the preservation of its beef, butter and fish in high temperatures. Belfast, too, had strong links with the Caribbean, supplying the coarse linen and shoes with which planters clothed their slaves. Some of these merchants, like the Blakes from Galway and Creaghs from Limerick, went on to settle in the Caribbean, a David Creagh purchasing a plantation in Barbados in the early 1700s that he equipped with more than 200 slaves bought for about £25 a head.[4]

When trade restrictions were eased in the late 1700s, Irish businessmen tried to get the country more directly involved in the slave trade, with a plan announced for the establishment of an 'African company' in Limerick in 1784. Six ships would be employed annually, carrying firearms, linen, cotton, soap, candles and even 'Dutch toys' to the slave coast of West Africa where, in true triangular-trade style, they would be exchanged for hundreds of slaves who would in turn be traded in the West Indies for sugar, coffee and other tropically grown goods. A similar proposal was mooted for Belfast a year later. Neither venture, however, took off, in part because of growing anti-slavery sentiment across the British Isles at the time, the radical Presbyterian watchmaker Thomas McCabe declaring of the Belfast plan: 'May God eternally damn the soul of the man who subscribes the first guinea.'[5]

And so, instead of helping carry ever more African slaves across the Atlantic to lives of bondage, Ireland played host to a wide array of anti-slavery speakers, from the famous freed slave Olaudah Equiano in the 1790s to Charles Lenox Remond, Douglass and others half a century later.

'Some Black O'Connell'
Douglass had arrived in Dublin – a cramped and crowded city of almost a quarter of a million souls – early on the morning of

Sunday 30 August, making his way with James Buffum past the liquor shops that surrounded the docks to a warm welcome at the home of James H. Webb, younger brother of the temporarily absent Richard D. Webb. The travellers seemed content, Douglass describing to Garrison how he was 'safe in old Ireland, in the beautiful city of Dublin' in the first of a series of letters charting his progress around Britain and Ireland published in the pages of the *Liberator*. His mind, however, was still full of the remarkable events on board the *Cambria*, a mix of righteous indignation and nervous energy coursing through his words. 'Yes, they actually got up a *mob* – a real American, republican, democratic, Christian mob,' he declared of the pro-slavery passengers. 'It is enough to make a slave ashamed of the country that enslaved him.'[6]

A few days later, Douglass and Buffum were ensconced in Richard D. Webb's home above the bookshop and printing business at 177 Great Brunswick Street (through the site of which a railway now runs). Douglass was right in the heart of the city, close to Trinity College Dublin around whose walls small bookstands vied for attention with women selling fruit. He was also just a short walk away from the old Irish Parliament where, fifty years earlier, the Irish politician Arthur O'Connor had made a powerful speech on Catholic emancipation that he had read many times in *The Columbian Orator*. The Parliament, however, once so central to the city's sense of fashion and political importance, was no more, abolished by the Act of Union of 1801, the long centuries of British rule taking new shape in the creation of the United Kingdom of Great Britain and Ireland. Its magnificent home on College Green had become a bank's headquarters, the old House of Commons gutted to make way for clerks and counters and men waiting around outside ready to hold horses as riders alighted.

The loss of its Parliament had been just one in a series of sharp socio-economic blows to Dublin, the wealth and grandeur of its late eighteenth-century pomp giving way to extreme poverty and decay. The scene was not unremittingly bleak, with Dublin Castle, the beating heart of the British administration in Ireland, still the setting for glittering balls and stylish soirées. Dublin also remained an important commercial city as well as the centre of Irish law, learning and medicine. Nevertheless, the sense of a city being abandoned to its poor, its wretched and infirm was unmistakeable, with many of the leading aristocratic families having decamped for London – their fashionable homes on the north side of the city falling into tenement use. The remaining gentry and affluent middle classes, meanwhile, had started to move out to new suburbs like Rathmines, perusing stories of their city's fall in the pages of its many newspapers.

As with every transatlantic crossing, the arrival of the *Cambria* had been eagerly awaited by the Dublin press. Their chief interest, however, lay not in the escaped-slave-turned-orator travelling on board but rather the prospect of war between America and Mexico. 'From what is contained in the files of American journals which we have received ... we are led to anticipate the breaking out of hostilities between the United States and Mexico,' reported the *Freeman's Journal*, which printed extracts from papers including the *New York Herald*. Long-standing tensions between the countries had been brought to a head earlier in the year by the American annexation of slave-owning Texas (an independent republic since 1836, when it won independence from Mexico). The papers were slightly premature in their predictions as war was not actually declared until May 1846. The fighting would last almost two years, American victory adding half a million square miles – including the present-day states of California, Nevada, Utah and New Mexico – to its territory.

Other items in that day's *Freeman's Journal* included an advertisement for the Ship Tavern, 5 Lower Abbey Street, where 'Gentlemen may dine on a variety of the Primest Joints for one shilling each ... from five to seven o'clock each day'. As an added attraction, an Irish Harper named Quinn also performed there each evening. Under the heading 'Board and Education for Young Ladies', a woman informed readers that she could accommodate 'Two or Three Young Ladies as Boarders, where they can finish their Education in every polite and useful accomplishment, consisting of French, Italian, Music, Drawing, &c, in a Private Family, on Moderate Terms'. There was a notice for an auction at 7 Rathmines Terrace of the extensive effects of 'the late Frederick Howard,

Esq.'. Still in the 'best state of preservation', these included 'seven elaborately-carved Antique Chairs, covered with needle-work', 'Feather Beds, Bolsters and Pillows' and a panoply of sofas, dressers, wardrobes, bookcases, blankets and carpets. Jobs, too, were being advertised, despite the poor economic situation, with an experienced flour miller required at one company and an 'accomplished' Catholic lady needed to work as a governess.

There was also a report of a talk given by the English botanist Thomas George Tilley to the Royal Zoological Society of Ireland, and an advertisement for the rather more intriguing sounding 'experimental' lecture by Thomas Adair on mesmerism and phreno-mesmerism, new therapeutic techniques involving hypnotism. Public lectures of this kind were extremely popular in nineteenth-century Britain and Ireland, and not just with the upper and middle classes. Indeed, throughout the British Isles, Mechanics' Institutes, Athenaeums and Literary and Scientific Societies – all boasting their own small libraries, museums and laboratories – opened up new worlds of culture and science to their artisan and working-class members.[7]

It is no surprise, therefore, that the young orator Douglass was thrust quickly onto the stage, stepping onto the platform of a small lecture room in the magnificent Royal Exchange on Dame Street (the present-day City Hall) on the evening of Wednesday, 3 September 1845, word of mouth alone ensuring that the venue (home to the regular meetings of the Hibernian Anti-Slavery Society) was crowded to excess. He spoke for about forty-five minutes, denouncing slavery as a system 'which made a chattel of a man ... which tore the husband and wife asunder ... and which deprived men of all their rights as human beings'. He also praised Daniel O'Connell, the tall, broad-chested folk hero who had waged and won the battle for Catholic emancipation in Ireland in 1829 – an immense success that enabled Irish Catholics to sit in Parliament and hold senior offices of state, rights long denied by the repressive penal laws. O'Connell had then emerged as one of the world's strongest campaigners against slavery in the 1830s, decrying the hypocrisy of the Declaration of Independence and promising to never 'pollute' his feet by treading on America's shores while slavery existed. Echoing the famous call from his Catholic emancipation campaign, he had also repeatedly urged 'some black O'Connell' to rise among the slaves and cry 'Agitate! Agitate! Agitate!'[8]

'Frederick is Very Popular Here'

With Webb to the fore, the Quaker element in the Hibernian Anti-Slavery Society was very strong. In fact, it had been a Quaker, Mary Peisley, who really introduced anti-slavery thinking into Ireland, publishing a pamphlet condemning Quaker slaveholders after a visit to North Carolina in the 1750s. With family letters constantly crossing the Atlantic, a significant number of Irish Quakers followed their American brethren in campaigning against slavery as the century progressed – publishing poems, pamphlets and books that revealed the sufferings of transported Africans in America. They were also involved in efforts to boycott sugar and other slave-produced goods. Indeed, it was soon said that the only two pictures commonly found in famously sparse Quaker homes were copies of Benjamin West's painting 'Penn's Treaty with the Indians' and the iconic image of the *Brookes* slave ship showing the appalling cramped conditions of the chained slaves held on board.[9]

Alongside Webb, other important members of the Hibernian Anti-Slavery Society included Richard Allen and James Haughton. Allen was a forty-two-year-old Quaker with his own tailoring and drapery store in Dublin city. Haughton, born into a Quaker family before joining the Unitarians, was about a decade older and owned a successful flour-milling business with his brother. As children Webb and Haughton had attended the famous Quaker school in Ballitore, County Kildare, imbibing the anti-slavery spirit of the schoolmaster Richard Shackleton, a forebear of the famous explorer Ernest Shackleton. They were now with Allen, soberly dressed, high-minded men, easily recognised on the streets of the city. Dubbed 'Anti-Everythingarians' by the *Dublin Evening Mail*, they campaigned on a number of causes besides slavery, including temperance, pacifism, prison reform and the abolition of capital punishment, Allen's deep and distracting involvement in so many philanthropic adventures almost costing him his business on a number of occasions. Their beliefs permeated the lives of their children, Webb's son Alfred describing how he and his siblings were often overheard playing with their toys and dolls: 'Now thee is going to a slavery meeting; now thee is going to a temperance meeting.'[10]

Young Alfred may even have attended Douglass's second Dublin lecture, held at an uncomfortably crowded Quaker Meeting House on Eustace Street in the centre of the city, another encouraging affair where Douglass's impassioned urging of the audience to make 'every American slaveholder, every American apologist of slavery, who set his feet upon our soil – *feel* that he was in a land of freedom, among a people that hated oppression, and who loved liberty – liberty for all; for the black man as well as the white man' elicited such loud applause from the predominantly non-Quaker audience he had to ask for quiet on account of the sombre nature of the venue.[11]

'Frederick is very popular here,' Buffum reported back to Boston, regretting that they had not brought over more copies of the *Liberator* and anti-slavery pamphlets like Theodore Dwight Weld's hugely influential *American Slavery As It Is*, a devastating documentation of the cruelties inflicted by the 'peculiar institution' assembled from the testimony of a thousand eyewitnesses (some former slaveholders), state legal codes and the South's own newspapers' accounts and advertisements. Nevertheless, Douglass's first weeks in Ireland were not without moments of awkwardness and controversy, a coruscating attack on American Methodists during another lecture in the Quaker Meeting House (held a day after his second talk at the Royal Exchange) getting him banned from the venue in another reminder of the innate conservatism of much of that body on both sides of the Atlantic.[12]

Douglass had actually been drawn powerfully to religion – particularly the Methodist faith so strong in the South – ever since Sophia Auld first read passages from the Bible to him. His reverence for religion, however, had fallen away once sent back to the Eastern Shore, where Thomas Auld and his wife Rowena prayed deeply every morning but still let their slaves almost starve.

Edward Covey, another pious Methodist, would smile at slaves on Sunday mornings on the way to church before whipping them the next day. Methodist ministers, meanwhile, encouraged slaves to look down upon their 'hard, horny hands' and 'muscular frames' as proof that God had adapted them to physical labour, while their white masters, 'who have slender frames and long delicate fingers', were designed for thinking. Douglass would parody these slavery-supporting southern ministers to great effect in speeches across Britain and Ireland, his gifts of mimicry and deep and dextrous voice coming to the fore as he spread out his arms, looked up at the ceiling and, in the manner of a minister addressing the black pews, intoned: 'And you too, my friends, have souls of infinite value – souls that will live through endless happiness or misery in eternity. Oh, labour diligently to make your calling and election sure. Oh, receive into your souls these words of the holy apostle – "Servants, be obedient unto your masters."'[13]

This quoting of the Bible (Ephesians 6:5) in support of slavery would have appalled John Wesley, the founding father of Methodism. Deeply committed to social justice, Wesley had attacked what he called 'this execrable villainy' in his *Thoughts upon Slavery* (1774) and other writings. Arriving in America during the Revolutionary era, Methodism's commitment to anti-slavery remained strong at first, preachers threatening slaveholders with excommunication if their slaves were not freed. The early years of the nineteenth century, however, saw the Methodist leadership start to accommodate slave-ownership. They did not want to damage the Church's appeal at a time when numbers in the South were growing impressively. Methodism, indeed, was particularly popular among wealthy southern slaveholders who, attracted by its evangelical dimension, began to play an ever-larger role in Church affairs. The question of slavery was relegated from a moral issue to a private matter between master and slave and southern ministers were even allowed to keep slaves. At the same time, many Methodists in the North continued to denounce slavery, with several ministers actively involved in the Underground Railroad. These tensions would lead to schism and the foundation of the Methodist Episcopal Church South in the mid-1840s.

Presbyterians and Baptists in America endured similar splits, but as the religion closest to Douglass's heart, Methodism was the one he attacked most vigorously in his speeches, which in Dublin had grown so popular they demanded a larger venue.[14]

'Mangled With the Lash'

The Music Hall on Lower Abbey Street – home in later years to the famous Abbey Theatre – was one of the main entertainment venues in nineteenth-century Dublin, playing host to a wide variety of concerts, shows and lectures. It had a capacity of more than 3,000 and was normally let, Douglass told Garrison, for 'about fifty dollars a night'.[15] The mercurial Webb, however, convinced the proprietor to donate it to the anti-slavery cause free of charge for a series of three talks by Douglass, beginning on the evening of Wednesday 17 September. Nevertheless, this was the first of Douglass's talks in Dublin to charge an entrance fee – an extremely reasonable 4d to the main body of the house and 2d to the gallery (a concert a few weeks earlier charged 6d for seats in the gallery).[16] The funds were needed to defray expenses incurred by the Hibernian Anti-Slavery Society, including placards and newspaper advertisements. The interest created by Douglass's earlier talks ensured a full house.

Douglass took to the stage at eight o'clock, launching immediately into the story of his life as a slave. Although far from the worst treated of slaves, his back had still been 'mangled with the lash'. Well versed in the art of capturing an audience's attention, he then lifted up a whip, some manacles and other instruments of torture used in the slave states, rattling them before the gasp-filled hall. Unafraid of controversy, he returned to the question of the American Churches and slavery. 'The word of God had been profaned ... to the purposes of slavery,' he declared, clergymen in America justifying the flogging of slaves with distorted quotes from the Bible. Almost all the main religious bodies were in some way culpable, Douglass argued, citing Baptists, Presbyterians and Congregationalists – the latter better known as Independents in Britain and Ireland at this time. Nevertheless, it was the Methodists who were again his main target:

The Methodists in America supported slavery, and when he exposed their conduct the other night to their friends in Dublin, he had the door of the Meeting House closed against him ... But whatever he might incur from them, he would not sacrifice his friends now in chains, and perhaps writhing under the lash while he spoke, to any fear of personal inconvenience ... While he lived, he would plead for those whom he left behind him in bondage.[17]

The relentless attacks on American Methodists were part of the abolitionists' plan to fracture relations between the American Churches and their British and Irish counterparts. They wanted to isolate and ostracise the slaveholding Churches and expose them to the moral glare of international public opinion. It was a valid tactic; the Churches in America genuinely craving respectability in world religious opinion and cherishing the dream of a worldwide Protestant federation. Douglass's criticisms certainly discomfited the Methodists in Dublin, many of whom had been to the fore of the efforts to abolish slavery in the West Indies in the early 1830s. The years since, however, had seen the Methodists, like other Protestant denominations in Ireland, grow more cautious in their relationship with anti-slavery, its divisiveness as a subject painfully apparent in the schisms renting the American Churches apart.

Douglass was back on stage a week later for another ninety-minute speech that melded his life story with more attacks on the hypocrisy of the American Churches. The constant talk of religion would not have bored Irish audiences, enmeshed as religion was in every facet of life in the country. The Catholics in the hall would certainly have enjoyed the denunciations of the Protestant denominations, and there were loud cheers when Douglass – conveniently overlooking the fact that its American leadership, including many Irish-born bishops, tacitly approved of slavery – declared that of all the Churches in America, only the Roman Catholic Church had never shut its doors to black worshippers. His final Music Hall speech – held a few days after he was the guest of honour at a special Lord Mayor's reception – was another sold-out affair, with his friends the Hutchinson Family joining him on stage, having travelled over from Liverpool to play a few concerts in Dublin. Once more, he brandished the chains and whips, calling upon the audience to help 'break the chains which bound the black man in America' to great applause.[18]

The speeches made a strong impact on the city, Douglass's positive reception on the streets matched in the pages of the capital's press. He had also broken out of the Quaker, anti-slavery, anti-everythingarian audience to reach a broader spectrum of the people, as evidenced by the thousands who crammed in to see him at the Music Hall. Many working men, indeed, had given up their own time to help set up the hall on the nights of his lectures. They had been moved by Douglass's eloquent testimony of the sufferings of slavery. But they had also come for excitement, Douglass always making sure to show whips or talk about beatings in vivid detail.[19]

Despite their staid credentials, the Hibernian Anti-Slavery Society had not been shy about pushing this element of the speeches either. 'The public streets are placarded with statements, setting forth that Mr Douglass has been a "slave," has *bona fide* felt the lash, &c.' wrote the young nationalist Thomas D'Arcy McGee in his 'Letter from Ireland' in the *Boston Pilot*. McGee had lived in America for a number of years and was far from enthusiastic about slave emancipation. He was certainly much more circumspect than O'Connell, who had continued to denounce slavery even though it harmed American support for his Repeal movement, the campaign to repeal the Act of Union that placed Ireland under direct British rule the latest and last of his long political career. Douglass would actually share a stage with the septuagenarian O'Connell on one of his final nights in Dublin, listening transfixed as the great orator declared himself the 'friend of liberty in every clime, class and colour', words the escaped slave would still be able quote decades later. Douglass then described to loud cheers how he had heard O'Connell's name in the 'curses of his masters' years earlier and immediately loved him, earning the sobriquet 'the black O'Connell of the United States' from the fabled 'Liberator' himself before travelling down the country, through Wexford and Waterford to Cork.[20]

'The Sufferings and Cruelties around Us'

The coach from Dublin to Wexford left Dawson Street every morning at seven o'clock, travelling through towns and villages like Bray, Arklow, Ferns (where it changed horses) and Enniscorthy. It was a ten-hour journey over roughly surfaced roads, the piles of luggage balanced precariously on top growing higher as more passengers climbed aboard. With the two-horse coach carrying anywhere between twelve and twenty tightly packed passengers at a time, motion sickness was a common complaint. The scenery, however, was quite beautiful en route, especially around the Glen of the Downs and the Vale of Avoca.

Douglass, Buffum and Webb were on their way to stay with Joseph Poole, a young Quaker cousin of Webb's in Wexford. They would stay with another branch of the Poole family in Waterford, Douglass delivering lectures in both cities and selling copies of the freshly printed first Dublin edition of his *Narrative*. Maria Waring, Webb's twenty-seven-year-old sister-in-law, travelled with them for part of the journey. Douglass was a 'fine man', she wrote to a relative soon afterwards. 'I wish thee could have heard him speak.' Waring had attended the World Anti-Slavery Convention in London in 1840 and would remain involved in the cause all her life. Nevertheless, as the coach bearing Douglass travelled down the east coast of Ireland, her mind turned to problems closer to home. 'It is unnatural and wrong to pass over the sufferings and cruelties around us for those that are at a distance. The humanity of those who do so is very questionable.'[21]

The propriety of asking an impoverished people to aid strangers thousands of miles away was an issue Douglass would have to confront throughout his time in Ireland, especially as the effects of a serious potato blight, the first reports of which had started to emerge while he was in Dublin, became ever clearer and ever graver, vast tracts of the population surviving on little more than potatoes with some buttermilk and herring for most of the year. More than half the crop, it was soon discovered, had been destroyed, heavy rains facilitating the progress of the disease. 'We deeply regret to say that the accounts reaching us, from all quarters, in regard to the failure of the potato crop are alarming,' wrote the *Wexford Independent*. 'Where potatoes were believed generally if not altogether safe a week or ten days past, it is now found that they are infected, and by entire masses become totally unfit for use.'[22]

Although the real impact of the blight would not be felt until the following spring, Douglass had already witnessed the extreme poverty in which many of the country's 8 million inhabitants lived, be it during city strolls down streets that were 'almost literally alive with beggars' or on longer walks through the Dublin hills with his new anti-slavery friends. Three decades of severe economic distress, dating back to the end of the Napoleonic Wars, had taken a heavy toll, and an Irish hut, Douglass declared, was the pre-eminent place in the world to observe 'human misery, ignorance, degradation, filth and wretchedness'. Echoing a passage from his *Narrative*, he described to Garrison how: 'Men and women, married and single, old and young, lie down together, in much the same degradation as the American slaves.' Douglass did not talk openly about the devastating scenes of poverty and penury he witnessed all over the country during his speeches in Ireland, but they made a deep impression. 'I am not only an American slave, but a man, and as such, am bound to use my powers for the welfare of the whole human brotherhood,' he would inform readers of the *Liberator*, coming to view his fight against slavery as part of a larger, global struggle against social injustice. 'I am not going through this land with my eyes shut, ears stopped, or heart steeled.'[23]

'A Girdle of Anti-Slavery Fire'

By the time Douglass, Buffum and Webb arrived in the southern city of Cork, they had been each other's constant companions for almost six weeks. The relationships had started to fray, Webb – who returned to Dublin almost as soon as he arrived in Cork – complaining to Maria Weston Chapman, one of the leading Garrisonians in Boston, of Douglass's rudeness to his cousin Elizabeth (Lizzy) Poole and sister-in-law Waring. 'They are both young women – sensible and comely. They walked with him and talked with him and treated him with respect and kindness and no condescension. Yet for some entirely groundless huff he took, he treated L.P. in such a contemptuous ... manner that I was and have ever since been perfectly indignant.' Not wanting to distract from the effort to raise the profile of the anti-slavery movement in Ireland, Webb had kept his counsel until Douglass left the country. Once unleashed, however, there was no holding back:

> In all my experience of men I have never known one ... so able and willing as he is to magnify the smallest causes of discomfort ... into insurmountable hills of offence and dissatisfaction. He is in my opinion ... the least likable and the least easy of all the abolitionists with whom I have come into intimate association. I think his selfishness intense, his affections weak and his unreasonableness quite extravagant when he is in the slightest degree hurt or when he thinks himself hurt.

Softly spoken in public, Webb clearly had a talent for invective with the pen.[24]

Although such strong criticisms from a man of Webb's moral stature cannot be ignored, it is difficult to reconcile them with the otherwise almost overwhelmingly positive response to Douglass in the country. Webb, in fact, believed all the praise Douglass received had gone to his head. It is also possible, however, that Douglass got a sense that he was being treated by his Quaker hosts with the kind of condescension he thought he had left behind him in America. 'The ladies had taken their exotic guest out on a leash, for all of Dublin to see. They thought it unseemly when he barked,' Douglass's biographer, McFeely, has observed of the incident with Poole and Waring. The latter, despite being hugely impressed by the escaped slave, would also describe him as a 'wild animal' in one conversation with Webb. Webb's wife, Hannah, meanwhile, would refer to Douglass as 'a child – a savage'.

Alert to any hint of patronising behaviour, Douglass may well have been somewhat sharp with his hosts in Dublin. Webb's response, however, was over the top. Indeed, it makes him seem as thin-skinned as he accused Douglass of being. James Haughton was probably somewhere closer to the truth, writing of Douglass:

'He is a fine, manly fellow, but like perhaps most of us, somewhat impatient of reproof.'[25]

Webb also informed Chapman that it had actually been Douglass's 'offensive and ungrateful' behaviour towards Buffum that first set him against the celebrated slave. There was certainly some tension between the two Americans, Buffum leaving Cork well before Douglass and travelling over to England where he met the Hutchinsons (who were still giving concerts around the north of England), shocking them with the news that he had had a 'falling out' with Douglass and 'could not stay with him any longer'. It is difficult to apportion blame. Perhaps Webb's judgements were correct, and Douglass was acting in an egotistical, high-handed manner with those around him. Or was the falling-out with Buffum simply the result of the friction that can arise between any two people thrown together for a long period of time in intense circumstances? It is also possible that deeper animosities were at work, as it may have been around this time that Douglass discovered that abolitionists in America had been plying Webb with letters urging him to keep a close eye on the escaped slave, lest he abandon the American Anti-Slavery Society for the more financially powerful British and Foreign Anti-Slavery Society. Was Buffum, then, the unfortunate close-at-hand target of the ire Douglass felt for the white Boston abolitionist grandees?[26]

Chapman received far more positive reports about Douglass from Isabel Jennings, the daughter of the Unitarian family with whom Douglass stayed in Cork. Douglass was a 'noble-minded' man who immediately felt 'like a friend'. Buffum, too, before he left, was much admired in the city. Despite the warm welcome, both men, Jennings wrote, were suffering somewhat, having felt 'the dampness of the climate very much'. The weather had certainly been poor, constant rain helping the spread of the potato blight. 'It has descended into the earth and is eating away the poor man's life while its leprous spots fester in his food,' wrote the *Southern Reporter*.[27]

As co-secretary of the Cork Ladies' Anti-Slavery Society, Isabel Jennings was a regular correspondent of Chapman's, especially around the time of the annual Boston Bazaar. 'Again we have the pleasure of sending through you, to the American Anti-Slavery Society, some articles for the Fair to be held in Boston,' a typical letter began. 'Many questions are asked as to whether plain or fancy work would be preferred? Little things for children or knitted ... articles? We would be glad to hear as many would do either with equal pleasure.' Showing that even good-hearted abolitionists were not beyond a little tax evasion, Jennings informed Chapman on one occasion that, in order to save on duties, the prices on the items sent over had been marked at a third of what they were expected to fetch. 'We were afraid to put too low a price lest suspicions might be aroused.'[28]

Thomas Jennings, Isabel's father, was the owner of a long-established company manufacturing vinegar, magnesia, mineral oil and non-alcoholic beverages like soda water. Business, however, was just one strand to this man's rich, multifaceted life. He had published some poetry in the 1820s, inspired, he told the editor of *Blackwood's Magazine*, by the death of the famous Irish boxer Dan Donnelly. He may also have lectured on phrenology – the now discredited 'pseudo-science' of measuring an individual's or indeed an entire race's intellectual capacities based on the dimensions of their skulls – in the 1830s and was certainly involved in any number of local groups, such as the Royal Cork Institution, together with broader humanitarian concerns like temperance and anti-slavery. His business partner, fifty-one-year-old Richard Dowden, was of a similarly active and philanthropic ilk, immersed in temperance, anti-slavery and a multitude of local boards and societies. Lord Mayor at the time of Douglass's visit, Dowden had studied medicine before being approached by the Jennings family to manage their business, even publishing a poem, again on Dan Donnelly, in the same issue of *Blackwood's*.[29]

Jennings lived with his wife and their eight grown-up children in a large house on Brown Street, just a few yards away from St Patrick's Street, the city's main thoroughfare where the bookshops Purcell & Co. and Bradford & Co. sold Douglass's *Narrative*. It was an extremely open-minded home, full of music, gossip and talk of the latest reforms, with one of Isabel's sisters, Jane, another prominent member of the Cork Ladies' Anti-Slavery Society and a brother, Francis, the author of numerous pamphlets on Irish social and economic issues. Douglass delighted in the free flow of talk and ideas around the Jennings' living room. (They certainly seem to have provided him with much more vivid company than Webb and his extended Quaker clan.) The admiration was shared. 'We are,' Jane Jennings wrote to Chapman soon after his departure, 'a large family, my mother, three brothers and five sisters, generally considered not easily pleased – but Frederick won the affection of every one of us.'[30]

Douglass enjoyed Cork so much that he stayed for almost a month – three weeks longer than originally planned. He delivered more than a dozen talks at venues ranging from small church halls to the sumptuous surrounds of the Imperial Hotel on the South Mall, the ubiquitous Isabel Jennings – 'Dear Isa' in the many letters they later exchanged – invariably close at hand, including for the appearance at the city courthouse on the afternoon of Tuesday 14 October that really introduced him to the people of Cork, the building 'densely crowded in every part' long before the meeting was scheduled to begin. Mayor Dowden, who, like his close friends and fellow Unitarians the Jennings, would be a constant presence during Douglass's stay, presided over the meeting, a series of anti-slavery resolutions passed before Douglass finally stepped forward to address the large audience, with a two-hour speech entitled 'I Am Here To Spread Light On American Slavery'.

'I stand before you in the most extraordinary position that one human being ever stood before his race – a slave,' Douglass began starkly. 'I have not been stripped of one of my rights and privileges, but of all. By the laws of the country whence I came, I was deprived of myself – of my own body, soul and spirit, and I am free only because I succeeded in escaping the clutches of the man who claimed me as his property.' He bore the 'marks of the slave-driver's whip' on his back, and would carry them to his grave. Much worse, however, than any physical pain was the manner in which slavery crushed the spirit of its victims, slaveholders enjoying the 'bloody power of tearing asunder those whom God had joined together – of separating husband from wife, parent from child, and of leaving the hut vacant and the hearth desolate'.

Quoting again Weld's great book, *American Slavery As It Is*, Douglass listed some of the gruesome punishments set down in law for slaves before turning his ire once more on the American Churches. 'In America, Bibles and slaveholders go hand in hand,' he declared powerfully. 'The Church and the slave prison stand together, and while you hear the chanting of psalms in one, you hear the clanking of chains in the other; the man who wields the cowhide during the week, fills the pulpit on Sunday. Here we have robbery and religion united – devils dressed in angels' garments.'

Douglass went on to treat the rapt audience to his stock impersonation of a southern minister. More seriously, however, he also explained, amid constant waves of applause, how the Irish could help put an end to slavery by lending the moral and religious influence they had over the American Churches to the abolitionist cause:

> We want to awaken the slaveholder to a sense of the iniquity of his position ... We want to encircle America with a girdle of anti-slavery fire ... We want Methodists in Ireland to speak to those of America, and say, 'While your hands are red with blood, while the thumb screws and gags and whips are wrapped up in the pontifical robes of your Church, we will have no fellowship with you, or acknowledge you as Christians.'[31]

He sat down to a standing ovation. The city was convinced.

'Stranger from a Distant Nation'

Despite – or possibly because of – the strong connection between the port of Cork and the Caribbean islands, the city had demonstrated a long commitment to anti-slavery activity, the Quaker influence once again looming large. In the mid to late 1700s, for example, Samuel Neale, a prominent Quaker merchant in the city, had acted as a link between the American Quaker Anthony Benezet and the Irish statesman and philosopher Edmund Burke when Benezet was trying to get British Parliamentary action on the slave trade. (Although not a Quaker, Burke had been educated at Ballitore School, maintaining lifelong friendships with Quakers like Richard Shackleton, the son of the school's founder.) More recent years had seen the establishment of the Cork Anti-Slavery Society (along with its female auxiliary) and, in something of a precursor to the modern free-trade movement, the setting up of a shop that sold sweets made from Indian rather than West Indian sugar. One local newspaper derided the 'good-natured jellies, warm-hearted ices, amiable tarts ... and philanthropic lozenges'. Nevertheless, all the talk of anti-slavery had been a cause of concern for those with business interests in the West Indies, who argued that the slaves were well treated and quite happy until outsiders started interfering on their behalf.[32]

The heavy Quaker involvement led to some tart observations that 'though they would not care a pin for us whites or our liberties yet the blacks across the sea are very precious'. It did not spare them, however, from Douglass's admonishments at the Wesleyan Chapel on St Patrick's Street, where he delivered another substantial two-hour lecture entitled 'Slavery Corrupts American Society and Religion'. The Quakers, he regretted to say, the recent split at the Indiana Yearly Meeting clearly in mind, had turned their backs on a proud anti-slavery history. Instead of being despised by the 'inhuman traffickers', as had formerly been the case, they were now spoken of by slaveholders as an 'excellent body'. Douglass's criticisms seem harsh given the continued deep involvement of so many Quakers in the anti-slavery movement and Underground Railroad, not to mention the support he had received from that body in Ireland. Nevertheless, anything less than the most wholehearted commitment to abolition was a failure in his eyes.[33]

Douglass's audiences in Cork were usually characterised as belonging to the most 'respectable' sections of society – an aspect Douglass always emphasised in letters to the *Liberator*, contrasting the high-level shows of support from lord mayors, aldermen and councillors in Ireland with the rebuffs abolitionists met from political leaders in most American cities. Nevertheless, his influence went deeper, the *Cork Examiner* writing approvingly of how the 'suffering poor', too, were 'thronging' to hear him speak. Furthermore, although there was some natural overlap in the speeches, Douglass made great efforts to keep his audiences interested and engaged, working on new angles and continuing the process of moving beyond mere personal testimony – an important step in light of the instructions he had received from white abolitionists in America earlier in his lecturing career: 'Give us the facts, we will take care of the philosophy.' He was also extremely adept at moulding his speeches to the different audiences, heaping effusive praise on O'Connell before the mainly Catholic courthouse crowd but not mentioning him once at the Wesleyan Chapel.[34]

Douglass's final public appearance in Cork came at a farewell soirée at the Independent Chapel on Monday 3 November, where a local poet, Daniel Casey, recited a poem that began:

> Stranger from a distant nation,
> We welcome thee with acclamation,
> And, as a brother, warmly greet thee –
> Rejoiced in Erin's Isle to meet thee.
>
> Then *Céad Míle Fáilte* to the stranger,
> Free from bondage, chains and danger.

Numerous other poems and songs celebrating Douglass were also composed around this time, some of which Isabel Jennings forwarded to Chapman in Boston for publication in the abolitionist press. She asked Chapman to send the poems to Douglass's wife Anna as well; 'He says that though she cannot read them she will love to look on them.'[35]

Douglass, his heart 'swelling with gratitude', left Cork a few days later, writing a letter of thanks to Dowden from Limerick, the next stop on his journey through Ireland. He was wearing a ring he had been given as a memento: 'I have it on the little finger of my right hand, I never wore one, or had the disposition to do so before, I shall wear this, and prize it as the representative of the holy feelings with which you espoused and advocated my humble cause.'[36]

'A Beautiful Sentimental Air'

With the rail network still in its infancy in Ireland, Douglass would have travelled to Limerick by the traditional coach route, through towns and villages like Charleville, Kilmallock and Bruff. This was good farming country, the east of Limerick lying right at the heart of the Golden Vale, Ireland's premier dairying terrain. With Webb in Dublin and Buffum in England, he was now travelling on his own, forging his own path both literally and metaphorically. Webb's hand, however, was still visible in some of the arrangements, Douglass staying with another of his relatives, Benjamin Clark Fisher, a prosperous sixty-three-year-old Quaker linen draper who had achieved some minor local celebrity when he introduced the first umbrellas into Limerick a few years earlier. Located just outside the city, 'Lifford' was another busy house, a majority of Fisher's twelve children (eleven daughters and one son) still living at home. One of the daughters, Susanna, was particularly active in the local anti-slavery group, her name appearing alongside those of 'Miss E. Poole' in Waterford, 'Mrs Allen' in Dublin and 'The Misses Jennings' in Cork on a list of women to whom donations for the Boston Bazaar could be sent, which was attached to the Dublin edition of the *Narrative*. It was also a beautiful home; another daughter, Rebecca, recalled how as children they kept a veritable menagerie of rabbits, pigeons, guinea pigs, hens, dogs, donkeys and horses in the seven acres of well-tended gardens and lawns.[37]

Although he stayed for nearly two weeks, Douglass has not left any detailed record of his time in Limerick. It was a small city, however, and we can assume he walked pretty much every inch of its streets, most likely in the company of Susanna Fisher or her sisters – the very fact he was not attacked or abused for walking alongside white women a revelation given his experiences in America. He might have started in the handsome Georgian Quarter before moving down through Rutland Street – where Benjamin Clarke Fisher had his shop – to the poorer districts around St Mary's Cathedral and King John's Castle, an area the English novelist William Makepeace Thackeray had described as 'a labyrinth of busy swarming poverty' during a recent tour of Ireland.[38]

Chaired by Benjamin Clarke Fisher, Douglass's first speech in the city took place at the Independent Chapel on Bedford Row on Monday 10 November, the celebrated escaped slave turning his attention almost immediately to the imminent admission of Texas into the Union as another slave state. America was not a true democracy, but a 'bastard republicanism', he declared. Not content with enslaving one sixth of its own population, it wanted to go further, stretching its 'long bony fingers into Mexico, and appropriating her territory ... in order to make it a hotbed of Negro slavery'. Mexico, with all her supposed 'barbarism and darkness', had abolished slavery after winning independence from Spain in the 1820s. It took the 'enlightened' and 'Christian' United States to stain again what had been 'washed' away. Mixing humour with seriousness in the style advised by *The Columbian Orator*, Douglass then raised laughter and cheers with his recollections of events on board the *Cambria* before ending with a flourish, brandishing once again the iron collar and fetters used to torture slaves, and recalling how his master Thomas Auld had whipped his disabled cousin Henny 'until the blood ran down her back' while quoting from the Bible. The meeting dispersed soon after, although not before more copies of the *Narrative* were sold.[39]

During the course of this talk Douglass also addressed some of the criticisms he had received on his travels through the country, in particular the argument that there were 'white slaves' in Ireland, struggling under the yoke of British oppression, who were much more in need of their countrymen's sympathies than black slaves across the ocean. 'When we are ourselves free,' the *Tipperary Free Press* had written, 'let us then engage in any struggle to erase the sin of slavery from every land. But, until then, our own liberation is that for which we should take counsel, and work steadily.'[40]

'But there was nothing like American slavery on the soil on which he now stood,' Douglass retorted strongly, drawing a clear divide between slavery and political oppression for the Limerick audience. 'Negro slavery consisted not in taking away any of the rights of man, but in annihilating them all – not in taking away a man's property, but in making property of him, and in destroying his identity – in treating him as the beasts and creeping things.'

The slave, Douglass continued, was told what to eat, what to drink, what to wear, who to speak to, when to work and even who to marry by his master. 'Could the most inferior person in this country be so treated by the highest?'[41]

This was one of the few times Douglass alluded in any way to Ireland's position under British rule during the tour. With British support deemed vital to the abolitionist cause, American activists were generally careful not to say anything negative about the country, Garrison once again being the iconoclastic exception to the rule and voicing support, for example, for O'Connell's (ultimately unsuccessful) Repeal movement. Garrison had even appropriated O'Connell's language – 'Repeal of the Union' – for his new campaign to get the anti-slavery states to secede from the American Union.[42] Douglass, however, was an unabashed Anglophile, an admirer of Shakespeare, Byron and Dickens whose view of Britain was shaped hugely by the lead it had taken in abolishing slavery in the West Indies. And so, while castigating American expansion into Mexico, Douglass, one writer has noted, 'conveniently overlooked' Britain's own imperialist manoeuvres, not least in the land upon which he then stood.[43]

Douglass was back at the Independent Chapel a few days later, warmly welcomed, no doubt, by the young minister there, Revd John De Kewer Williams, a graduate of Highbury College in London, a dissenting academy with a long anti-slavery tradition.[44] He then found himself surrounded by a host of local dignitaries, businessmen and religious leaders on a platform at the Philosophical Rooms on Glentworth Street for an anti-slavery soirée marking his departure from the city. Following a toast by Mayor Francis P. Russell, Douglass rose to loud cheers from the more than 400-strong audience, praising the Irish people for having helped free the slaves of the West Indies, but also reminding them that there were another 3 million slaves in America seeking their support, crying out 'come and help us'. Nevertheless, this was a shorter, gentler meeting, a celebratory farewell rather than a rallying call, Douglass thanking the city for its hospitality: 'Whether home or abroad he would never forget the very kind manner he was received in Limerick.' The meeting concluded around eleven o'clock with a number of those present singing songs. Buoyed by the convivial mood, Douglass joined in, singing 'a beautiful sentimental air', the name of which, unfortunately, was not furnished in reports.[45]

Douglass left for Dublin the next day, travelling north to Belfast, the last stop on his Irish tour.

'The Chattel Becomes a Man'

Belfast was a city on the rise when Douglass arrived in early December 1845, its thriving port surrounded by linen mills, foundries, warehouses and busy shipbuilding yards. It was also a predominantly Protestant city with a deep attachment to the Act of Union. Like many travellers before him, Douglass was quick to note the differences between the industrially vibrant north and the largely agricultural south. His explanation, however, as to why this was the case was extremely reductionist and crude. Belfast's early adaption to cotton manufacture during the Industrial Revolution and close proximity to the industrial heartlands of Britain – the north of England and central Scotland – do not get a mention. Instead, Douglass blamed religion, food and genes for the south's poverty and apparent backwardness:

> The south is Roman Catholic; its people live mainly on potatoes; and the population is purely Irish ... no people can be strong and flourish upon a single article of diet ... In fact, it does not appear that oneness in population, oneness in the matter of religious belief or oneness in diet is favourable to progress.[46]

Douglass would have been surprised to learn that reliance on the potato was almost as strong in the north as in the south, leading to what has been termed a 'hidden famine' in Belfast a few years later. He was on surer ground discussing slavery, as evidenced by the great success of his talks. 'Well, all my Books went last night at one go,' he wrote delightedly to Webb, the day after his first lecture in Belfast, a talk he had nearly missed owing to snow and ice on the way up from Dublin. 'I want more. I want more,' he continued, the initial run of 2,000 almost sold out and talks already underway for a second edition.[47]

Held before a crowded Independent Chapel on Donegall Street on Friday 5 December, Douglass's first talk in Belfast had begun with a standard recapitulation of his life story. Chaired by the Lord Mayor Andrew Mulholland, a wealthy industrialist, it was then enlivened with an extended, humorous account of his journey across the Atlantic, the crowd roaring with laughter as Douglass mimicked the slaveholders on board saying 'Oh! I wish I had you in New Orleans'. For the benefit of the largely Protestant audience, there was a pointed reference to how 'John Bull' – in the person of Captain Judkins of the *Cambria* – had put the slaveholders in their place. He concluded amidst cheers, imploring the people of Belfast to 'rise up' and 'tell the Americans to tear down their star-spangled banner, and, with its folds, bind up the bleeding wounds of the lacerated slaves'.[48]

Webb dispatched another fifty copies of the *Narrative*, but this was quickly dismissed as inadequate. 'I shall probably sell them all on Tuesday night,' Douglass replied, referring to his planned appearance at the Wesleyan Methodist Church – the fair-minded Methodists of Belfast opening their doors despite letters of warning from co-religionists in Cork and Dublin. He wanted fifty more, at least; sales of the book were so strong that he even had the luxury of buying a new watch, 'a right down good one', for £7 10s, a watch that would last his whole life, a permanent reminder of his journey through Ireland. 'I swell, but I think I shall not burst,' he wrote a little mischievously, aware no doubt of Webb's belief that his success was going to his head.

The letters between Douglass and Webb around this time show relations were still strained. Nevertheless, Douglass promised to take Webb's advice as to being prompter in replying to letters from his supporters. There were also touches of kindness, Douglass asking Webb to thank one of his brothers for the gift of a blanket that had been 'of great service' to him in the northern chill and wishing for a 'speedy deliverance of Mrs Webb and [Webb's son] Richy from their cold'. Douglass had also met Maria Webb, a Quaker cousin of his publisher's in Belfast. Like so many other members of the family, Maria Webb had been in London for the World Anti-Slavery Convention in 1840, describing Garrison at the time as 'one of God's nobility'. She was just as impressed with Douglass, helping establish the Belfast Ladies' Anti-Slavery Society after one of his talks.[49]

Douglass was writing from a comfortable room in the Victoria Hotel on Donegall Street, the central thoroughfare where so many of the churches and meeting houses of the intensely religious city were also found. He was also entertaining – not entirely happily – a constant stream of visitors, the Belfast Anti-Slavery Society putting him up at the hotel instead of someone's home for the express purpose of making him accessible to the public. 'They have gained their purpose thus far ... everyone that hears me seems to think he has a special claim on my time to listen to his opinion of me, to tell me just how much he condemned and how much he approved. Very well, let them come. I am ready for them though it is not the most agreeable.'[50]

Douglass would give several more talks over the Christmas season, the reports of which were mixed in among advertisements for Christmas presents like Charles Dickens's new story *The Cricket on the Hearth* – passages of which, incidentally, were read aloud to the Hutchinsons on Christmas Day in Manchester. Douglass's trenchant attacks on the American Churches had led to something of a smear campaign, with suggestions he was an imposter and not really a slave circulating through the city. The deeply conservative *Banner of Ulster*, founded by the Presbyterian minister Revd William Gibson, also took offence. Mary Ireland, however, a teacher at the Belfast Academical Institution, described how an 'intense interest' had been 'excited' by his oratory, and that there was 'scarcely a lady in Belfast who would not be anxious to join in any means calculated to promote the enfranchisement of the deeply injured Africans'. His *Narrative* was also the inspiration for a poem by Frances Brown – 'The Blind Poetess of Ulster' – called 'The Land of the Slave'.[51]

Douglass sailed for Scotland during the first week of 1846, carrying a beautiful new gilt-edged Bible – a 'golden gift', as he called it, from the Belfast Anti-Slavery Society – together with a newfound sense of self. 'I seem to have undergone a transformation,' he wrote to Garrison of his time in Ireland. 'I live a new life.' Douglass had been away from America for four and a half months, and although there were times when he thought fondly of her 'bright blue sky ... grand old woods ... fertile fields ... beautiful rivers ... mighty lakes ... and star-crowned mountains', such reveries never lasted long, the escaped slave remembering how 'with the waters of her noblest rivers', the tears of his 'brethren' were 'borne to the ocean', while her 'most fertile fields' drank daily 'of the warm blood of my outraged sisters'. In the South, Douglass wrote, he had been a slave, 'thought of and spoken of as property'. In the North he had been a fugitive slave, liable to be 'hunted at any moment like a felon' and hurled back into the 'terrible jaws' of slavery. 'But now behold the change!' Douglass exclaimed. 'Eleven days and a half gone, and I have crossed three thousand miles of the perilous deep. Instead of a democratic government, I am under a monarchical government. Instead of the bright blue sky of America, I am covered with the soft grey fog of the Emerald Isle. I breathe, and lo! the chattel becomes a man.'[52]

3

'SEND BACK THE MONEY'

'It is quite an advantage to be a nigger here,' Frederick Douglass wrote from Scotland in late January 1846. 'I find I am hardly black enough for British taste, but by keeping my hair as woolly as possible I make out to pass for at least a half a Negro at any rate.' The easy, jocular tone came from the confidence he felt at having made a real mark on the country in so short a time. 'Old Scotland boils like a pot,' he declared proudly. The reason? The powerful new catchcall with which he was assailing the Free Church of Scotland: 'Send Back the Money.'[1]

Thomas Chalmers, the sixty-five-year-old leader of the Free Church, an evangelical Presbyterian denomination that had recently broken away from the Church of Scotland in a schism known as the 'Great Disruption', was a deeply moral, intellectual man, regarded by James McCosh, the philosopher, Free Church minister and future president of Princeton University, as the greatest preacher the country ever produced, his followers carried along to the close of his sermons 'by a torrent which they could not resist, and to which they enthusiastically yielded'. Dedicated to alleviating the plight – physical and spiritual – of the urban poor in Scotland, he had also written a pamphlet criticising slavery in the West Indies. Chalmers's preference, however, had been for gradual rather than immediate emancipation of the slaves, emphasising the 'sacredness' of property in British law. It is unsurprising, therefore, that he had little hesitation in accepting tens of thousands of dollars in donations from slaveholding states when the newly established Free Church embarked on fundraising campaigns among Presbyterians in America in late 1844, the monies needed to build new churches and look after the almost 500 ministers and their families who had given up their positions in the established church on a point of principle – the issue, essentially, of how much influence the state should wield in church affairs. 'I do not need to assure you how little I sympathise with those who – because slavery happens to prevail in the Southern States of America – would unchristianise that whole region,' he informed a correspondent in South Carolina.[2]

Abolitionists on both sides of the Atlantic were appalled, believing the Free Church's actions gave succour to the slaveholding South at a time when they were attempting to isolate and ostracise the region. Chalmers, a former Professor of Divinity at the University of Edinburgh among other prestigious posts, responded in a formal letter stating: 'Slavery, like war, is a great evil ... Yet destructive and demoralising as both are ... it follows not that there may not be a Christian soldier, and neither does it follow that there may not be a Christian slaveholder.' A number of anti-slavery societies republished Chalmers's letter in order to refute it, including the Belfast Anti-Slavery Society. Indeed, it had been in Belfast that Douglass first addressed the Free Church issue, the deep religious links between that city and Scotland ensuring a lot of support for Chalmers and, subsequently, disquiet when the escaped slave implored him to 'send back the blood-stained money'.[3]

Douglass would carry these words across to Scotland, his tour of the country beginning in Glasgow – the port city on the River Clyde that had perhaps benefited most from the country's involvement in the slave trade while at the same time doing the greatest amount to bring about its abolition.

'Sterling Anti-Slavery Men'
Although a few high-profile legal cases, including that of Joseph Knight, the slave whose quest for freedom culminated in the ruling abolishing slavery in Scotland in 1778, brought the

experiences of some of their number into the public sphere, the majority of slaves in Scotland lived lives on the margins.[4] Small in number and brought over for the most part from the West Indies, they worked as domestic servants, cooks and coopers, usually only coming to attention when they ran away or were about to be sold, like nineteen-year-old 'Peggy' – 'a good house wench and washer and dresser' – advertised for sale in the *Edinburgh Evening Courant* in 1766 together with her infant child.[5] Their stories, however, were but one manifestation of Scotland's long relationship with slavery, especially in the century between the Act of Union in 1707 – which officially opened up the colonies to Scots merchants and entrepreneurs – and the abolition of the slave trade in 1807, years when tens of thousands of Scots, mostly young men, crossed the Atlantic, covering the land of first the tobacco-rich Chesapeake and then the sugar islands of the Caribbean with names they carried from home.

Compared with the thousands of journeys begun from English ports like Liverpool and Bristol, the number of ships leaving Scotland to participate directly in the ferrying of captured Africans across the Atlantic was relatively minor, about 30 over the course of the eighteenth century, carrying 4,000–5,000 slaves in total. Nevertheless, slavery and the slave trade seeped into every aspect of Scottish life, every strata of Scottish society: from the penurious highland youth forced to work as an indentured servant in the West Indies only to die from some tropical disease within a year to the politician Henry Dundas, whose efforts in support of the pro-slavery lobby in the 1790s helped kill off the anti-slave trade campaign for a generation; from the rum-soaked slave drivers utterly dehumanised by constant recourse to the whip to Janet Schaw, the self-proclaimed 'Lady of Quality', cataloguing in inane detail the meals prepared for her during a tour of Antigua and St Kitts while blithely dismissing the suffering endured by the slaves; and from the legions of professionals 'seduced', as Sir Tom Devine has put it, by the reputation of the slave colonies for making easy money to plantation owners like George Munro raping twelve-year-old slaves in Berbice (part of modern-day Guyana).[6]

Slavery created macabre scenes on the coast of Africa, where the Scottish slave trader Richard Oswald fitted out his fort, or 'slave factory', on Bunce Island in Sierra Leone with its own small golf course, forcing the African caddies to dress in tartan loincloths. Back home, it bought vast estates for families like the slave-trading Malcolms of Poltalloch, before being invested in more respectable businesses like shipyards and insurance. It also transformed cities across the country, the trade in tobacco, sugar, cotton and rum turning Glasgow, in particular – 'proclaimed that they were built by money wrung out of the blood and sweat of the negroes of Jamaica, St Vincents, etc.' – into a thrusting crush of shipyards, factories, foundries and engineering works so that by the time of Douglass's visit it had strong claim to the title of 'Second City of the Empire'.[7]

Douglass stayed with William Smeal, a prosperous fifty-three-year-old Quaker grocer who lived in the Gallowgate area of the city, not far from the grand townhouses of wealthy merchants that lined the riverfront, including those of the families of the old 'tobacco lords' who had made their fortunes before the American Revolution, when Glasgow was the centre of the world's tobacco trade. He was just as close to the squalid tenements that were a near-inevitable corollary to the rapid growth and economic success of so many of Britain's leading industrial cities, Glasgow's infrastructure failing abysmally to keep pace with a rapidly rising population as people came from the surrounding countryside and further afield in search of work, one official report describing it as perhaps the filthiest city in the kingdom. Douglass would not have been spared the squalor as he was shown around the city by Smeal and other 'sterling anti-slavery men' like Andrew Paton, a forty-one-year-old businessman who had earlier been deeply involved in the agitation for the era-defining Reform Act.[8]

A bespectacled, frock-coated figure carrying a walking stick in a picture taken in the 1860s, Smeal, his nose disfigured either from birth of through some unknown accident, had been deeply involved in the anti-slavery scene for many years, publishing pamphlets on the topic and attending the World Anti-Slavery Convention in London in 1840. He had earlier helped found the

Glasgow Anti-Slavery Society in 1822, the effort to bring about the abolition of slavery in the West Indies reigniting a movement that had lain dormant from the high point of 1807, mainly because of the Napoleonic Wars and the major social upheaval of the post-war years. His brother Robert – with whom he published the Quaker monthly the *British Friend* – and daughter Jane were also involved in the campaign, the Glasgow group proving itself one of the most active societies in Britain in the decade leading up to the abolition of slavery in the West Indies.

Although Quakers had been unusually absent from Scotland's leading anti-slavery lights before the Smeals, the country had still played a vital role in the late eighteenth-century anti-slave trade campaign, the philosophers Adam Smith and David Hume giving firm moral and economic foundations to the growing anti-slavery mood of the time and the Inveraray-born Zachary Macaulay, a one-time book-keeper at a sugar plantation in Jamaica, becoming an important ally of William Wilberforce and Thomas Clarkson. Father of the writer and historian Thomas Babbington Macaulay, the elder Macaulay was a particularly strong influence on John Murray – or 'honest John Murray' as Douglass called him.[9] A tall, gaunt figure in his fifties by the time the famous escaped slave made his acquaintance, Murray, like Macaulay, had witnessed slavery up close, travelling to the West Indies for his health and working as a builder in St Kitts for several years before returning to Scotland 'poor in pocket, but rich in abolitionism'.

Married to his childhood sweetheart Anna and working variously as a spirits merchant and surveyor for the Forth and Clyde Canal before settling down as collector of canal dues in Bowling Bay near Glasgow while raising three children, Murray had been an important member of the Glasgow Anti-Slavery Society. With Smeal, he was then to the fore of the establishment of its more radical successor, the Glasgow Emancipation Society, in late 1833, their attention turning to the problem of slavery the world over at a time when many other anti-slavery organisations across Britain and Ireland were starting to dissolve, considering their work complete with emancipation in the West Indies.[10]

William Lloyd Garrison was another major influence on Murray, the power of his trenchant articles, editorials and pamphlets convincing the leading members of the Glasgow Emancipation Society to focus their attention on America, in the belief that it was there that the biggest blow against worldwide slavery could be struck. This was not a popular stance in a city whose large textiles industry depended on slave-grown cotton from the southern states. Pro-slavery forces were still strong, not least in the business community and newspapers like the tri-weekly *Glasgow Courier*, edited for much of the 1820s and 1830s by James McQueen, a former overseer at the Westerhall plantation in Grenada, and William Motherwell, a staunchly conservative poet and antiquarian who attacked Catholic emancipation and the Reform Act with as much vigour as he assailed abolitionists. McQueen, a skilled polemicist, had also taken on the influential liberal monthly the *Edinburgh Review*, accusing it of spreading lies and misinformation in his pamphlet *The West India Colonies*, a work with which the Barbadian legislature was so pleased they awarded him £500 for defending West Indian interests.[11]

The close connection between Scottish and American Churches also saw many significant Glaswegian figures who had supported the abolition of slavery in the West Indies keep their distance from the new society, a trend that became more pronounced after the split in American anti-slavery circles in the early 1840s and Garrison's unwavering insistence on 'No Fellowship with Slaveholders'. Garrison, by this stage, would have received positive reports about the Glasgow abolitionists from James McCune Smith, the free black doctor who had studied in the city. Smith was the first African-American ever to earn a medical degree, sailing over to the University of Glasgow – an institution with a proud history of accepting students based on talent rather than background – as a precociously talented nineteen-year-old after being rejected by a number of American universities. Heavily involved during his sojourn in the city with the Glasgow Emancipation Society, whose members helped fund his education, Smith joined the American Anti-Slavery Society as soon as he returned home in 1837. Garrison cemented the alliance between the two groups in 1840, travelling up to Glasgow after attending the World Anti Slavery Convention. He was greeted warmly and it was not long before Catherine Paton, sister of Andrew, was sending over boxes of materials for the Boston Bazaar.[12]

In later years, Smith would author a warm memorial to Murray, the 'great friend of the slave' who 'never made a speech of one minute long', preferring instead to work unheralded in the background, writing reports and organising meetings.[13] Douglass had no such qualms about standing forth before the public, taking to the stage of the recently built Glasgow City Halls on the evening of Thursday 15 January. Introduced by the Revd George Jeffrey, who had just read his *Narrative* that day, Douglass told the crowd he was glad to be in Scotland, 'where no blood-hound could be set upon his track'. In America, that so-called 'land of the free' and 'home of the brave', there was not one spot on which he could stand without fear of capture. 'Wherever the twenty-six stars [signifying the twenty-six states that made up the United States at this time] shone on the blue ground of the American flag, there he was liable to be made a slave … There was no mountain so high, no valley so deep, and no spot so sacred as to give security to the slave.' Even at Bunker Hill, he told his audience, the site of the battle that was such a potent symbol of American freedom, he was liable to 'be secured and dragged back to the man who claimed to hold him as his property'.

Douglass turned next to Sir Charles Lyell, the highly esteemed Scottish professor of geology whose recently published account of a tour of the United States had emphasised the 'cheerful' nature of the well-fed slaves.[14] Lyell, a friend and teacher of Charles Darwin, had stayed in the grand homes of several wealthy slave-owners, walking the plantations with the refined ladies of the houses and dining at their full tables where he was served by well-dressed slaves. His 'love' of these slave-owners, Douglass argued, had 'misled' him as to the true character of slavery. 'He spoke of the contentment and happiness of the slaves,' Douglass scoffed. 'He might as well speak of the happiness and contentment of the drunkard lying in the ditch.' Douglass would criticise Lyell, whom he accused of trying 'to throw a mask over slavery', in a number of other speeches. His attacks met with some success, the *Southern Literary Messenger*, a monthly arts review published in Richmond, Virginia, and edited at one stage by a young Edgar Allan Poe, noting a few years later how the professor's travelogues did not find much favour in Britain, as they did not appeal to the 'Frederick-Douglass philanthropists'.[15]

Playing on the intense religiosity that coursed through Scottish society, Douglass next described how the 'slave-mother, for teaching her child the letters which composed the Lord's Prayer, could be hung up by the neck till she was dead', remarks that brought forth fervent shouts of 'Shame'. As to the question of why he had travelled over to the British Isles, he answered that 'England and Scotland had something to do in the enslaving of his race' and so he had come over to 'ask them to lend a hand in destroying' the system they had helped set up. More positively, he said he wanted to 'encircle' America 'with a cordon of Anti-Slavery feeling – bounding it by Canada on the north, Mexico on the West, and England, Scotland and Ireland on the east, so that wherever the slaveholder went he might hear nothing but denunciations of slavery, that he might be looked down upon as a man-stealing, cradle-robbing and woman-stripping monster and that he might see reproof and detestation on every hand'.

Towards the end of his two-hour talk, Douglass alluded to how the Churches in America were guilty of supporting slavery, how the ministers 'held the keys of the dungeon in which the slave was confined'. He did not, however, discuss the Free Church at this widely publicised first major public appearance in Scotland, which was more of an introduction to the abominable realities of slavery in America. That would change during the next stage of what would turn out to be an almost five-month tour of the country.[16]

'Their Hands are Full of Blood'
From Glasgow, Douglass made his way north-east through wintry countryside to Perth, a large town in the shadows of the Ochil Hills that had become something of a draw for literary-minded tourists since the publication of Walter Scott's *The Fair Maid of*

Perth (1828), one of the last instalments in the writer's Waverley series of novels, a number of which, including *Rob Roy*, contained subtle references to Scotland's role in the slave trade. Although not on the tourist trail, Douglass was a huge admirer of the great Scottish author who had died in 1832. The connection, of course, went deeper still, with one of the characters in Scott's 1815 poem *The Lady of the Lake* – 'the black Douglas' – providing the inspiration for the escaped slave's name.

Douglass was travelling with James Buffum, the pair having made amends in a series of letters over Christmas 1845. They were soon joined by another American, Henry C. Wright, a forty-eight-year-old former missionary turned radical abolitionist and pacifist who had spent much of the previous two years touring the British Isles trying to generate support for Garrison's 'disunion' campaign, whereby the anti-slavery states would secede from the Union. Douglass had known the somewhat cantankerous Wright in America. Nevertheless, in a move seen as a step away from the Garrisonian fold, he had rejected the opportunity to combine efforts with him in Ireland a few months earlier, informing his Irish publisher Richard D. Webb that 'I by no means agree with him [Wright] as to the importance of discussing in this country the disunion question, and I think our difference in this matter would prevent that harmony necessary to success.'[17] The Free Church, however, was an issue on which they could – and would – work well together.

Wright, the author of innumerable books and pamphlets, including *A Kiss for a Blow*, a collection of stories designed to teach children how to resolve quarrels with acts of love and kindness, had actually been touring the small towns and villages around Perth just before meeting up with Douglass, declaring the area a 'strong hold of the Nons, as the Frees are here called'. He had also coined the phrase 'Send Back the Money' long before Douglass arrived in the country and may have been annoyed at the way it only captured the public imagination when uttered by the famous escaped slave. If so, he hid his feelings well, extolling Douglass's value to the cause in a letter to the *Liberator* after a series of four anti-slavery meetings – including one said to have been held before an audience of 3,000 – had left Perth 'thoroughly convulsed'.[18] Such open letters, however, like Douglass's own vivid communiqués across the Atlantic, were minor propaganda pieces in themselves, written for public consumption and determined to show the movement in its best light.

A few days later, the abolitionist trio were in Dundee, a city on the east coast of the country whose rapidly growing textile industry was the subject of regular comment in its papers, with flax of 'good quality and colour' commanding a 'full price' around this time. It was also an industry heavily dependent on poorly paid women and children labouring long into the night. Indeed, it was probably some of these penurious workers the *Dundee, Perth and Cuper Advertiser* of 30 January had in mind when it complained about the 'neglect' on the part of many parents in failing to get their children vaccinated for smallpox despite a recent outbreak in the city, the paper failing to take into account the simple lack of time such constant toil left for visits to the local infirmary. Less dangerous than smallpox but still worthy of complaint in the same day's paper were the poorly fastened window shutters that made shopping or even walking down footpaths a hazardous enterprise on many streets; another column, meanwhile, carrying news of the publican John Watt being sentenced to twenty days' imprisonment for 'keeping an uproarious house'.

Although Douglass stayed at the Royal Hotel in the centre of the city, it is also likely he spent time with supportive ministers like the Revd George Gilfillan of the United Secession Church, yet another of the myriad Presbyterian denominations in Scotland. A friend of Edinburgh-based Thomas De Quincey, author of the controversial but influential *Confessions of an English Opium-Eater*, the still just thirty-three-year-old Gilfillan was a prolific writer himself, especially of poems and works of literary criticism. Conscious of the manner in which authors like Lyell attempted to sanitise the image of slavery, Gilfillan would go on to author a pamphlet that argued no number of 'good' masters could ever mitigate its horrors. However, he was equally keen to show that slavery could not break the human spirit of the slaves, stating: 'You have seen in Frederick Douglass a man whom slavery has not nipped.'[19]

Douglass delivered four talks during this stay in Dundee, the first two of which were so 'fearfully crowded' the remainder had to be ticketed. Framing his comments once again to the Scripture-loving sentiments of his audience, Douglass began his 30 January lecture at the Bell Street United Presbyterian Chapel with an extended quote from the Bible (Isaiah: 4–20), an excoriating passage that went in part: 'And when ye spread forth your hands, I will hide mine eyes from you: yea, when ye make many prayers, I will not hear: your hands are full of blood.' Revelling in the vividness of that final phrase, he went on to declare: 'I should find it impossible to draw a more graphic picture of the state of the Churches in the United States than is drawn in these lines from the holy prophet Isaiah ... Their hands are full of blood.' All the Churches, he said, were guilty. His main targets that evening, however, were the leaders of the Free Church, who had come 'from this land, the inhabitants of which are distinguished by their love of freedom – a land whose every hill has been made classic by heroic deeds performed by her noble sons – a land whose every brook and river carry the songs of freedom as they pass to the ocean' to collect money to build churches from those whose hands were 'full of blood'. The ordinary Free Church members, he hoped, when 'they looked up to their meeting-houses and reflected that they were built with the price of blood, would yet compel their clergy to send back the blood stained money'.

Towards the end of the speech, Douglass held up a copy of the *New Orleans Picayune* from the summer of 1845 that contained a positive passage on Chalmers (*The Columbian Orator* having long ago placed a premium on such gestures). He then turned the page, contrasting the panegyric on Chalmers, 'the eloquent Scotch divine', with the reward notice for two runaway slaves:

Phil, aged about 40 years, dark complexion; has a deep scar on (perhaps) his left hand, and a piece off one ear.
   Sam, aged about 20 years; has a scar on his chin, several lumps on his neck and back, and walks rather lame.

It was with the owners of these unfortunate slaves, Douglass declared, that Chalmers 'had struck hands ... in Christian fellowship', the attack on the Free Church finally beginning in earnest. He then concluded to great cheers: 'Let the people of Scotland arise, and show the Free Church that they did not represent them. Let the voice of public opinion compel that church to send back the money.'[20]

Amidst the cheers there were also a few hisses, Dundee home to the forty-two-year-old Revd George Lewis, one of the most popular and prominent Free Church leaders. The main figure in the fundraising tour, Lewis had actually condemned slavery as 'the foul spot in the condition of the United States' in his account of his journey, words Buffum would delight in quoting back in other meetings. Lewis even went so far as to write: 'We have no hesitation in pronouncing slaveholding a sin, and calling on all slaveholders to abandon it.' Nevertheless, whether from genuine belief or mere tactical expediency in light of the Free Church's acceptance of money from slaveholders, he went on to assert that 'we have as little [hesitation] in pronouncing those men foolish and unwise who would proscribe and cast out of the Church those who, like Abraham, have been born and bred to the evil'.[21]

To Douglass, this was mere sophistry, similar to the efforts of those who sought Biblical justification for slavery in the story of St Paul returning the runaway slave Onemisus to his master (Philemon 1:10–16) or in the oft-repeated claim of Chalmers that slaveholders in the South were compelled by law to hold onto their slaves. This last assertion was utterly untrue, even if many slave states – especially in the Deep South – made manumission an awkward and expensive legal process and even put responsibility for the good behaviour of freed slaves on their former masters or forced former slaves to leave the state within a certain period of time of being freed.

'A Voice on Thunder Borne'

After a comfortable stay at the Royal Hotel in Dundee, Douglass and Buffum travelled further up the east coast to Arbroath, another town built largely around the textile industry, though fishing and shipping were also on the rise following the recent construction of a new harbour. Arriving on the afternoon of Tuesday 10 February, they found the local churches closed to them, the ministers wary of the emerging controversy caused by the heavy criticisms of the Free Church. Unperturbed, Douglass spoke at the Trades Hall before what the *Arbroath Guide* claimed to be 'hundreds of townspeople', one of whom, James Anderson, a businessman and lay religious leader, was so impressed that he interrupted the talk to offer the escaped slave the use of the town's Abbey Church.

'I am here to speak for those who cannot speak for themselves, to plead the cause of the perishing slave, and to arouse the energies, excite the sympathies, and obtain the aid and co-operation of the good people of old Scotland in behalf of what I believe to be a righteous cause – the breaking of every yoke, the undoing of heavy burdens, and letting the oppressed go free,' Douglass declared before a 'densely crowded' Abbey Church a few nights later, naming during the course of the speech a number of ministers from various religious denominations who supported him, including one, Dr Michael Willis, from the Free Church. Willis, however, a member of the Glasgow Emancipation Society, was the exception to the rule in a Free Church leadership cadre that focused in the main on seeking justifications for their actions, or 'lowering the standard of Christianity', as Douglass perceived it, 'so that the vilest thief, the foulest murderer ... may claim to be a Christian'. It was this heresy, he said, that now held 'in chains three millions of men, women and children in the United States', going on to demand that 'as light can have no union with darkness' so 'a Free Church should have no fellowship with a slave church'. He closed the meeting, the admiring *Guide* reported, by making the 'welkin' ring with shouts of 'Send Back the Money' from the audience.[22]

From Arbroath, Douglass set off on a criss-cross tour of Scotland that lasted all through the spring. Travelling usually with Buffum or Wright, he delivered sometimes near-nightly speeches – usually free – at Montrose, Ayr, Greenock and numerous other towns and villages, sharing stages with mayors, religious ministers and business leaders. In Aberdeen, the reaction was similar to Arbroath, the people wary at first – Douglass recording that they were 'as hard as the granite of which their houses are built' – but then flocking to hear him speak. In Ayr, the Cathcart Street Church was 'crowded in every part', pews and passages alike heaving with people. In Paisley, he filled the Abbey Close Church several nights over before speaking until near midnight at the Exchange Rooms during another visit, his praise of key British anti-slavery figures like Wilberforce and Clarkson eliciting loud cheers – though, as has been noted, the fact that he did not mention prominent Scotch abolitionists like William Dickson, James Stephen and Zachary Macaulay shows perhaps a gap in his knowledge of the history of the movement.[23]

Addressing crowds that could reach into the thousands, Douglass was no ordinary travelling speaker. Nor was his tour any ordinary tour, the *Arbroath Guide*, for example, stating that the 'sensation' created by his speeches had 'rarely if ever' been surpassed. The simple fact that he was discussing religion, a subject at the core of the nineteenth-century Scottish soul, was one of the reasons for his success, the 'Send Back the Money' campaign benefitting from the still-raw controversy caused by the establishment of the Free Church, a genuinely momentous event that split families, friends and communities. The *Dundee Courier* attributed the large turnout at his first talks in that city in part to 'the novelty of a slave addressing a Scottish audience'. More than that, however, he was a dominating physical presence and a poised and polished performer able to bring audiences close to tears with graphic accounts of whippings but also get their spirits to soar with pulsating oratory that convinced his listeners they had a genuine part to play in the freeing of three million slaves in America, that actions in Greenock, Galashiels or Kelso could reverberate through the plantations of Virginia, Louisiana and Georgia. He certainly pricked the conscience of the anonymous Dundee woman who wrote a reproachful letter to Chalmers thanking 'God in Mercy' for sending 'these men [Douglass and Buffum] to shew me my transgressions, by telling me what my sisters are suffering pent up in chains, bloodhounds their guardians, iron collars their necklaces, whips instead of the strong arm of a man to lean on or ward off ill'.[24]

It was not long before Douglass's efforts were celebrated in verse, an eight-page booklet of poems and song inspired by his tour being published in Edinburgh around this time. One such poem included the following lines:

Send back the Money! Send it back!
'Tis dark polluted gold;
'Twas wrung from human flesh and bones,
By agonies untold:
There's not a mite in all the sum
But what is stained with blood;
There's not a mite in all the sum
But what is cursed of God.

A song entitled 'O For Good Luck To Our Coffers', meanwhile, had a verse that went:

The worthy Free Priest was pleas'd to allow,
That all the Slaveholders were Christians now;
The Doctor he bless'd them for what they had paid,
And wish'd them success in their Slaveholding trade.

Another, based on old Scottish tune 'My Boy Tammy', imagined a scene between 'Tammy' – Thomas Chalmers – and 'Mother Kirk'. Written in the colloquial style, one verse alluded directly to Douglass:

I've heard a voice on thunder borne,
My Boy Tammy;
I've seen the fingers rais'd in scorn,
My Boy Tammy;
Heaven rings wi' DOUGLASS' appeal,
An' thrills my heart like burnin' stell,
An' conscience racks me on the wheel,
You've wranged – ye've grie'd your Mammy![25]

Douglass's speeches during this part of the tour touched on many issues, including the recent annexation of the Republic of Cracow, the last vestige of an independent Poland, by the 'bloody and despotic' powers of Austria, Russia and Prussia, an act roundly condemned by liberals across Britain and to which he had been clearly paying attention.[26] In another, Douglass noted the more personally pertinent fact that Thomas Auld, a private man wearying of being caught up in public controversy, had signed over his ownership of the troublesome slave to his brother Hugh, who had apparently promised to 'spare no pains or expense' to regain possession of his 'poor property'.[27] The speeches always came back, however, to the Free Church, Douglass describing, for example, to a 1,200-strong audience at a ticketed talk at George's Chapel in Dundee the scene if that city's own George Lewis – whom Douglass had challenged to a public debate – had paid a call to the Eastern Shore home of his then-master Thomas Auld during the Free Church's fundraising tour in 1844:

Sir, I can almost imagine I see Brother Lewis calling on the slaveholder. I can almost go down south, and see him, when I was a slave, calling on my old master, Mr Thomas Auld (who would be a very likely party to call on), with his subscription paper. When Brother Lewis knocks at the door, I answer, and he asks, 'Well, my lad, is your master in?' (Laughter.) 'Yes, Sir.' Well, he walks into the house, sees my master, and introduces himself thus (for my ear would be at the keyhole immediately on the door being shut) – 'My object in making this call this morning is to see if you would do something for the cause of religious freedom in Scotland. We have been labouring some time back, and have undergone severe struggles, for Gospel freedom in Scotland, and we have thought it right to call upon you, as a benevolent man and as having means to bestow, to see what you can do for us.' My master would reply, 'Brother Lewis, I deeply sympathise with your efforts; and as I see the cause recommended by Deacon such-a-one, I would like to have my name down with his. I'll tell you what I will do. I have a fine young Negro who is to be sold, and I will sell him tomorrow and give you a contribution to the cause of freedom … Come about nine o'clock, brother, and I will see what I can do for the cause of freedom in Scotland.' (Laughter and cheering.)

The morning comes, and the breakfast hour, and Brother Lewis also. (I have a son named Lewis, but I think I'll change his name.) (Applause.) The Bible is given to Brother Lewis, and he reads, 'Blessed are the poor in spirit – Blessed are they that give to the poor,' and so on. All goes on delightfully. Brother Lewis prays, and after prayer sits down and partakes of the bounties produced by the blood of the slave, watered by the sweat and enriched by the blood of the half-famished Negro. (Applause.) Brother Auld orders the carriage to be brought round to the door – I am tied to the carriage and taken away, as I have seen often done: I am on the auction block, and the auctioneer is crying 'Who bids for this comely stout young Negro? He is accustomed to his work, and has an excellent trade on his hands.' Well, 500 dollars are bid. Oh, how Brother Lewis's eyes twinkle! (Laughter.) The auctioneer continues – 'This is not half the value of the Negro; he is not sold for any bad quality. His master has no desire to get rid of him, but only wants to get a little money to aid the cause of religious freedom in Scotland.' (Laughter.) Another flame of light from Brother Lewis's eyes. 600 hundred dollars are bid. Once, twice, thrice, is said by the auctioneer, and I am sold for 600 dollars.

The speech nearing its conclusion, Douglass turned mantra-like to the invocation 'Send Back the Money' in his denunciations of the Free Church and the excuses they lined up for slaveholders:

When the Free Church says – Did not Abraham hold slaves? The reply should be, Send back the money! (Cheers.) When they ask did not Paul send back Onesimus? I answer, Send you back that money! (Great cheering.) That is the only answer which should be given to their sophistical [sic] arguments, and it is one which they cannot get over. (Great cheering.) In order to justify their conduct, they endeavour to forget that they are a Church, and speak as if they were a manufacturing corporation. They forget that a Church is not for making money, but for spreading the Gospel. We are guilty, say they, but these merchants are guilty, and some other parties are guilty also. I say, Send back that money! (Cheering.) There is music in that sound. (Great cheering.) There is poetry in it.[28]

'A Glib-Tongued Scoundrel'

'The agitation goes nobly on ... The very boys in the street are singing out "*Send back that money*,"' Douglass had written triumphantly to Webb after one of his first talks in Dundee, the uneasy pair maintaining links on account of preparations for a new edition of *Narrative*, the first of which had almost sold out, earning, the publisher estimated, upwards of £150 for its author, a hugely significant amount, albeit one that had to support both Douglass in Britain and his family in America. The reaction, however, was not all positive, the conservative *Scottish Guardian* calling him 'the black' and sneering that if 'American slavery' was abolished 'tomorrow' and the abolitionists lost their 'trade' Douglass would have to return 'to his more important duties as a chimney sweeper'. Another writer, having already derided Douglass's audiences as 'old women of both sexes', went on to wonder disbelievingly if the escaped slave's demand for the Free Church to send back its money should extend to all the Scottish plantation owners and businessmen who had made fortunes from slavery and the slave trade, a comment that brings to mind the ongoing debate about the need for Britain to pay reparations to Caribbean countries like Jamaica. The Free Church leaders had also gone on the attack, the Revd John MacNaughton of Paisley calling him an 'ignorant runaway slave, who had picked up a few sentences which he was pleased to retail up and down the country' before expressing surprise that the citizens of the town had paid to hear him speak. The Free Church also got its paper, the *Northern Warder*, to accuse Douglass of being in 'the pay' of the Church of Scotland, 'sent for and hired by them', a charge the escaped slave robustly denied, stating explicitly at the beginning of several talks that he had no intention of offering any opinion as to the right or the wrong of the establishment of the Free Church.[29]

'For the purpose of disparaging my mission and invalidating my testimony, the grossest representations and the darkest insinuations have been resorted to on the part of the great defender of the Free Church, the *Northern Warder*,' Douglass told an audience in Dundee, the city in which the paper – an eight-page weekly costing 4½d – had been established in early 1841, right in the midst of the tense religious disputes that would give rise to the 'Great Disruption'. Denied a right of reply in its columns, he hit back from the lectern. He had support from the *Dundee Courier*, whose editor accused his counterpart at the *Warder* of having 'Jesuitised desperately, and tortured Scripture cruelly, to prove the innocence of the Free Church in the matter of the slave-money', the two newspapers carrying over a rivalry that had begun on religion into a new sphere, the *Warder*, for its part, labelling the *Courier* the 'literary common-sewer' of the city. 'The *Courier* will be read on the other side of the Atlantic with the warmest emotions of gratitude by the Abolitionists,' Douglass declared, 'and while the *Warder* may congratulate itself on the support it gains to the Free Church from human fleshmongers, a more satisfactory compensation will be afforded to my excellent friend the Editor of the *Courier* by the warmest gratitude of three millions of bondsmen.'[30]

'I remember, when a little boy of only a few years, passing along the streets with my father one Sunday on his way to Gilfillans Church … and seeing on the walls large posters bearing the words "Send Back the Money!"' wrote Thomas Yule Miller, a journalist in later years at the *Courier*. 'What these words meant puzzled me, and in reply to my query my father said the Free Kirk ministers had run away with money which did not belong to them,' the author continued, the clear recollection of the scene more than sixty years after its occurrence a sign of the impression Douglass's campaign had made on the country.[31] He was making an impression further afield, too, an anti-slavery supporter from Bristol writing in mid-February: 'We are looking forward with great interest to a visit from Frederick Douglass next month; he seems to be exciting a great sensation wherever he appears.' Eager by this stage to hear Douglass for themselves, abolitionists south of the border would have to wait longer than expected, Buffum explaining:

'We make slow headway – we are detained in the place where we go much longer than we expected, owing to the increased interest in the question of the Free Church and its taking the slaveholders' money.'[32]

America, too, was getting caught up in Douglass's tour, the *New York Herald*, the incredibly popular tabloid, and the *New York Daily Express*, edited by the future Congressman James Brooks, 'denouncing me as a glib-tongued scoundrel' for attacking the country's institutions before foreign audiences, the escaped slave told a crowd in Paisley. Support, however, came from Horace Greeley, founder and editor of the *New York Tribune*, one of the great newspapers of the time. Douglass replied from Glasgow, thanking Greeley for the 'deep and lively interest' he had taken in 'the cause of my long neglected race'.[33]

Douglass was also corresponding with Maria Weston Chapman in Boston around this time, confidently asserting in a letter in late March that she would soon see 'proof' of his success in an increased number of donations for the next Boston Bazaar. The main thrust of this letter, however, was his anger with her for instructing Webb to, in Douglass's words, keep a 'watch' over him, lest he be 'bought up by the London committee', a reference to the well-funded British and Foreign Anti-Slavery Society, the organisation behind the World Anti-Slavery Convention in 1840 and to which the anti-Garrisonian American and Foreign Anti-Slavery Society, as its name suggests, was closely aligned. 'If you wish to drive me from the Anti-Slavery Society, put me under overseership and the work is done,' he warned, deliberately using terminology with clear connotations of masters and slaves.[34]

Douglass had probably learned of this injunction while still in Dublin, Webb, as was his somewhat injudicious habit, reading aloud letters from abolitionists in America to his small circle of anti-slavery friends without checking them beforehand. If so, it is unclear as to why the escaped slave held his counsel for so long. Perhaps it was only with the success of the tour of Scotland that he felt confident enough to snap back at one of the major figures in the movement, the firm and flinty Chapman, a recently widowed merchant banker's wife who had been deeply involved in abolition since the early 1830s, her 'silvery voice and blonde ringlets', one writer noting, making her seem more a 'socialite' than the 'shrewd commander' she would prove to be during many tense stand-offs with anti-abolitionist mobs around New England.[35] Whatever the reason for the delay, the incident hurt Douglass deeply, dealing a significant blow to his trust in the American Anti-Slavery Society and its white Boston grandees.

'I Used To Think I Was a President'

Douglass had written to Chapman from the town of Kilmarnock – the home of Johnnie Walker, the man behind the famous whiskey – in late March. A day later he was back in Paisley, travelling the 20 miles to deliver a well-attended talk entitled 'Temperance and Anti-Slavery' at the town's Secession Church. Although still somewhat wary of distracting from the anti-slavery cause by speaking publicly on other subjects – especially as the clarity of his 'Send Back the Money' message had proven so effective – Douglass made an exception for temperance, the two movements long synonymous with each other on both sides of the Atlantic. In America, indeed, there was a sense that temperance was essential to black elevation. 'Wherever it can be said that the free blacks are a sober, industrious and intelligent people, capable of self-government, the only argument in favour of slavery falls to the ground,' wrote the black newspaper owner Stephen Meyers, a contemporary of Douglass's. Northern free blacks had also been among the first to form temperance groups in the country in the early nineteenth century. In the South, meanwhile, as Douglass knew only too well, masters dulled the spirits of slaves by plying them with alcohol on Sundays or holidays like Christmas.[36]

'I knew once what it was to drink with all the ardour of an *old soaker*,' Douglass, a teetotaller by this stage for almost eight years, admitted to his audience in Paisley, recalling his time as a lowly field hand on the Eastern Shore. 'I lived with a Mr Freeland who used to give his slaves apple brandy. Some of the slaves were not able to drink their own share, but I was able to drink my own and theirs too. I took it because it made me feel I was a great man. I used to think I was a president.'

It was not long, however, before Douglass saw through the apparent acts of kindness for what they really were: another way to keep the minds of slaves away from thoughts of freedom. He began to view temperance as an important step on the path to emancipation, declaring in Paisley, 'I am a temperance man because I am an anti-slavery man.'

A few weeks earlier, Douglass had addressed the topic of temperance at a meeting in Glasgow City Halls organised by the Scottish Temperance League, a large gathering that had attracted advocates of the cause from all over the country and even the north of England, some groups organising special trains for their journeys. He had also given a few talks on the subject in Ireland, where the movement was in the midst of an extraordinary upsurge in popularity under the leadership of the Franciscan priest Fr Theobald Mathew, the so-called 'Apostle of Temperance'. Douglass was greatly impressed with Mathew, certainly much more so than the six Scottish ministers he dined with one night in Perth, all of whom, he thought, set a bad example for their congregations by drinking too much whiskey or wine. Nevertheless, drunkenness remained rife in Ireland, Douglass believed, blaming it almost entirely for the country's poverty, a superficial judgement that suggests no matter how fond the escaped slave became of the country, he did not really attain any deep understanding of its social and economic problems. He would similarly blame alcohol – spirits in particular – for Scotland's woes, asserting 'that nine-tenths of the crime, misery, disease, and death, of these lands is occasioned by intemperance'.

Douglass had been thrilled at the openness with which he was received by temperance organisations in Scotland and Ireland, most white temperance groups in America refusing membership to free blacks. 'He might be a Webster in intellect, a Channing in literature, or a Howard in philanthropy, yet the bare fact of his being a man of colour, would prevent him from being welcomed on a temperance platform in the United States,' Douglass stated, referring to the towering American politician Daniel Webster, the influential Unitarian writer William Ellery Canning and the eighteenth-century philanthropist and prison reformer John Howard. Political, literary and cultural allusions of this sort were a common facet of his lectures, subtly showcasing the breadth of his learning. For Scottish audiences in particular there were several mentions of the great poet Robert Burns, the revered 'ploughman' whose *Collected Works* was one of Douglass's foundation texts, purchased soon after his escape from slavery and later handed down to his son Lewis, the escaped slave even paraphrasing a line – 'the De'il has business on his hands' – from 'Tam O'Shanter' in one attack on Chalmers.[37]

While still travelling with Buffum, Douglass made a pilgrimage to the town of Ayr, 'famous', he wrote in a letter published in the *New York Tribune*, 'for being the birthplace of Robert Burns, the poet, by whose brilliant genius every stream, hill, glen and valley in the neighbourhood have been made classic'. The abolitionists had been met off their coach by Revd Renwick, at whose meeting house they were to lecture that evening, before being escorted the three miles to the site of the Burns Monument, a striking 70-foot high Grecian-style temple surrounded by manicured gardens that had been built on the banks of the River Doon in early 1820s.

'The banks of the "Doon" rising majestically from the sea toward the sky, and the Clyde stretching off to the highlands of Arran, whose dim outline is scarcely discernible through the fog by which it is almost constantly overhung, makes the spot admirable and beautifully adapted to the Monument of Scotland's noble bard,' wrote Douglass near-reverentially. 'In the Monument there is a finely executed marble bust of Burns – the finest thing of the kind I ever saw. I never before, looking upon it, realised the power of man to make the marble speak. The expression is so fine, and the face is so lit up, as to cause one to forget the form in gazing upon the spirit.' There were also life-size sandstone statues of some of the characters from Burns's most famous poem, including 'Souter Johnny' and the eponymous 'Tam O'Shanter' in an adjoining Statue House, as well as a Bible in a glass case and a lock of hair from Mary Campbell, the 'sweet Highland Mary' who died from typhus at a young age after inspiring many of his greatest works.

A radical whose political outlook was formed during the era of the American and French revolutions, Burns had published an anti-slavery poem, 'The Slave's Lament', in 1792, the first verse of which read:

> It was in sweet Senegal that my foes did me enthral,
> For the lands of Virginia, -ginia, O:
> Torn from that lovely shore, and must never see it more;
> And alas! I am weary, weary O:
> Torn from that lovely shore, and must never see it more;
> And alas! I am weary, weary O.

Nevertheless, like many young Scots before him, a financially troubled Burns had been tempted to make a career in the West Indies just a few years previously, accepting a post as a book-keeper on a sugar plantation in Jamaica just before the publication of his first volume of poems brought surprise success and financial freedom.

En route to the monument, Douglass had been thrilled to meet Burns's last surviving sibling, Isabella Begg, a 'spirited looking woman' in her mid-seventies who lived in a nearby cottage. He had also met two of her daughters, the poet's nieces, their 'jet black eyes' sparkling 'with the poetic fire which illuminated the breast of their brilliant uncle'. Kind words were exchanged and some letters in Burns's own handwriting passed around for the American visitors to examine, the family having grown accustomed by this time to entertaining Burns-loving guests from all over the world. Caught up in the emotion of the moment, Douglass tried to link their lives, describing how the poor, self-educated Burns had lived in the midst of a 'bigoted' clergy who 'looked upon the ploughman … as being little better than a brute' before he broke loose – like Douglass – 'from the moorings which society had thrown around him'.[38]

'Two Fair Quakeresses'
'I am now in Edinburgh,' Douglass wrote to his abolitionist friend Amy Post in America on the afternoon of Tuesday 28 April, his peregrinations through Scotland having finally brought him

into the heart of its capital city. Like Glasgow, Edinburgh had benefitted significantly from the slave trade, with leading figures from its important financial sector, for example, having invested heavily in slave ships over many years. Douglass, however, was more concerned in this letter with noting how Edinburgh was the 'most beautiful' city he had ever seen, emphasising not just its buildings but its 'picturesque position' in the midst of several surrounding hills. Buffum was still with him, sitting close by 'near the fire' of the hotel room they were sharing. Resting up against the window, meanwhile, was George Thompson, the radical English politician who had met up with them in Glasgow a few days earlier. A Liverpudlian firebrand whose 'glorious spirit' Asa Hutchinson – who had already met him in London – would extol, Thompson was well known to American anti-slavery activists from a tumultuous lecture tour that had brought him face-to-face with snarling pro-slavery mobs across the North in the mid-1830s. Wright, too, would soon rejoin his abolitionist companions, having spent some time lecturing further south, near the border.

Apologising to the forty-three-year-old Post for not writing sooner, Douglass blamed 'the press of immediate engagements'. The effort had been worthwhile, however, the whole country 'in a blaze of anti-slavery excitement in consequence of our exposures of the pro-slavery conduct of the Free Church of Scotland'. The assault would continue in venues across Edinburgh, Douglass telling a 2,000-strong audience in the Music Hall in George Street, all of whom paid 6d for tickets to hear him speak, that the Free Church, having given a 'respectability to slavery in America which it never before enjoyed', now had to take its share of responsibility for the 'tears and agony of the slave' and for 'the crime – the deep, black, damning crime – of the blood-polluted man-stealer'.[39]

While staying originally at the York Hotel in the centre of the city, Douglass also spent time at 5 South Grey Street, the home of William Smeal's daughter Jane. Married since 1840 to the Quaker shawl manufacturer John Wigham, forty-five-year-old Jane had been enmeshed in the anti-slavery cause all her life, establishing the Glasgow Ladies' Emancipation Society in the early 1830s and co-authoring an 1838 pamphlet, *Address to the Women of Great*

Britain, that urged women to speak out in public on the issue of slavery and organise more of their own anti-slavery societies – controversial sentiments at a time when male abolitionists on both sides of the Atlantic, including the wealthy businessman Lewis Tappen, founder of the anti-Garrisonian American and Foreign Anti-Slavery Society, claimed their 'dignity' and religious beliefs precluded them from sharing public stages or working on committees with women, taking refuge in St Paul's injunction in the *First Epistle to Timothy* (1 Timothy 2:12): 'But I suffer not a woman to teach, nor to usurp authority over the man, but to be in silence.' Even the otherwise admirable abolitionist, the polyglot Elizur Wright, editor, mathematician, inventor and 'father of life insurance' in the United States, commented crudely that he was 'opposed to hens crowing' and thought 'the tom turkeys ought to do the gobbling'.[40]

In Edinburgh, Jane joined forces with her spirited stepdaughter Eliza (John Wigham's first wife, also Jane, having died in 1830) to make the city's Ladies' Anti-Slavery Society one of the most ardently Garrisonian that side of the Atlantic. Just twenty years old at the time, Eliza had already travelled down to the World Anti-Slavery Convention in London in the summer of 1840, where the disappointment of being denied entry into the main conference hall (like all female delegates) was leavened by meetings with the pioneering American women's rights activists Lucretia Mott and Elizabeth Cady Stanton. The following years would see Jane and Eliza Wigham organise contributions for the Boston Bazaar amongst numerous other anti-slavery activities, complaining at one point to Maria Weston Chapman that marking the prices on the items was the most 'disagreeable' aspect of the task and dating their letters in the distinctive Quaker fashion, with '11th month 21st 1844' signifying 21 November 1844. With Douglass by their side, the 'two fair Quakeresses', tightly bonneted no doubt but carrying spades in their hands, then seem to have scaled the heights of Arthur's Seat to carve out the phrase 'Send Back the Money' in the grass of the craggy hill overlooking the city.[41]

Although affiliated to the more conservative British and Foreign Anti-Slavery Society, John Wigham, Jane's husband, was also involved in the anti-slavery scene, as were two of his sons, Henry and John, the latter of whom would go on to a successful career as an engineer and inventor of gas lighting for lighthouses. Elsewhere in the city, the Salisbury Road Wighams, the family of John Wigham's cousin (another John), were just as well known for their anti-slavery activity and philanthropy, the extended Wigham clan, indeed, one of the key Quaker families in the British Isles, with family connections stretching from Edinburgh and Aberdeen to Newcastle and Dublin. Mary Welsh was another vital figure in the Edinburgh anti-slavery group, having previously played host to Wright during his solo lecture tours as well as helping organise contributions for the Boston Bazaar with her close friends the Wighams. A regular correspondent with Chapman, she wrote to Boston again in the middle of May, revelling in the 'set of glorious meetings' held across Edinburgh attacking the Free Church and its raising of money in the slaveholding South. 'George Thompson, Frederick Douglass, James Buffum & H. C. Wright have done wonders in opening the eyes of the public to this enormous iniquity,' Welsh continued. 'Never was there such excitement created as at present & there is no doubt but great good will be the result.'[42]

The concerted attacks certainly had an effect, with some uncomfortable questioning from members at the Free Church's General Assembly held at the Canonmills Hall in Edinburgh in late May – one session of which Douglass and Thompson managed to gain admittance to, leading to tense moments with the Revd Robert Candlish, Chalmers's able and experienced deputy, the aging leader himself absent through illness. Nevertheless, Douglass's claim that the church's members were leaving it 'like rats escaping from a sinking ship' was utterly unfounded. Their moral authority questioned, the Free Church had also started to strike back against the rival churches it saw as facilitating the attacks by opening up their pulpits to Douglass, Thompson and others, accusing the Rose Street Missionary Society, at whose Rose Street Secessionist Chapel Douglass spoke at least twice, of accepting £500 from the owners of the Goshen Esate in Jamaica, owners who had 'pocketed their share of the TWENTY MILLIONS' compensation paid to

West Indian slaveholders. The Revd John Aikman, meanwhile, was accused of building the Independent Church on Argyle Square with money inherited from his slave-owning father, a claim entirely without foundation, though the fact Aikman had once owned a slave while living in Jamaica and that his uncle Alexander, King's printer in Jamaica, had received almost £7,000 for more than 350 enslaved people under the 1833 Act, allowed the *Witness*, the Edinburgh-based Free Church organ, to continue to link it with money derived 'from the foul hands of the slave-dealer'.[43]

In later years, Douglass would acknowledge the eloquence and intellectual keenness of Free Church leaders like Chalmers, Candlish and the Revd William Cunnigham, admitting the battle over the 'Send Back the Money' campaign had been 'a hard-fought one'. He has also been criticised for the intensity of his attacks, which were sometimes quite personal in nature – producing a slave collar at one talk and envisioning it around the necks of Chalmers's own daughters – and left the Free Church leaders no room for compromise or dignified retreat. They were, after all, far removed from one-dimensional villains of the piece, with Chalmers's genuine anti-slavery feelings seeing him invited to an American Anti-Slavery Society meeting not long before the fundraising controversy broke out. It had also been none other than George Lewis, the Free Church minister lampooned by Douglass in speeches in Dundee, who had led the complaints when a black passenger on board the *Acadia* – the vessel in which he was returning to Scotland following the successful fundraising campaign in America in 1844 – was denied entry to the saloon by the ship's captain – the same Captain Charles Judkins generally lionised by Douglass for his actions on board the *Cambria* a year later (see page 43). Approaching the summer of 1846, however, Douglass saw no place for nuance in the great fight against slavery, continuing to attack the Free Church even after he left Scotland and travelled down to London.[44]

4

'A NEGRO HERCULES'

'I take up my pen to give you a hasty sketch of five days' visit to this great city,' Frederick Douglass wrote to William Lloyd Garrison from London on Saturday, 23 May 1846. Staying at George Thompson's handsome South Kensington home – at the site of which a blue heritage plaque commemorating the escaped slave's tour can now be found – he had been caught up in a whirl of sightseeing and speechmaking, including a morning's walk around the grounds of Cremorne Gardens, a new attraction on the banks of the Thames near Chelsea that would prove a haven for a generation of Victorian day-trippers. 'I was admitted without a whisper of objection on the part of the proprietor or spectators,' Douglass noted pointedly, galleries and museums in even the supposedly 'free' northern states in America often closed to black visitors. 'Everyone looked as they thought I had as much right as themselves, and not the slightest dislike was manifested toward me on account of my Negro origin.'[1]

Through Thompson, Douglass also gained admittance into the gallery of the House of Commons, where for more than three hours on the afternoon of Wednesday 20 May he watched on as the Tory Prime Minister Sir Robert Peel, the Whig Leader of the Opposition Lord John Russell and others – including Thomas Wakely, the Radical MP and founder of the *Lancet* medical journal – debated a bill to ameliorate the working conditions in the country's lace factories, where thousands of children, some as young as six, toiled nightly. A subsequent visit allowed Douglass to observe Benjamin Disraeli, the then rising star in the Tory ranks. 'I watched him narrowly when I saw him in the House of Commons, but I saw and heard nothing there that foreshadowed the immense space he at last came to fill in the mind of his country and the world,' Douglass recalled many years later, his disapproval of some of the future Prime Minister's policies perhaps colouring his assessment. Escorted into the resplendent House of Lords by the Whig elder statesman Lord Lansdowne, Douglass was much more impressed with the strongly abolitionist Lord Brougham. 'He struck me as the most wonderful speaker of them all,' Douglass wrote of the flamboyant but now largely forgotten Scottish politician, one of the leading reformers of the age and a prominent figure in several Whig governments.

How he was ever reported I cannot imagine. Listening to him was like standing near the track of a railway train, drawn by a locomotive at the rate of 40 miles an hour. You are riveted to the spot, charmed with the sublime spectacle of speed and power, but can give no description of the carriages, or of the passengers at the windows. There was so much to see and hear ... that when this strange man sat down you felt like one who had hastily passed through the bewildering wonders of a world's exhibition.[2]

Douglass praised the 'respectful manner' in which the British politicians debated each other in his letter to Garrison. But he was also quick to point out that he had nothing to compare it to, for if he had ever tried to enter Congress in Washington as he had the Commons in London 'the ardent defenders of democratic liberty would at once put me into prison'. This contrasting of 'monarchical freedom' with 'republican slavery' was a regular trope of Douglass's tour, designed to shame America into action on slavery. Its constant invocation, however, obscured Britain's deep slavery past, London in particular playing an unparalleled role in the development of the international slave trade from the mid-1600s, the strong tides of the Thames carrying off ships of first the Royal Adventurers into Africa and then the Royal African Company on journeys to trade goods for captured Africans who would then be carried over to America and the West Indies. With the 'Royal' prefix coming from the role of King Charles II and his brother the Duke of York in its founding, the Royal African Company carried more Africans into slavery than any other British company, about 150,000 men, women and children between the 1670s and 1730s, many of whom had the company's initials 'RAC' branded onto their chests as they were corralled into slave pens on the west coast of Africa.[3]

Although overtaken by Bristol and Liverpool as the country's premier slave-trading port during the course of the eighteenth century, a natural corollary of London's long involvement in the slave trade was a rise in its own black population, be they servants brought back from the West Indies, runaways eking out a living playing music on the streets, sailors who had worked for the Royal Navy or black loyalists who resettled there after the American War of Independence. London became Britain's – if not Europe's – black capital, though exact figures are impossible to pin down. A number of its black citizens even attained celebrity in the Georgian era, from the bare-knuckle fighter Bill Richmond to the freed slave turned best-selling author Olaudah Equiano, and from the rakish Julius Soubise to the famous writer Samuel Johnson's Jamaica-born servant and surrogate son, Francis Barber. Nevertheless, London remained the financial hub of the international slave trade, insurers like Lloyds and banks like Barings gleaning enormous profits from the trade in slaves from their inceptions. Abolition – either of the slave trade or of slavery in the West Indies – did little to curtail this element of their businesses, with the Havana-based J. C. Burnham, one of Douglass's fellow passengers on board the *Cambria*, likely to have been travelling to London to arrange loans with Barings, the bank having made a determined effort to increase its presence in Cuba – where slavery still flourished – from the 1830s.[4]

By the time of Douglass's arrival, London had been totally transformed by its exposure to slavery – physically, economically and psychologically. It had proven a source of immense wealth for merchants and professionals as well as of more humdrum employment for innumerable workers in industries like shipbuilding, ironmongery, weaving and distilling. The constant traffic to and from Africa and the West Indies also made the world seem smaller to Londoners, while new flavours transformed the city's palate and young black servants became fashion accessories for its aristocrats, to be included in family portraits by artists like Sir Joshua Reynolds. Slavery worked its way into the capital's favourite books, like Laurence Stern's *The Life and Opinions of Tristram Shandy, Gentleman,* and was the genesis behind great feats of engineering like the vast West India Docks, now the site of Canary Wharf. Slavery-tainted philanthropy also underpinned the establishment of institutions like the National Gallery and the Tate Museum. Slavery reached into Parliament, too, with large numbers of slave-owners holding seats in both the Commons and the Lords, including Sir John Gladstone, father of the future Prime Minister William Gladstone. Its influence was still evident, had he cared to notice, on the day of Douglass's first visit to Westminster, with Joseph Brotherton, for example, one of the speakers Douglass praised, having earned his fortune in the Manchester cotton trade, an industry utterly dependent on imported slave-grown cotton. Another speaker, Sir John Cam Hobhouse, a close friend in his youth of Lord Byron, perhaps Douglass's favourite author, came from a family of Bristol merchants whose wealth could be traced back to the slave trade.

Despite this, London was a city overwhelmingly associated with opposition to slavery in the broader public mind, the very name attached to William Wilberforce and his abolitionist accomplices – the 'Clapham Sect' – taken from the area of the city in which they held their first meetings. More recently, it had been the scene of the first World Anti-Slavery Convention, organised by the then newly formed British and Foreign Anti-Slavery Society and held over the course of ten intoxicatingly debate-filled days in the Freemasons' Hall in the summer of 1840, the still-recent ending of apprenticeship in the West Indies inspiring delegates with a genuine belief that they could rid the world of slavery.

'The Everyday Fruits of American Slavery'

Following on closely from the final defeat of the apprenticeship system in the West Indies, the establishment of the British and Foreign Anti-Slavery Society had signalled the beginning of a new phase in the British anti-slavery movement, the focus turning from the emancipation of slaves in the British Empire to those worldwide. Founded by Joseph Sturge, a wealthy Birmingham-based Quaker who had been involved in the movement for many years, sharing stages with anti-slavery luminaries like Wilberforce in the 1820s and touring the West Indies under an assumed name in an attempt to discover the true workings of apprenticeship in the 1830s, it had followed the example of earlier anti-slavery organisations by setting up a network of branches across the country before really announcing its presence with the World Anti-Slavery Convention, the opening session of which would be captured on canvas by the artist Benjamin Robert Haydon, the large painting hanging today in the National Portrait Gallery.

Celebrated in verse by John Greenleaf Whittier, the great American anti-slavery poet who became a close friend, Sturge, in his early fifties by the time of Douglass's tour, combined his leadership of the British and Foreign Anti-Slavery Society – which continues to exist today as the NGO Anti-Slavery International – with roles in the Peace Society and numerous other reform organisations. A stoutly built figure with a brow and forehead one early biographer likened to Napoleon Bonaparte's – 'broad rather than high' – Sturge was not, however, so forward-thinking on matters of gender equality, his denial of entry to the main hall of the proceedings to female delegates at the World Anti-Slavery Convention (relegating them instead to the distant pews of the public galleries) leading to a serious dispute with Garrison. The rupture was never repaired, Sturge siding openly with – and donating hundreds of pounds to – the New York abolitionist Lewis Tappen's more socially conservative American and Foreign Anti-Slavery Society after the split in the American anti-slavery movement in 1841, the break so bitter it saw Garrisonians level the religiously charged accusation of 'apostasy' at their new rivals. Sturge also supported James G. Birney's Liberty Party, the short-lived political organisation that had itself emerged from the split, dismissing Garrison as the leader of a 'very small' band to an anti-slavery activist in Bristol while insisting that the 'finest minds' among the abolitionists in the United States all 'ranged themselves under the "Liberty" banner'. To Garrisonians like the Irish publisher Richard D. Webb, meanwhile, Sturge was 'snuffling, secretive, bigoted, and destitute of magnanimity', a man who ran his organisation like a despot, using his immense wealth to cow opponents and brooking no dissent.[5]

Despite these tensions, Douglass had travelled down to London to attend the annual convention of the British and Foreign Anti-Slavery Society, much to the chagrin of staunch 'old organisationists' who believed it amounted to consorting with the enemy. Douglass stood his ground. 'I have no confession to make or pardon to ask for my conduct in the matter,' he wrote brusquely to Maria Weston Chapman afterwards, stating he was not 'carried there by what you term "money temptations"' but rather the advice of Thompson, the clear lack of trust carrying their tense relationship close to the point of rupture. Heavily reliant on sales of his book (which while strong could not be guaranteed) to fund both the tour and his family back home, Douglass was not uninterested in money and had a growing sense of his worth. His principles, however, were not for sale.[6]

The meeting itself, held at noon on Monday 18 May, was a disappointment, for although Douglass was well received, the attendance was poor, apparently because it clashed with a number of other philanthropic gatherings. Nevertheless, impressed by Douglass, Sturge immediately set about organising a bigger public speech for later in the week. Held at Finsbury Chapel, a now-demolished Independent chapel built by the abolitionist Scottish minister Alexander Fletcher in 1825, it was this near three-hour speech – 'An Appeal to the British People' – that really introduced the escaped slave to the capital, published in detail in major newspapers like Charles Dickens's new journalistic venture the *Daily News* and later as a pamphlet.

'The condition of a slave is simply that of a brute beast,' Douglass declared to the almost 3,000-strong audience crowding the central London venue almost to the point of suffocation soon after taking to the stage at eight o'clock on the evening of Friday 22 May. 'He is a piece of property – a marketable commodity ... to be bought or sold at the will and caprice of the master who claims him to be his property.' Slavery attacked minds, Douglass went on, forbidding slaves from learning how to read or write. It attacked souls, he continued, denying them the right to marry or access to the Bible. It also attacked bodies, with the whip, the chain, the gag, the thumb-screw, the cat-o'-nine-tails and the bloodhound all turned on the flesh of slaves.

Douglass did not wish to dwell, he said, on 'the physical evils of slavery'. Nevertheless, he felt it was important to let the slaveholders of America know that 'the curtain which conceals their crimes' was being lifted:

> We want them to know that a knowledge of their whippings, their scourging, their brandings, their chaining, is not confined to their plantations, but that some Negro of theirs has broken loose from his chains – has burst through the dark incrustation of slavery, and is now exposing their deeds of deep damnation to the gaze of the Christian people of England.

If anyone doubted the veracity of his words, he suggested they read Dickens's *American Notes*, the author's account of an 1842 visit to the United States that contained a scathing chapter on slavery. Continuing the literary theme he also quoted part of Whittier's poem *Expostulation*:

> What, ho! our Countrymen in chains,
> The whip on woman's shrinking flesh,
> Our soil yet reddening with the stains,
> Caught from her scourging warm and fresh.

Douglass then described a possibly apocryphal but still deeply moving scene at a slave auction, where a black man and woman – man and wife in their eyes – were up for sale:

> The man and woman were brought to the auctioneer's block, under the sound of the hammer. The cry was raised, 'Here

goes; who bids cash?' ... The woman was placed on the auctioneer's block; her limbs, as is customary, were brutally exposed to the purchasers, who examined her with all the freedom with which they would examine a horse. There stood the husband powerless; no right to his wife; the master's right pre-eminent. She was sold.

He was next brought to the auctioneer's block. His eyes followed his wife in the distance; and he looked beseechingly, imploringly to the man that had bought his wife, to buy him also. But he was at length bid off to another person. He was about to be separated from her he loved forever. No word of his, no work of his, could save him from this separation. He asked permission of his new master to go and take the hand of his wife at parting. It was denied him. In the agony of his soul he rushed from the man who had just bought him, that he might take a farewell of his wife; but his way was obstructed, he was struck over the head with a loaded whip, and was held for a moment; but his agony was too great. When he was let go, he fell a corpse at the feet of his master. His heart was broken. Such scenes are the everyday fruits of American slavery.

Douglass went on in a similar vein, detailing more horrific scenes that brought deep gasps from the crowd before skilfully bringing the narrative back to the role of the Churches in slavery, the issue he would return to again and again throughout the tour:

I have to inform you, that the religion of the southern states ... is the great supporter, the great sanctioner [sic] of the bloody atrocities to which I have referred. While America is printing tracts and Bibles; sending missionaries abroad to convert the heathen; expending her money in various ways for the promotion of the Gospel in foreign lands, the slave not only lies forgotten – uncared for – but is trampled underfoot by the very churches of the land.

'Why we have slavery made part of the religion of the land,' he continued, amid loud shouts of 'Shame' aimed at the guilty

American ministers. 'Yes, the pulpit there stands up as the great defender of this cursed *institution* ... Ministers of religion come forward and torture the hallowed pages of inspired wisdom to sanction the bloody deed ... Instead of preaching the Gospel against this tyranny, rebuke and wrong, ministers of religion have sought ... to throw in the background whatever in the Bible could be construed into opposition to slavery and to bring forward that which they could torture into its support.'

For Douglass, this collusion was the 'darkest feature of slavery', the most difficult to confront because it led to the charge that he was attacking religion, led to cries of 'infidel' being hurled at him, Garrison and the entire American Anti-Slavery Society. 'But I cannot be induced to leave off these exposures,' he asserted. 'I love the religion of our blessed Saviour ... It is because I love this religion that I hate the slaveholding, the woman-whipping, the mind-darkening, the soul-destroying religion that exists in the southern states of America ... Loving the one I must hate the other.'

Towards his conclusion, Douglass brought the part his audience – as consumers – continued to play in the subjugation of his race uncomfortably close to home, highlighting how when 'cotton gets up in the market in England, the price of human flesh gets up in the United States'. However, he also emphasised the incomparable moral influence the country exerted on America:

The power I exert now is something like the power that is exerted by the man at the end of the lever; my influence now is just in proportion to the distance that I am from the United States. My exposure of slavery abroad will tell more upon the hearts and consciences of slaveholders, than if I were attacking them in America, for almost every paper that I now receive from the United States comes teeming with statements about the fugitive Negro ... and saying that he is running out against the institutions and people of America.

Douglass denied the charge that he was attacking America. 'What I have to say is against slavery and slaveholders. I feel at liberty to

speak on this subject. I have on my back the marks of the lash.'
He spoke out, he said, because to 'expose' slavery was to 'kill' it.
'The slaveholders want total darkness on the subject,' he continued
to prolonged cheers. 'They want the hatchway shut down, that
the monster may crawl in his den of darkness, crushing human
hopes and happiness, destroying the bondman at will, and having
no-one to reprove or rebuke him. Slavery shrinks from the light,
it hateth the light ... lest its deeds should be reproved.' Returning
to an image he had already called forth in Ireland and Scotland,
he then declared:

> I want the slaveholder surrounded, as by a wall of anti-slavery
> fire ... I want him to feel that he has no sympathy in England,
> Scotland, or Ireland; that he has none in Canada, none in
> Mexico ... I would have condemnation blaze down upon him
> in every direction, till, stunned and overwhelmed with shame
> and confusion, he is compelled to let go the grasp he holds
> upon the persons of his victims, and restore them to their
> long-lost rights.

Douglass ended with a forceful denunciation of the Free Church
of Scotland – exhorting the 'Christians of England' to unite and
call out 'Send Back the Money' – finally sitting down to prolonged
cheers from the immense audience, many of whom seemed
gratifyingly young and new to the cause, no doubt going on to buy
copies of his *Narrative* which were on sale at the door.[7]

'Rumours of War'

Douglass had not been idle between these two anti-slavery
appearances, delivering another three talks in three days to
enraptured audiences across the capital, his growing stature as
an orator ensuring his services were in high demand during this
period of the year when many philanthropic and reform-minded
organisations gathered in London for yearly conventions. The
evening of Tuesday 19 May, for example, found him addressing
a 'large and excellent' meeting of the London Peace Society – a
group founded in the aftermath of the Napoleonic Wars and

whose current members included the ubiquitous Sturge. Douglass discussed the possibility of war between Britain and America over Oregon, the vast area of land in the Pacific Northwest that was at the centre of a tense territorial dispute territory between the two powers, the Hutchinson Family even blaming the 'rumours of war' for poor reviews of their performances in London earlier in the year. It was a topic abolitionists on both sides of the Atlantic had been trading views on for many months, wary, for the most part, that overly aggressive statements in Congress would precipitate a conflict neither government particularly desired. Douglass hoped war could be avoided, he said, even though he had been accused of trying to incite trouble between the countries, many commentators believing such a conflict would result in the emancipation of American slaves. 'I believe this would be the result; but such is my regard for the principle of peace ... that were I to be asked the question as to whether I would have my emancipation by the shedding of one single drop of blood, my answer would be in the negative,' he announced, adhering – for the time being – to the firm Garrisonian stance against violence.[8]

A couple of days later, Douglass spoke before a largely working-class audience (including a full row of coal porters) at the fourth anniversary meeting of the National Temperance Society, held at what he called the 'far-famed' Exeter Hall, the beautiful, Corinthian-columned building on the north side of the Strand that was synonymous with Wilberforce's old Anti-Slavery Society. To Douglass's delight, the extremely wealthy and influential Sturge declared he would not support the proposed World's Temperance Convention in London if slaveholders were allowed to attend, threatening to withhold the £50 he had planned to donate. His threat worked, the World's Temperance Convention being held within a few months – but without any slaveholders. Other potential donors had followed his example at the meeting, the feeling of 'No Union with Slaveholders' growing ever-stronger to Douglass's mind. 'American slaveholders must prepare,' he wrote excitedly, 'not only to be excluded from the communion of British Christians, but peremptorily driven from the platform of every philanthropic association. Let them be hemmed in on every side. Let them be placed beyond the pale of respectability, and, standing out separated, alone in their infamy, let the storm gather over them, and its hottest bolts descend.'

The evening of Wednesday 20 May, meanwhile, had seen Douglass deliver a speech to the Complete Suffrage Association (another Sturge-backed group) at the Crown and Anchor Tavern, a famous venue in the bustling Strand area of the city, one that had been playing host to radical meetings for more than fifty years, the now-twenty-eight-year-old escaped slave adding his name to the long list of oratorical luminaries like Charles James Fox and William Hazlitt to grace its rooms. 'I am persuaded that, after the complete triumph of the Anti-Corn Law movement, the next great reform will be that of complete suffrage,' he wrote to Garrison in the aftermath of the talk, though the strength of the campaign to extend the right to vote was seen most clearly not in the Sturgian organisation he addressed but rather in the power and popularity of the Chartists, the working-class movement built around the 'Six Points' – including universal male suffrage and the secret ballot – of the 'People's Charter' of 1838. 'The battle will be hot, but the right [cause] must triumph,' Douglass continued. Nevertheless, coming from a so-called democracy that enslaved a sixth of its population, he was also well aware that universal male suffrage did not necessarily equate to enlightened policies. 'God grant that they may make a better use of their political freedom, than the working people of the United States have hitherto done!' he wrote of the British working class. 'For, instead of taking sides with the oppressed, they have acted the unnatural and execrable part of the vilest oppressors. They stand forth in the front ranks of tyranny, and, with words of freedom on their deceitful lips, have given victory to a party [the Democrats], the chief pride, boast and glory of which is that of having blasted one of the fairest portions of our common earth with slavery.'[9]

A perennial source of debate, the Corn Laws Douglass referred to in his correspondence with Garrison were a set of prohibitive duties that had been placed on imported corn since the end of the Napoleonic Wars and that had returned to the top of the political agenda during the 1840s against a backdrop of economic distress across Britain and Ireland. Opponents of the duties, including the middle-class pressure group the Anti-Corn Law League and the recently established *Economist* magazine, blamed them for keeping the price of bread artificially high to the benefit of large (often Tory) landowners while supporters, known as Protectionists, argued that they protected British farmers from having their produce undercut by cheap foreign imports. The Protectionists also joined forces with some tenant farmers to present themselves as defenders of traditional rural society, the question of repeal becoming a proxy for any number of overlapping debates: protectionism versus free trade, the aristocracy versus the people, rural versus urban.

Protectionism was assumed to be a central tenet of the governing Tory Party policy. Privately, however, the Prime Minister, Peel, had long held doubts about the value of the Corn Laws. As indications of his weakening resolve seeped out into the public arena the debate grew ever more strident. Powerful voices including the writers Thomas Carlyle and Dickens came out in support of repeal, the latter weaving the free-trade ideas of the Anti-Corn Law League into *The Chimes*, his tale of a starving farm labourer, Will Fern, and a tyrannical landlord, Sir Joseph Bowley. (*The Chimes* was Dickens's second Christmas book, but did not match the success of its predecessor, *A Christmas Carol*.) The Protectionists hit back with a propaganda machine of their own, backed by popular magazines like *Blackwood's* and *Fraser's*, both sides holding mass rallies and mobilising forces across the country. Across the Atlantic, abolitionists like Garrison, who covered the issue in detail in the *Liberator*, saw the campaign as yet another manifestation of the 'spirit of reform' that seemed characteristic of the age. Others developed a harsher economic critique in which the Corn Laws played a central role in upholding slavery, by excluding free-grown American corn from Britain while allowing the untrammelled importation of slave-grown cotton.[10]

It was against this frenzied backdrop that *The Times*, the leading paper of the age, had stunned readers with the announcement of Peel's final conversion to repeal on 4 December 1845. 'The decision … is no longer a secret. Parliament, it is confidently reported, is to be summoned for the first week in January; and the Royal Speech will ... recommend an immediate consideration of the Corn Laws, preparatory to their total repeal.' John Bright, MP for Durham and one of the leading opponents of the Corn Laws, was so excited he wrote 'the reading of the article has almost made me ill – what a glorious prospect is now before us'.[11] Less glorious was the reaction within Tory ranks, the party splitting irreparably between Protectionists and Peelites.

With his Cabinet divided, Peel offered his resignation to Queen Victoria, the twenty-six-year-old monarch who, under the influence of her even younger German husband Prince Albert, had come to regard the Prime Minister affectionately despite initially fraught relations. The Whig opposition, however, under Lord John Russell, proved unable to form a government, forcing Peel to stay in place for six months to see the measure through. When the Corn Laws were finally repealed in June 1846, Peel travelled immediately to Osborne House (then in the midst of a Prince Albert-overseen redevelopment) on the Isle of Wight, tendering his resignation to a Queen still recuperating from the birth of her fifth child. Russell, at the second time of asking, formed a new Whig government, a number of whose members, including the new Prime Minister himself, had been part of the great reforming ministry of Lord Grey that abolished slavery in the West Indies.

Despite this pedigree, one of Russell's first acts would have severely detrimental effects on the West Indies' new freed people, the government's decision to lower the tariffs that had long protected colonial sugar from cheap slave-grown competition from countries like Cuba and Brazil leading Thomas Clarkson's wife, Catherine, to describe British abolitionists as 'drooping just now' in an early August letter. They were not overly surprised, however, the sugar duties – in tandem with the Corn Laws – having become an increasingly bitter subject of debate in recent years. Influential politicians decried the way in which the artificially high price of sugar denied ordinary British citizens an article that had become 'a necessary of life'. It was 'the only little luxury that many families can enjoy,' one MP declared. 'It renders palatable their rice, their crout [cabbage], their gruel, their indifferent tea or coffee.' Russell, too, had made his position clear as early as 1841, painting a patently false picture of newly free slaves enjoying lives of plenty on idyllic small farms in the West Indies while industrial cities like Bolton were beset by poverty. 'I do not think that we should be justified in giving our attention exclusively to their [freed blacks'] interests ... whilst the people of this country were suffering from want of the common comforts of life,' he had declared to the Commons, the former slaves slowly morphing in public discourse from figures of sympathy to unworthy beneficiaries of British munificence.[12]

Hindered by dissent within its ranks, the anti-slavery movement in Britain, many of whose members were ideologically committed to free trade, failed to wage any meaningful campaign against the equalisation of the sugar duties – the announcement of which was apparently met with celebrations on the streets of Havana. The results, however, were exactly what those opposed to the measure – including Sturge – expected, George Blyth, a missionary in the West Indies, describing a few years later how most of the farms and plantations there were on the verge of ruin. 'I hope the Anti-Slavery Friends will continue to advocate the cause of the Emancipated class,' he continued. 'If the present state of things continues they will sink, as certainly as a sailor goes down with his foundered vessel. The grand experiment which has blessed these colonies with freedom must fail and the whole mass of the population will be involved in difficulties as distressing as those which lately desolated Ireland.'[13] Britain's conscience was clear, however. Having paid £20 million to free the West Indian slaves, it did not seem to believe its responsibilities stretched any further.

Another link to the reforms of the early 1830s, the famously bellicose Lord Palmerston, serving as Foreign Secretary for the third occasion, had a particularly strong reputation on anti-slavery, receiving a congratulatory address from the British and Foreign Anti-Slavery Society for the 'eminent services' he had given the cause. A senior politician at the time of the war of 1812 (something of a misnomer, seeing as it lasted until 1815), the last conflict between the two countries, he was also unashamedly anti-American, constantly condemning his Tory predecessor Lord Aberdeen's conciliatory policies towards the

United States in Parliament and through the pages of the so-called 'Palmerstonian press'.[14] Nevertheless, as a seasoned hand at the Foreign Office, the sixty-one-year-old Palmerston knew well the difference between sound bites in opposition and the realities of wielding power. Consequently he supported the Oregon Treaty, which had been concluded by Aberdeen just a few weeks after Douglass discussed the issue in London. He also followed a steadfast policy of non-interference in the Mexican-American War, which had finally broken out after many months of aggressive American posturing, disappointing those abolitionists like the Unitarian minister Samuel J. May (whose young niece Louisa May Alcott would go on to author *Little Women*), who saw British intervention in support of Mexico as the certain prelude to the fall of slavery in America.[15]

'Rather Absurd In Their Over-Attention'

While the New York-based May was dispatching letters across the Atlantic decrying the Mexican-American War, Douglass was writing home to his wife Anna with a life-changing plan. For months supporters in Britain had been encouraging him to relocate there permanently, some, including Sturge, even raising money to help pay the costs of such a move. By the middle of the summer, Douglass was convinced. It is not hard to see why, feted as he was by all classes of society and revelling in the freedom of movement and mind afforded by being out of the oppressive political climate of the United States. He was also concerned that his increased fame (notoriety in the South) had made it too dangerous to return, particularly with his new owner Hugh Auld apparently determined to recapture him should he ever set foot again in America. Douglass had scoffed at his transfer from one brother to another in speeches across England and Scotland. 'He ought to have given me to his brother when I should have been of some service to him,' he joked of his former owner Thomas Auld, 'but he had made him a present of a person 3,000 miles off.'[16] Alone with his thoughts, however, the threats may have begun to feel real.

Douglass's dreams of a new life in Britain did not last long; his wife Anna – who, being illiterate, like the majority of

African-Americans at the time, had her husband's letters read out to her by friends – refusing to countenance the move. Life in Lynn was not easy, Anna taking on piecework for a shoe factory to help pay the bills while continuing to look after a household and raise four young children without her partner. Nevertheless, she at least had a strong black community around her for support, her eldest daughter, Rosetta, recalling in an affectionate memoir published many years after her death how friends and neighbours would come around and help with the 'household duties' on the mornings of local anti-slavery meetings in order to ensure her mother's attendance, for although not a public figure with great speeches reprinted in the *Liberator* Anna was still deeply involved in and committed to the cause.[17] In Britain, all these networks would be gone. Even more so than in America, Anna, a proud black woman wrapped up in the rhythms of African-American life, would be reduced to a mere appendage of her husband, the great man whose anti-slavery work had seen him work closely with white people for many years and who she must have known from newspaper clippings sent home was at that very moment exciting the attention of white women at speeches across the British Isles, leading Webb to wonder callously how Douglass would bear the sight of his wife when he returned to America given all the 'petting' he received from elegant ladies that side of the Atlantic.[18]

Anna's illiteracy and low public profile made her an easy target for comfortable, well-educated white men like Webb who knew nothing of the strong spirit underpinning her placid demeanour, knew nothing of the resourcefulness displayed in helping Douglass escape Baltimore or the bravery required to follow him north on her own to the dangerous (for all African-Americans) streets of New York before launching their new lives in New Bedford. However, there was some truth to the 'petting' comments, Douglass inspiring near devotion in women's anti-slavery groups across Britain and Ireland, many of which, for example in Belfast, were set up in the immediate aftermath of his talks. He was a brilliant, charismatic speaker and it is easy to see why they were enraptured. He was also a powerfully attractive man – a female audience member once describing how the 'play of his fine features made a little thrill run through me'[19] – which led to a great deal of prurient speculation about the sexual component of his friendships with white women. Isabel Jennings, to whom Douglass had been exceptionally close in Cork, was quick to quash any hints of impropriety, writing to Chapman that he 'evinced the highest regard for his wife and children' at all times and avoided 'confidential conversations with young ladies', even though one or two were 'rather absurd in their over-attention'. The Bristol eye doctor John Bishop Estlin – who in due course would open his home to the escaped slave – concurred: 'You can hardly imagine how he is noticed – *petted* I may say by *ladies*. Some of them really a little exceed the bounds of propriety, or delicacy, as far as appearances are concerned; yet F. D.'s conduct is most guardedly correct, judicious & decorous.'[20]

While de rigueur for the time, the condescending newspaper accounts of the 'crowded' female galleries or 'numerous' ladies present at Douglass's speeches across Britain and Ireland do a great disservice to the vital role women played in the anti-slavery movement on both sides of the Atlantic, stepping out of their supposed private 'sphere' to provide formidable leaders like Maria Weston Chapman in America and Jane and Eliza Wigham in Britain. For many – the 'great silent army' of volunteers and fundraisers[21] – the simple act of signing a petition or knitting an article for an anti-slavery fair was revelatory, allowing them to claim a space in their nation's political life they had hitherto been denied, one writer even describing how these women made fabric their 'arena for the battle' with American slavery, 'every stitch contributing funds to end its horrific hold over 3 million black bodies'.[22] Others like the famous Grimké sisters in America (inspirations for Sue Monk Kidd's recent best-selling novel *The Invention of Wings*) went further, taking to the stage to denounce slavery in an era when a woman's appearance on a public platform still had the potential to cause a riot, yet more putting their lives at risk when they formed a bodyguard around George Thompson after one of his lectures in Boston in 1834 turned violent, similar scenes playing out across the northern states throughout the 1830s and 1840s.

'I belong to the women,' Douglass would declare before an audience at the grand Horticultural Hall on Tremont Street in

Boston many years later. He was certainly always much more comfortable opening up to women than to men, a characteristic picked up by British abolitionists like Estlin – 'I doubt if he forms intimacies much with gentlemen' – and traced back by many commentators to his deep attachment to his grandmother Betsey Bailey. Women, indeed, played an instrumental part at every step on his path to freedom, from the young Lucretia Auld arranging his transfer across the Chesapeake to Sophia Auld teaching him to read, and from his then-fiancé Anna funding his escape to New York to the protection he told the Horticultural Hall crowd he received from the brave 'women of old Massachusetts' during his first years on the anti-slavery trail. It is little surprise, therefore, that he would prove a staunch supporter of the women's rights campaign in the second half of the nineteenth century, a campaign founded and led, to a large degree, by women who had cut their activist teeth in the anti-slavery movement.[23]

'Send Back the Nigger'

While the question of relocation was still unresolved, letters between Douglass and his wife taking about two weeks each to cross the Atlantic, the escaped slave continued to tour, criss-crossing Britain and Ireland all through the summer. From London he returned to Scotland, tackling the Free Church again in a series of speeches at the Music Hall in Edinburgh alongside Thompson, who would also receive the Freedom of the City around this time. Back in England, Douglass spoke, among other venues, at the Ebenezer Chapel in Birmingham, where he was joined on stage by Sturge and the seventy-eight-year-old Richard T. Cadbury, *paterfamilias* of the famously philanthropic Quaker clan. The start of July, meanwhile, found him in Liverpool attending the Hutchinson Family's final concert before their return to America, the musical family, together with Douglass's abolitionist cohort James Buffum, sailing home, appropriately enough, on the morning of 4 July, on board the *Cambria* with Captain Judkins again at the helm.

After some embarrassingly small audiences at the beginning of their tour, the final few months had been hugely successful for the

Hutchinsons, with even the initially harsh critics of the *Times* and the *Spectator* succumbing to the charms and musical abilities of the siblings from 'the Mountains of the old Granite State', the 'little Yankee girl' Abby, 'dressed in a plain shot-silk gown, without a single ornament', standing 'in the midst of her sturdy brothers' on stage. In Manchester, they filled the nearly 5,000-capacity Free Trade Hall for two 'farewell' concerts, earning £200 in the process each night. Alexander Ireland of the *Manchester Examiner* got to know them well during their sojourn, recalling happily the commingling of 'apprentice lads and milliner girls' with 'parsons and politicians' at their concerts. He also travelled to Liverpool to see them off, finding himself seated next to Douglass at a post-concert party.[24]

'The appearance of this man is destined to form an era in the history of American slavery,' Ireland wrote presciently. 'He is tall, and of great muscular strength; indeed, he might serve as a model for a Negro Hercules,' the journalist continued, Douglass's powerful black body a source of fascination for men and women alike, in private correspondence and the pages of the press. Not all such commentary, however, was supportive, Douglass taking exception to a description of him as 'an excellent specimen of the Negro' in an article in the conservative *Cork Constitution* in the autumn of 1845. 'He was familiar with such epithets in America, and cared little for what their public journals said,' Douglass told a public meeting in the city soon afterwards. 'But in Cork, in a place of Enlightenment, he was not prepared for such language from a public journal; it looked like a good advertisement from a slave trader.'[25]

Douglass would have to deal with worse when he returned to Ireland in July 1846, travelling to Belfast at the same time that the annual Presbyterian Assembly was being held in the city. The County Down-born Revd Dr Thomas Smyth of Charleston, South Carolina, a friend of Thomas Chalmers who had returned home to deal with an inheritance, was also present, complaining about the city being in a complete 'hub-bub' over Douglass and of being denied entry into the Assembly in response to calls for it to break fraternal relations with its American brethren. Hurt and angered by the manner in which he had been received, Smyth spread a rumour that Douglass had been seen leaving a brothel in Manchester, a monumentally damaging slur in a city as pious as Belfast, 'Send Back the Nigger' placards appearing on the streets, posted either by Smyth or some of his supporters.[26]

Although the threat of legal action wrangled a public apology out of Smyth, the affair, combined with Anna's now-known refusal to move to Britain, clearly affected Douglass, who, frustrated and worn-down, blamed 'the foul slanders of this Revd man-stealer' when apologising to Isabel Jennings – his 'Dear Isa' – for being rude and abrupt in a previous letter. 'No man hath power over the spirit,' he had continued. 'He must submit to its magic sway with the same resignation that the weather-beaten Mariner does when dashed upon the waves of the storm-tossed ocean. I would be always pleasant and agreeable if I could be, but so I cannot always be. I cannot be always upon the mountain top, no more than I can be always in the tranquil shade of the valley. I have my times and seasons like everybody else. You told me nothing new, when you told me that I was imperfect.'[27]

With Buffum and the Hutchinsons departed, the year that he was meant to have been away coming to an end and still no certainty about when or if he would return to America, Douglass was also suddenly deeply homesick, dreaming of and writing to his friend William A. White, the black abolitionist who had been by his side when attacked by an anti-abolitionist mob in Pendleton, Indiana, a few years earlier. 'William, do you think it would be safe for me to come home this fall?' he asked plaintively. 'Would master Hugh stand much chance in Mass[achusetts]? Think he could take me from the old Bay State?' To a Buffalo-based friend, he wrote: 'I wish I could see you this morning, could press your generous hand and hear your friendly voice.'[28]

Faltering in spirit and facing another extended period of time away from his family, Douglass would soon be revived, however, by the appearance of Garrison, the editor of the *Liberator* making his way across the Atlantic to join the escaped slave on his tour through Britain.

5

'FRIENDS OF FREEDOM'

'Never did I behold so gorgeous a sight as was presented by the shipping in the harbour,' wrote William Lloyd Garrison of the scene as he arrived into Liverpool on board the *Britannia* on the afternoon of 31 July 1846, the day after the opening of the new Albert Dock by the eponymous royal. While impressed by the thousands of flags 'of all colours, shapes and nations' still 'floating in the breeze' and 'meeting the eye in every direction', the American editor, an ardent republican, was quick to pour scorn on the public's 'loyal delirium'. Somewhat harshly, Garrison dismissed Albert as 'a harmless, well-behaved, good-looking young man', little more than an 'appendage to the throne'. He was on surer ground when suggesting Albert's appearance in the city was aimed at least in part at 'gratifying public curiosity', the British people at large idolising Queen Victoria but still unsure about her German-born husband.[1]

Married to Victoria for more than six years by this stage, Albert had actually made his first major public speech at an anti-slavery event in the summer of 1840: the first public meeting of the esteemed abolitionist Sir Thomas Fowell Buxton's Society for the Extinction of the Slave Trade and for the Civilisation of Africa. Partly, this was because it was easier for royals – then as now – to avoid controversy by addressing international moral concerns rather than controversial domestic issues. However, it was also a sign of his genuine conviction that slavery was a 'stain upon civilised Europe' as well as a 'state of things so repugnant to the principles of Christianity'.[2] Albert had been extremely nervous about the speech – delivered when he was just twenty years old to a crowd of more than 4,000 in a language that was not his first – memorising it by heart, practising it over breakfast with Victoria and keeping a copy in the bottom of his hat while he spoke.

Its success, however, encouraged him to stay involved in the cause, even giving his name a year later to one of the ships that took part in an ill-fated expedition up the River Niger, one that planned to mix missionary work with the development of agriculture and other trades – Buxton's 'Bible and plough' approach to eradicating the internal slave trade in Africa.

Victoria, too, was seen as a friend of the movement, especially by the legions of female anti-slavery activists who had petitioned her on the question of West Indies 'apprenticeship' soon after she ascended to the throne. Diplomatic decorum, however, perforce kept her from engaging with the topic too openly. It also meant there was little chance   should she or Albert have wished it – of meeting Frederick Douglass, a high profile fugitive slave, after all, in a country with which Britain was ostensibly on good terms.

There were no such issues with another American in the midst of a hugely successful tour of Britain: 'General' Tom Thumb, the eight-year-old dwarf whose manager, the pioneering (and incredibly exploitative) showman P. T. Barnum, was also a distant cousin. Victoria, indeed, would arrange three private shows with the child performer whose real name was Charles S. Stratton and whose acts, including song and dance routines and sketches where he dressed up as Napoleon Bonaparte and other famous figures, were the most popular of the year, drawing tens of thousands of aristocrats, artists and ordinary theatregoers alike to the grand Egyptian Hall in Piccadilly in central London. Charles Dickens was a definite fan, cajoling even friends like the world-renowned Shakespearean actor William Macready to join him at performances. Benjamin Robert Haydon, however, the artist who had painted the opening session of the World

Anti-Slavery Convention a few years earlier and whose nearby exhibition was all but ignored, was deeply unimpressed. 'They rush by thousands to see Tom Thumb. They push, they fight, they scream, they faint. They cry help and murder! And oh! And ah!' the debt-laden painter confided bitterly to his diary, just weeks before committing suicide. Similar scenes had been repeated across the country, the 'General' even performing in cities like Perth, Dundee and Exeter shortly before or just after Douglass. Getting measured at a tailors on Regent Street at the beginning of the year, Asa Hutchinson had been given a sense of the 2-foot-tall performer's immense success: 'Little "Tom Thumb's" clothes were made there. I saw a pattern of his hanging up in the shop. Wolf [the tailor] told me that Tom's father had already made by him 40,000 pounds in this country and Barnum three times that sum.'[3]

Victoria also attended a Royal Command Performance by the popular American minstrel group the Ethiopian Serenaders at Arundel Castle in Sussex, the 'blackface' group having spent much of the year performing to great crowds three nights a week at St James's Theatre in London before embarking on a provincial tour, filling the days between appearances with private shows for aristocrats like the Duke of Devonshire. (A few years earlier, they had performed at the White House for President John Tyler.) Whether performed by travelling American troupes or British or Irish impersonators, minstrel shows of this sort would prove a perennially popular feature of the Victorian stage, a programme for a Virginia Minstrels show in Dublin in 1844, for example, promising the audience views of the 'sports and pastimes of the Virginia Coloured Race, through the medium of Songs, Refrains and Ditties as sung by southern slaves'. The *Edinburgh Evening Post*, meanwhile, would lavish praise on the 'American nigger minstrelsy' of the Serenaders when they performed in that city.[4]

For British and Irish audiences of the era, including Victoria and Albert, there was no hypocrisy in enjoying minstrel shows at the same time as supporting anti-slavery, for although generally portraying black people in a childish light, they were not as overtly racist as they would become in later years. Many of the shows, indeed, were anti-slavery in sentiment, encouraging audiences to sympathise with the plight of the oppressed slave even as they lampooned black people. Douglass, however, was contemptuous of these 'blackface' performers, rebuking a local actor for performing 'Jim Crow ... apes of the Negro' during one of his speeches in Limerick. Despite his annoyance, Douglass could be just as quick to trade in stereotypes, joking to English audiences about the possibility of abolitionists adopting the motto of the Irishman 'Pat', who, 'upon entering a Tipperary row', declared: 'Wherever you see a head, hit it!' He could also be extremely crude in comments about the 'savage' and 'wild' Native Americans.[5]

The aforementioned Macready, playing Hamlet at the Surrey Theatre around the time of Douglass's tour, had also donned blackface on stage on a number of occasions, albeit for the more artistically acceptable reason of performing *Othello*. The great tragedian did not, however, have the Shakespearean audience all to himself in 1846. The celebrated American actresses Charlotte and Susan Cushman – joining Douglass, the Hutchinson Family, Tom Thumb, the Ethiopian Seranaders and others in a veritable American invasion of the British stage – undertook their own extensive tour of Britain that year and earned rave reviews for their performances in *Romeo and Juliet*; Charlotte, as was common in the gender-fluid theatre of the time, playing the male lead.

'The Central Point of Human Existence'

Garrison's journey across the Atlantic had been exhausting, a problem with the ship causing a delay at Halifax, Nova Scotia, and seasickness confining him to his berth for much of the remainder of the passage. His spirits were revived by the sight of Henry C. Wright and Richard D. Webb waiting among the crowd at the docks in Liverpool. The three friends embraced warmly before repairing to Brown's Temperance Hotel in Clayton Square, where they were soon joined by other anti-slavery activists from across Britain and Ireland, all of whom were anxious to meet their revered but rarely glimpsed American leader. A few days later, they travelled en masse to London, taking lodgings and talking anti-slavery long into the nights.[6]

'This, you know, is my third visit to London,' Garrison wrote almost immediately to his pregnant wife Helen, whom he was already missing deeply. 'If, at first, its vastness and splendour overwhelmed me, my astonishment is rather increased than diminished, the more I attempt to take its dimensions, and look into its wonders.' Quoting Isaiah 40:17, he went on:

> There are two positions in which I feel myself 'less than nothing, and vanity' – a mere mote in the sun-beam – on the Atlantic ocean, and in London, the central point of human existence ... The throng of people is immense, without end, go where you will ... The Thames ... presents a curious spectacle, at all hours. In addition to the multitude of vessels from various parts of the globe, the river is crowded with steamers of all sizes and descriptions, gliding up and down with great velocity, and carrying multitudes of people, who are enabled to travel a long distance for a mere trifle. Nothing can be more animating or picturesque than to stand on any one of the fine bridges which span the Thames, and look up and down the river, to see the innumerable conveyances which are flying in every direction. As for the streets in London, their name is legion, and in length many of them seem interminable. Yet, huge as is the city, and complicated as are its arrangements and mysterious as are its modes of existence, everything goes on with a regularity and precision truly marvellous. There is no violent collision – scarcely any jostle – the mechanism is perfect, 'like clock-work' – and no one is allowed or expected to interfere with another.[7]

Garrison was troubled, however, by the 'immense number' of prostitutes on the streets. 'They are of all grades in appearance, from the most fashionably dressed to the most ragged,' he wrote to Helen. 'They are very importunate to all passers-by, often taking them by the arm, and frequently accosting them in a familiar manner. Hence, there is a perpetual temptation, and a very formidable one, held out, especially to young, unmarried men, to be licentious. In fact, personal purity on the part of married men, I am told, is scarcely regarded at all, taking them in a mass.'

Garrison, of course, was more than adequately endowed with the 'personal purity' needed to withstand such propositions, describing to his wife how he had to jump onto a passing omnibus to escape the attentions of one particularly forthright 'young lady' outside the Mansion House. Nevertheless, clearly sympathising with the woman's plight, he continued:

My heart sunk within me to think of the horrid fate of that unfortunate creature. She seemed to me like one just entering on her frightful career. I thought of her as a sister – as *my* sister – seduced, it may be, by some villain, who had pledged to her eternal fidelity. I thought of her as a daughter – as *my* daughter – once the hope, the pride, the ornament of the family circle – now a castaway, and forever shut out from virtuous society. To think of such a one selling her body nightly, for a few shillings to furnish her with bread – no matter to whom, provided she can obtain the price! What unutterable loathing must possess her soul – and yet, so inexorable is society, this she must do, or die of starvation on the streets. O, horrible doom![8]

'The Real Friends of Emancipation'

Like Douglass before him, Garrison stayed at George Thompson's 'handsomely furnished' South Kensington home. 'He is still the same loving, faithful friend – the same playful, mirthful, entertaining companion – the same modest, unpretending man – the same zealous and eloquent advocate – the same warm and sympathising friend of suffering humanity – that he was eleven years ago, when he was in our country,' the editor wrote, the genuineness of his feelings evident in the fact that this description came in a private letter to his wife rather than a piece for the *Liberator*. Nevertheless, the remorselessly pure Garrison still found time to chide his host slightly for having started taking snuff:

'Like all snuff-takers, he uses it almost unconsciously. Of course, I have borne my testimony against his box and its contents. He has too much good sense to take offence, and too much honesty to attempt to extenuate his conduct; so he simply smiles, and hears me with all kindness.'[9]

Garrison also travelled down to Gravesend in Kent for a night, where Thompson's wife and children – four girls and two boys (one of whom was named Garrison after the editor) – had been enjoying a short summer break. Previously the den of 'sailors' and 'lewd women', it had recently been transformed into a pleasant resort, Garrison joining the Thompsons on a 'beautiful' walk through the nearby Rosherville Gardens – another popular Victorian amenity like Cremorne lost to time and changing styles. Jenny Thompson looked 'quite as young as she did when in Boston,' Garrison commented to his wife. The children, however, Garrison found remarkably quiet. 'Far too much so, for me,' he wrote, longing for 'an hour's frolic' with his own boisterous boys and girls.[10]

Garrison and the whole Thompson clan returned to London the next morning. By this stage, Douglass, too, was in the capital, having travelled down from Scotland to join forces with his mentor. Almost immediately he found himself the centre of controversy at the World's Temperance Convention. Organised by the National Temperance Society – a body Douglass had addressed a couple of months earlier – this was the first temperance gathering of its kind. Billed as a global affair, it was, in reality, almost entirely Anglo-American in complexion – the only 'world' that really mattered to this conclave of illustrious English-speaking Christians, the indissoluble bonds linking the two countries referred to explicitly and poetically in the American reformer Elihu Burritt's introduction to its published proceedings, a piece that did not doubt their duty to remake the world in their image. 'Two great nations, planted in the two hemispheres that they might move the world with their progress and pervade it with their peace, had been newly united by the very ocean that divided them,' Burritt stated, acknowledging the transformative effect of recent advances in steam-powered travel. 'They were daily approaching each other, and, by their increasing mutual proximity, were drawing all men, and tribes, and tongues into one compact family circle, within the compass of a common civilisation and Christianity.' Even in times of war, the connections had been strong: 'Whilst the men of Old England and the men of New England were engaged in deadly strife on Bunker Hill and Monmouth, the wives, and mothers, and fathers of the latter were, perhaps, reading by firelight in their humble homes, the works of [Richard] Baxter and [John] Bunyan, and feeding their souls and the spirits of their religious devotions with the words that burned on the lips, and the thoughts that breathed in the lines, of the old English divines.'[11]

Lymen Beecher, the septuagenarian 'father of temperance' in America, was among the large number of delegates to travel from the United States, religious reformers in the main who saw alcohol at the root of much of the poverty and violence in the world. (Beecher was also the father of Harriet Beecher Stowe, the author who would soon burst to fame with the publication of the anti-slavery novel *Uncle Tom's Cabin*.) There were, however, no slaveholders present. Joseph Sturge had made this a stipulation of his financial contributions to the conference.

Nevertheless, anxious to avoid any distractions from the gathering's core concern and wary of the ineffable ability of slavery to stoke division – especially among Americans – Sturge had also called on all participants to refrain from discussing the topic. The chairman of the convention concurred, urging the need 'to preserve as much unanimity as possible' because 'the eye of the world is upon us'.[12]

Held over the course of five days from 4–8 August in the stately surrounds of the Covent Garden Theatre, the convention was a largely self-congratulatory affair, with papers read, statistics quoted and motions promoting the reduction of the sale and use of alcohol moved and seconded. Douglass punctured the mood on the third day, when, chafing at the praise being heaped on American temperance groups, he drew attention to the manner in which they excluded black people. His words – which did not make it into the official convention proceedings – caused an immediate stir, with some delegates crying 'go on, go on' while others – 'the American delegates on the platform' – demanded he 'sit down' and complained that he was insinuating temperance societies in the United States supported slavery.

The aftermath of this contretemps saw a sharp epistolary exchange between Douglass and Revd Dr Samuel Hanson Cox, a Presbyterian minister from New York and delegate in London. Writing to the *New York Evangelist*, Cox, a much-admired orator who had earlier helped found New York University, described how the 'glorious unity' of the event had been ruined as soon as Douglass, 'the coloured abolition agitator and ultraist', took to the stage, the word 'ultraist' a clear sign of his allegiance to the Tappenite American and Foreign Anti-Slavery Society. 'He lugged in anti-slavery or abolition, no doubt prompted to it by some of the politic ones, who can use him to do what they would not themselves adventure to do in person,' Cox continued, his comments indicative of the bitterness with which the supposedly irreligious Garrison was looked on by many in America, even otherwise worthy abolitionists, as Cox truly was, having had his house and church attacked during anti-abolitionist riots in New York in the 1830s.

Douglass replied with a letter of his own, which was soon published as a pamphlet. Defending himself at first from Cox's 'misrepresentations', he explained (not entirely accurately, given that he was not an official delegate) how he had been 'the recognised representative of the coloured population of the United States' at the convention and thus had every right to speak up for them. 'It would have been quite easy for me to have made a speech upon the general question of temperance, carefully excluding all reference to my enslaved, neglected and persecuted brethren in America,' he continued. 'But to have pursued such a course, would have been selling my birthright for a mess of pottage – would have been to play the part of Judas.' More provocatively, he speculated whether the fact that Cox had been made to share a platform with a 'Negro, a fugitive slave' was the real cause of his anger. 'I do not assert this positively – it may not be quite true. But if it be true, I sincerely pity your littleness of soul.' Turning to Cox's supposed history of support for anti-slavery, he then declared with finality: 'But, Sir, you are not an abolitionist, and you only assumed to be one during your recent tour in this country, that you might sham your way through this land, and the more effectually stab and blast the character of the real friends of emancipation.'[13]

Writing to his wife, Garrison, who like Douglass attended the convention, was scathing of the whole proceedings, quickly perceiving that 'the same spirit which controlled the anti-slavery convention in 1840' had 'entire mastery over this' and that free discussion was 'out of the question'. Nevertheless, it gained attention in *The Times* and other leading dailies. Douglass, meanwhile, featured prominently in the *Illustrated London News*'s coverage of the event, pictured both on his own and as part of a wider group.

The same issue that carried these pictures also had an advertisement for the sale of 'New Albert Cravats' from William Whitelock's establishment on the Strand, the Queen's husband subtly insinuating himself into the consciousness of the country. A man of sartorial influence, he has also been credited with popularising the frock coat.[14]

The following week's *Illustrated London News* showed scenes from the Kaffir Wars in southern Africa – a series of conflicts between European settlers and African tribes now known as the Xhosa Wars. There was also a brief mention of a new organisation called the Anti-Slavery League.

'No Apology for Slavery'

Almost as soon as they had gathered together in London, Garrison, Douglass and their supporters had started to formulate plans for a new anti-slavery organisation to rival the British and Foreign Anti-Slavery Society, launching the Anti-Slavery League at a crowded meeting at the Crown and Anchor Tavern on the Strand on the evening of Monday 17 August, the now demolished venue once 'famous as the headquarters of agitation' in the city. It was a tumultuous six-hour affair that ended past midnight, with Garrison, Thompson (the organisation's president) and Douglass all to the fore, the latter's speech 'one of his very best efforts'. Dissent came from Sidney Morse, editor of the *New York Observer* and brother of the inventor (and, in an earlier career, noted portrait painter) Samuel B. Morse, as well as the Revd John Howard Hinton, a Baptist minister in London who spoke up in support of the anti-Garrisonian American and Foreign Anti-Slavery Society. The controversial American mesmerist (an early form of hypnosis) Robert H. Collyer, meanwhile, insisted the United States could settle its own 'internal affairs without foreign aid' before being shouted down by the audience (all of whom had paid 6*d* to attend) for derogatorily referring to Douglass as 'that coloured man'.[15]

Several of the following day's papers carried positive reports of the meeting, the *Morning Chronicle* – chief rival of *The Times* – including the three founding principles of the Anti-Slavery League:

> First – That slave-holding is, under all circumstances, a sin of the deepest dye, and ought to be immediately abandoned.
> Secondly – That the members of this league shall consist of all persons subscribing to the foregoing principles, without respect of country, complexion, or religious or political creeds.
> Thirdly – That the sole object of the league shall be the overthrow, by means exclusively moral and peaceful, of slavery in every land, but with special reference to the system now existing in the United States.

Across the Atlantic, the *Liberator* was unsurprisingly fulsome in its praise of the new body, one that would provide 'a bond of union' between the 'true abolitionists' of the old world and the new. This was vital, the paper continued, for no matter how loud American protestations to the contrary, public opinion in the 'mother-country' still held a 'mighty influence' on the United States. 'Though the connection with her is no longer *colonial*, it is still, in a very important sense, *provincial*. She is our metropolis after all, to which we look for the fashion of our thoughts as well as of our coats.'[16]

With placards for the event having encouraged all Americans in London to attend, the Boston-based evangelist Revd Edward N. Kirk had also been present at the launch of the Anti-Slavery League. He soon 'found the atmosphere too warm', however, Garrison wrote, and departed. Like many other American ministers, the forty-three-year-old Kirk – dressed in surviving portraits in the evangelist's uniform of cut-away tail-coats, white shirts and high collars – had crossed the Atlantic for the dual purpose of attending the World Temperance Convention – where he had been to the fore of those shouting Douglass down – and the Evangelical Alliance. Attended by over 900 delegates (clergymen and laymen) and held over the course of a fortnight in late August and early September at the Freemasons' Hall in Great Queen Street in London, the latter was a long-planned meeting aimed at cementing the ties between the increasingly influential evangelists on both sides of the Atlantic. Instead, Douglass's agenda-setting tour turned it – like the Free Church of Scotland fundraising campaign and the World Temperance Convention beforehand – into another theatre in which the fractious debate over slavery could be played out, the efforts of a number of British delegates (including friends of Douglass's like the Belfast-based Revd Isaac Nelson) to get the new body to ban slaveholders from membership leading to days of tense arguments before the matter was indecorously put to 'Committee' in order to save face.[17]

The abolitionists were quick to turn the controversy to their new organisation's advantage, holding a 6,000-strong public meeting at Exeter Hall where Douglass accused the American ministers at the Evangelical Alliance of having 'hoodwinked' and 'misled' their British brethren, and at which a large amount of money was raised for the Anti-Slavery League. Although some of the harsh words aimed at the clergymen led to complaints that the meeting was more 'anti-clerical' rather than 'anti-slavery', the characterisation of the Evangelical Alliance as a weak, conniving, slavery-supporting organisation took hold in the public consciousness, with many newspapers, national and local, noting little else except its fudged stance on slaveholders. Delegates like the Revd John Fenwick of Newcastle also resigned from the body in protest at its refusal to bar slaveholders while respected voices like John Burnet, the Independent minister in Camberwell in south London, declared: 'The judgement of the Alliance is not the judgement of England.'[18]

Loath to see their great gathering so openly traduced, members of the Evangelical Alliance responded in kind. They held public meetings across the country, including in Aylesbury, the county town of Buckinghamshire, where Sir Culling Eardley Smith, a well-known religious reformer and founder member of the Alliance, claimed – to the Glasgow abolitionist Andrew Paton's disgust – that worthy Christians in America could 'in spite of themselves' become 'unwilling' holders of slaves. In Norwich, meanwhile, the Revd W. M. Clarke, a black minister from Washington, DC, defended the Alliance's stance on slavery, stating: 'The object of the Alliance was to promote Christianity, and if this object were attained, that of itself would tend more than anything else, to check slavery.' Echoing the words of the Free Church leader Thomas Chalmers a few years earlier, he also insisted that he would be 'departing from the spirit of the gospel' if he were to 'unchristianise' all those connected with slavery in America. He then took refuge in the fallacious but oft-repeated claim that it was against the law in America to free slaves, an assertion that drew forth from the audience boos, hisses and cries of 'No apology for slavery'.[19]

'England's Best Production'

Away from the stages of Exeter Hall and the Crown and Anchor Tavern, Garrison used his time in London to renew some old acquaintances, spending, for example, a number of days with the Quakers William and Mary Howitt, a then well-known literary couple whom he had first met around the time of the World Anti-Slavery Convention in 1840 and who numbered the finest writers of the era among their closest friends, from William Wordsworth to Elizabeth Gaskell, and from Lord Tennyson to Elizabeth Barrett Browning, the great poet who opposed fiercely the slavery on which her family's fortune had been made. Though largely forgotten today, William Howitt, in his mid-fifties by this stage, was the author of innumerable books on history, literature, travel, nature and religion, among other topics. Karl Marx, living in near penury and pawning the family gold in Brussels in the summer of 1846, was among his many admirers, later quoting *Colonisation and Christianity* approvingly in his groundbreaking first volume of *Capital*. Mary Howitt, meanwhile, who was about seven years younger than her husband, was a prolific translator and poet, best known for the still-popular children's rhyme *The Spider and the Fly*.

Douglass, too, got to know the Howitts, accompanying Garrison to their large, secluded home in Lower Clapton, where a row of elm trees at the front gave way to a long lawn and 'creeper-festooned walls' at the back as well as a meadow through which ran the Lea, a tributary of the Thames. Mary interviewed the two American abolitionists at length for biographical sketches that would be published in the *People's Journal* – a new politically progressive journal – before being published as pamphlets. 'Such men ennoble their age and the country,' she wrote of Garrison. Douglass, meanwhile, was 'a noble human being'. The Americans certainly made a deep impression, Mary writing (more than a shade condescendingly) to her sister: 'I am just now deeply interested in the anti-slavery question, the real thorough Abolitionist view which would cut up the crying sin root and branch, and spare none of its participants ... I can talk of nothing but the "dear blacks".'[20]

Mary Howitt conducted similar interviews with the Hutchinson Family, who had visited The Elms, as the Howitts home was called, on a number of occasions earlier in the year. She would pen a poem in their honour, called 'Band of Young Apostles'; they in turn setting the words of *The Spider and the Fly* to song. According to John Hutchinson, the Howitts were 'England's best production ... full of enthusiasm, love and faith', their home in east London ever-open to 'friends of freedom', including, at the time of Douglass's visits, the young German poet

Ferdinand Freiligrath, whose political radicalism had forced him into exile.[21] Freiligrath, whom the Howitts had gotten to know during their years living in Germany at the start of the decade, would have been well versed in the topic of slavery, having forged a deep friendship with the American poet Henry Wadsworth Longfellow while the latter was recuperating from an illness in a spa at Marienberg on the Rhine a few years earlier. Best known for the legend-making 1861 poem 'Paul Revere's Ride', Longfellow, the most popular American poet of his era, was also the author of a small but powerful collection entitled simply *Poems on Slavery*, the closing verse of which, 'The Warning', is now read as a foreshadowing of the American Civil War.

'William and Mary Howitt were among the kindliest people I ever met,' Douglass recalled many years later, their interest in America and 'well-known testimonies against slavery' making him feel 'much at home with them'. It was also while staying with the Howitts that Douglass met 'the Swedish poet and author' Hans Christian Andersen, whose early work Mary Howitt – a specialist in Scandinavian literature – had translated. 'He, like myself, was a guest, spending a few days,' Douglass wrote. Nevertheless, the escaped American slave spent little time with the slightly built author of such famous fairy tales as *The Princess and the Pea* and *Thumbelina*, separated both by a language barrier – 'his bad English, and my destitution of Swedish' – and Andersen's solitary personality. 'He was singular in his appearance, and equally singular in his silence. His mind seemed to me all the while turned inwardly. He walked about the beautiful garden as one might in a dream.'[22]

Douglass and Garrison also spent a number of relaxing days at the Muswell Hill home of William Henry Ashurst, a prominent fifty-four-year-old Unitarian solicitor and radical who schooled his children – one son and four daughters all close in age to the escaped slave – so thoroughly in the ways of reform that they became notable activists in their own rights. Like their close friends the Howitts, the Ashursts had first met Garrison at the time of the World Anti-Slavery Convention in 1840, William going on to contribute regularly to the *Liberator* under the pseudonym

Edward Search. Again like the Howitts, their London home was a veritable melting pot of artists and agitators of all stripes, earning their circle of friends the sobriquet the 'Muswell Hill Brigade'. Douglass's first visit appears to have been on the afternoon of Sunday 23 August, a large social gathering with guests including the noted Unitarian minister William J. Fox that ended after dinner with those present 'rolling balls on the greensward', a reference, it seems, to a game of boules.[23]

Although the date is not specified, it was also at Muswell Hill – that 'beautiful home', Garrison would write, 'where so many of Freedom's exiles from the Continent always found ... the most generous hospitality' – that the two American abolitionists met the Italian nationalist Giuseppe Mazzini, London at the time a haven for radicals seeking shelter from the autocracies of continental Europe. It was a coming together that would have a strong effect on Garrison. The editor of the *Liberator* and the prison-scarred Mazzini would enjoy a deep friendship for the remainder of their lives, Garrison writing a warm introduction for a book – edited by one of Ashurst's daughters – of Mazzini's writings many years later.[24]

As well as old friends, Garrison was eager to meet any figures of consequence who could give support to the anti-slavery cause, breakfasting on one of his first mornings in the city with the distinguished Swedish professor of anatomy Anders Retzius and the young Bristol-based Dr Agustin Prichard, whose membership of various medical organisations would soon bring him into contact (sometimes conflict) with the then newly emerging field of anaesthetics. Encouraged by Prince Albert's interest in matters of medical progress, Victoria would go on to use chloroform for her final two labours in 1853 and 1857, fashionable London soon following suit in spite of objections from medical journals like *The Lancet*.[25]

Together with Douglass and Thompson, Garrison also took breakfast with the widely travelled and slightly wild-haired Radical politician John Bowring. 'He was full of interesting information, and had a charming way of imparting his knowledge,' Douglass wrote. 'The conversation was about slavery and about China, and as my knowledge was very slender about the "Flowery Kingdom" and its people, I was greatly interested in [his] description of the ideas and manners prevailing among them.' Douglass was particularly taken by the apparently widespread use of the 'doctrine of substitution' in the country, which went so far that people 'sometimes procured others to suffer even the penalty of death in their stead'. The abolitionists in turn made a good impression on Bowring, the MP for Bolton, who would later serve as Governor of Hong Kong, quickly agreeing to support the Anti-Slavery League.[26]

A newspaper man himself, Garrison was also keen to cultivate contacts in the press, strongly believing in the power of the fourth estate to mould 'public sentiment' on the question of slavery. He began with the conductors of journals that while relatively small in circulation were influential in the dissenting denominations so long the bedrock of the anti-slavery movement in Britain. These included the Independent minister and future MP Edward Miall of the *Nonconformist* and the Cork-born Revd William Hincks of the *Inquirer*, a weekly Unitarian magazine that exists to this day, the latter promising 'to do all that he can to promote the League, both in his private capacity, and as an editor'. Garrison also received backing from the London bi-weekly the *Patriot*, even though its editor, Josiah Conder, was close to Joseph Sturge, the American buying 300 copies of the edition that contained the Exeter Hall speeches against the Evangelical Alliance for dissemination among supporters in England and the United States. John Saunders of the *People's Journal*, the publication to which William and Mary Howitt (as well as Mazzini) were regular contributors, was another, assuredly more natural supporter.[27]

Although not on a par with his far more famous and less controversial compatriot Ralph Waldo Emerson's gaining entry into the editor's room of *The Times* a few years later, Garrison also met Douglas Jerrold, the acerbic but deeply compassionate leading writer for the popular satirical magazine *Punch*, a publication, the American editor wrote, that had 'consecrated the somewhat dangerous weapons of wit and satire, and the perilous art of caricature, to the cause of humanity'. The forty-three-year-old

Jerrold, who also edited two weekly journals carrying his highly regarded name, *Douglas Jerrold's Shilling Magazine* and *Douglas Jerrold's Weekly Newspaper*, publications Garrison described as 'of a graver character' to *Punch* but 'equally on the side of the people', received his fellow editor warmly. 'He promised to give us a helping hand for [slavery's] overthrow, and has since manifested his sincerity in copying various articles from the *Liberator* into his magazine.'

Another day, Garrison had a 'pleasant interview' with John Forster, the editor of the *Daily News*, the new paper established by Dickens at the beginning of the year that had already given a good deal of coverage to Douglass's tour. 'It will be in his power, and from what fell from his lips it will be his wish, to inform the public mind ... of the workings of slavery in America, and the success of the anti-slavery movement,' Garrison wrote, noting also how Richard D. Webb would 'cull' articles from the *Liberator* and other anti-slavery papers for insertion in its columns. Disappointingly, Dickens himself, who had earlier taken his wife and children to a Hutchinson Family concert, was absent in Europe, writing *Dombey and Son* while holidaying with his family in Lausanne, Switzerland. Deeply engaged in the slavery question, he would have been keen to meet the visiting American abolitionists. He certainly admired Douglass's writing, sending a copy of the *Narrative* to his friend Macready when the actor was about to embark on a tour of America a couple of years later. George Cruickshank, however, the illustrator who brought so many of Dickens's most famous characters vividly to life, did see Douglass in action, a drawing of his portraying the escaped slave addressing a well-appointed English audience appearing in an anti-slavery almanac a few years later.[28]

'The Same Great Chain of Oppression'

With the implacably anti-slavery tone of sections of *American Notes* and his follow-up 1844 novel *Martin Chuzzlewit*, large parts of which were set in America, leading to widespread condemnation across the South, it is no surprise Dickens was extremely popular with African-American readers. Nevertheless, his work as a whole continued to be enjoyed in large numbers in the South throughout this period, readers in the largely agrarian, slaveholding states revelling in not just his humorous prose and finely drawn characters but also his condemnations of the industrial capitalism that had taken hold of both Britain and the North. Indeed, it was a regular trope of apologists for slavery to favourably contrast the lot of their own contented, well-fed slaves with benighted factory workers across the Atlantic, a print by the American artist John Haven entitled 'Slavery As It Exists in America/Slavery As It Exists in England', for example, depicting in one panel a group of slaves dancing joyously at the end of their short working day while in another, stooped, gaunt figures emerge from a seventeen-hour shift at an English cloth factory (see plate section).[29]

Notwithstanding the crude attempts of southern propagandists to hide the inhumanity of slavery behind the injustices of free labour capitalism, the societal ills depicted in Dickens's work were very real, leading in part to a huge rise in support for the working-class Chartist movement through the late 1830s and early 1840s. Douglass and Garrison, the latter of whom gave significant coverage to Chartist meetings in the *Liberator*, would quickly become acquainted with some its leaders – or at least the leaders of its 'moral force' faction, as opposed to 'physical force' proponents like Feargus O'Connor and the mixed-race William Cuffay, shared organisational values trumping shared slave heritage in this instance. 'I shall derive great assistance from the co-operation of William Lovett and Henry Vincent,' Garrison, a 'moral force' man to the core, wrote to his wife Helen. 'They are true men, who will stand by us to the last – men who have been cast into prisons in this country, and confined therein (the former one year, the latter twenty months) for pleading the cause of the starving operatives in this country, and contending for universal suffrage. Such men I honour and revere.'[30]

The ties between the two radical reform bodies seemed strong, with Garrison greeted by a 'thunder-storm' of applause when he addressed a Chartist meeting in London, Vincent – whose powerful speeches saw him labelled 'the young Demosthenes of English Democracy' after the ancient Greek orator – taking a part in the Anti-Slavery League and the gentle forty-six-year-old Lovett writing of slavery as 'a link in the same great chain of oppression which binds all multitudes in all countries and climes'. The warm personal connection, too, was clear, Lovett describing 'a very delightful evening' where 'Douglass, who had a fine voice, sang a number of Negro melodies, Mr Garrison sang several anti-slavery pieces, and our grave friend, H. C. Wright, sang an old Indian war-song'.

Nevertheless, attempts to address the deep-seated issue of poverty brought difficulties for Douglass. Genuinely moving from the position of a single-issue reformer to a broader humanitarian conception of the fight against slavery as part of a larger, global struggle against injustice, he sympathised deeply with the plight of the urban poor in England. But he was also repeatedly compelled to challenge efforts to draw some sort of moral equivalency between 'chattel slavery' and so-called 'wage slavery', describing in one meeting how 'some persons had asked why American slavery was agitated [for] in England' when a form of 'slavery' already existed there. 'If there was slavery in England, let it perish! If there were oppression, he hated oppression! If there were tyranny, he hated the tyrant! Whatsoever he could do he would to wrest from the hand of the tyrant his bloody power!' Douglass thundered in response. '[But] there was no slavery in England, and were the poorest peasant asked to change his lot, he would scorn to give up his liberty for that of slavery!'[31]

'You remind me of the poor, in this country,' he wrote in a similar vein in response to a letter from the Lynn Anti-Slavery Sewing Circle. 'I thank you for it,' he continued, promising that they could rely on him 'as one who will never desert the cause of the poor, no matter whether black or white'. Again, however, he was insistent: 'We have poverty here, but no slavery; we have crime here, but no slavery; we have suffering here, but no slavery, and in all this, England has a decided advantage over America.'[32]

If the Chartist connection created some tension for Douglass, an unalloyed highlight of the tour was the 20 August journey he made with Garrison and Thompson to the grand Ipswich home of the aged abolitionist Thomas Clarkson, whom he anointed 'the last of the noble line of Englishmen who inaugurated the anti-slavery movement for England and the civilised world – the lifelong friend and co-worker with Granville Sharp, William Wilberforce [and] Thomas Fowell Buxton'. Clarkson's poor health meant it was just a short visit. Nevertheless, the sense of awe was still palpable in his words when Douglass later described how the seriously ill and practically deaf Clarkson had clasped his two frail hands around one of the escaped slave's and in a 'tremulous' voice said: 'God bless you, Frederick Douglass! I have given sixty years of my life to the emancipation of your people, and if I had sixty years more they should all be given to the same cause.'

Carrying a copy of the pamphlet *Hints for the American People in the Event of a Dissolution of the Union*, the final work the octogenarian Clarkson would ever complete, the three visiting abolitionists left Playford Hall, the Elizabethan mansion Clarkson shared with his wife Catherine just outside of Ipswich, 'with something of the feeling with which a man takes final leave of a beloved friend at the edge of a grave'.[33] The sense of foreboding proved accurate, Clarkson dying just over a month later, on 26 September, *The Times* in common with all the leading papers of the day carrying the news amid heavy black borders. The *Liberator*, meanwhile, reproduced an old sonnet by the poet laureate Wordsworth, a lifelong friend of the deceased abolitionist (even though his own anti-slavery feelings were never more than lukewarm).

> To Thomas Clarkson
> On the Final Passing of the Bill for the Abolition of the Slave Trade
> March 1807
>
> CLARKSON! it was an obstinate hill to climb:
> How toilsome – nay, how dire – it was, by thee
> Is known; by none, perhaps, so feelingly:
> But thou, who, starting in thy fervent prime,

Didst first lead forth that enterprise sublime,
Hast heard the constant Voice its charge repeat,
Which, out of thy young heart's oracular seat,
First roused thee. O true yoke-fellow of Time,
Duty's intrepid liegeman, see, the palm
Is won, and by all Nations shall be worn!
The blood-stained Writhing is forever torn;
And thou henceforth wilt have a good man's calm,
A great man's happiness; thy zeal shall find
Repose at length, firm friend of humankind!

6

'THE LION OF THE OCCASION'

On the afternoon of Friday, 28 August 1846, an elaborate, centuries-old ceremony saw the mysteriously named 'Black Rod' – a senior Parliamentary official – knock on the door of the House of Commons before leading its members into the House of Lords amid loud hurrahs, elaborate bows and the ostentatious doffing of hats. The extravagantly be-wigged and be-robed Lord Chancellor then read out a statement from Queen Victoria reviewing the year's main events – including the repeal of the Corn Laws and the settling 'in a manner consistent with national honour' of the Oregon question – before officially proroguing Parliament for two months. Normally, Victoria would have delivered this message herself. She seems to have disliked the ceremony, however, and soon ceased to attend entirely. Her successors have followed suit, and so, while the monarch of the day continues to appear and speak at the State Opening of Parliament, the formal winding up of Parliamentary sessions is left to the members of a Royal Commission.[1]

With Parliament in recess and the 'Season' – that summertime swirl of banquets, balls and great sporting occasions like the Derby – coming to an end, thoughts turned to the holiday destinations favoured by the country's elite, especially France, the *Illustrated London News* filling it pages with pictures of British tourists visiting sights in Boulogne or reposing in plush Parisian cafés. The Queen, three months after giving birth to her fifth child, was travelling with her husband around the Isle of Wight, Jersey and Guernsey in their new yacht, rather unimaginatively named the *Victoria and Albert*. The rise of the railways, meanwhile, made excursions to the Lake District and seaside towns like Blackpool attainable even to those of more modest means, the publisher George Bradshaw issuing his first railway guides and the travel company Thomas Cook starting to expand from its temperance festival origins to tours of Scotland and beyond around this time. (A temperance campaigner in Market Harborough in Leicestershire, Cook's first organised tours had been aimed at getting children out of Leicester during the alcohol-fuelled excesses of race week.[2])

Frederick Douglass and William Lloyd Garrison – joined on and off by George Thompson – were also on the move, taking their anti-slavery crusade out of the metropolis and into the towns and cities of provincial England, an exhilarating if physically draining journey that began in Bristol, another port city deeply connected with the slave trade. Already the scale of invitations to give talks had seen the editor inform his wife that he would not be returning home until the 19 October sailing of the *Britannia*, two weeks later than originally planned.[3]

'The Holy Cause'

Douglass and Garrison arrived at Bristol railway station in the early evening of Monday 24 August, the journey from London taking them through rolling West Country hills dappled with fabulous mansions built from the proceeds of slavery, Bristol having long served as the hub of the powerful West India planter interests. They were met off the train by John Bishop Estlin, a sixty-year-old eye surgeon of national renown who conveyed them directly by phaeton (a light horse-drawn carriage) to the spacious 47 Park Street home he shared with his twenty-five-year-old daughter Mary, his wife Margaret having died many years earlier. The guests barely had time for dinner before the house was filled, the abolitionists of the city having waited months for a first glimpse of the famous escaped slave. As early as March, indeed, Mary Estlin had written to Maria Weston Chapman about what she then presumed would be Douglass's imminent visit, adding she had already sold 150 copies of his autobiography.[4]

The elder Estlin, the son of a highly regarded Unitarian minister, was one of Bristol's most respected citizens, combining a lucrative medical career with a lifetime's dedication to philanthropic causes, including the establishment of a free eye clinic for the city's poor. He was also drawn to anti-slavery, publishing a pamphlet on American slavery full of praise for the American Anti-Slavery Society just a few months before Douglass's visit and maintaining a long transatlantic correspondence with the American abolitionist Samuel May Jr., a Unitarian minister who toured Britain in 1843 and whose Massachusetts home formed part of the Underground Railroad.

Returning to Bristol after an extended 1832 sojourn on the Caribbean island of St Vincent to restore his health, Estlin had actually authored an article for the Unitarian magazine the *Christian Reformer* any pro-slavery propagandist would have been proud of, emphasising how the 'physical condition of the slave ... was superior, in many respects, to that of large numbers of the poorer classes of his own countrymen'. Explained away by an early biographer as a consequence of Estlin's having not yet fully 'sounded [the] depths' of the slavery question, this was in truth an unsurprising point of view for a man born and brought up in a city suffused with the planter mindset, a city that was still holding large pro-slavery meetings in the last weeks before the passage of the Slavery Abolition Act 1833. It may also be a sign that the arguments of pro-slavery lecturers like the future Tory MP Peter Borthwick had hit their mark, the West India lobby having matched the abolitionist movement almost speech-for-speech in the year leading up to the passage of the epochal legislation. Time, thought and the influence of May, however, had brought Estlin around to the Garrisonian way of thinking – though the inherently conservative nature of his character was still evident in his attempts to get the Irish publisher Richard D. Webb to edit some passages in Douglass's *Narrative* about slave-breeding, for fear such 'disgusting details' would put people 'in this part of the world' off reading the book.[5]

Mary Estlin embraced the anti-slavery cause even more thoroughly than her father, becoming a leading member of the Bristol and Clifton Ladies' Anti-Slavery Society, which, though officially an auxiliary of the British and Foreign Anti-Slavery Society, had turned quite Garrisonian in outlook after May's visit to the city, sending large quantities of articles to the Boston Bazaar in 1844 and 1845. Together with Mary Carpenter, a fellow Unitarian whose whole family were involved in social causes, Mary Estlin had taken the lead in this aspect of the society's work, writing in one letter to Chapman how she was 'very glad to hear that the Bristol contributions sold well'. Indeed, it was in part to raise the profile of the Bazaar that her father had authored his recent pamphlet, describing in its introduction how he hoped it would engage the 'sympathy' of the city in 'the holy cause' in which the American abolitionists were 'labouring with self-sacrificing zeal and untiring devotedness'.[6]

While Garrison spent his first night in Bristol with the Estlins, Douglass stayed at the home of their wealthy Quaker friend George Thomas, the founder of Bristol General Hospital who, John Estlin wrote to May, 'would not allow my monopolising both'. Douglass was back at Park Street the next morning for a busy breakfast with more of the ophthalmologist's friends before Mary Estlin escorted him to the nearby Blind Asylum, where visually impaired people were trained for employment in crafts such as basket- and mat-making – examples of which they would soon send to the Boston Bazaar. The 'pupils' there, 'about 60 men, women & children', had had his *Narrative* read aloud to them. 'Their delight was extreme to <u>feel</u> him & question him. I think F. D. will never forget the scene,' John Estlin wrote to May, the underlining of 'feel' suggesting they actually placed their hands on Douglass's striking face and features.[7]

From the Blind Asylum, Douglass made his way to an afternoon meeting at the Victoria Rooms, a handsome Greek revival-style building that had opened in 1842 – the foundation stone having been laid on Queen Victoria's birthday in 1838. John K. Haberfield, the popular mayor, took the chair, noting Douglass's *Narrative* had been 'extensively read in this city', but also intimating that some still doubted it could have been written by a slave – a sign of lingering prejudice. Garrison spoke first before Douglass took to the stage, acknowledging it was difficult for many in England to believe what he said about the horrors of slavery, because they 'had heard of America, 3000 miles off, as the land of the free and the home of the brave', as 'the asylum where the oppressed of all nations on the face of the globe' went to find refuge. He then explained how the abolitionists wanted to 'humble' the slaveholder. 'They knew that the only chance of saving him from himself was to humble him, and they believed that the best way of doing it would be to exclude him from the communion of the church – to set the brand of Cain upon him and mark him out as a vagabond.'

His well-honed ability to engage audiences to the fore, he pointed to a child near the front the crowd as he exclaimed: 'And was he not a vagabond – when he would, without remorse, steal yon bright-eyed boy … tear him from his mother's arms … doom him to slavery … and force him to drag his chains and fetters under the degrading torture of the lash?' The boy was white, but the point was made. And besides, Douglass suggested to the crowd, the slaveholder 'would steal white men as readily as a man who stole a black horse would not scruple to steal a white horse'.[8]

Douglass sat down to 'long-continued cheering', wrote a local paper, the *Bristol Mercury*, describing also how despite his generally 'quiet and subdued' manner there were 'occasional tones in his voice – not unlike the low growl of the lion – which hint at "something dangerous" and which would seem to indicate that he is a man not to be trampled on with impunity'. Mary Carpenter, meanwhile, could not remember a speech of such 'powerful reasoning … touching appeals, keen sarcasm & graphic description'. Garrison, however, was not quite so satisfied with the event, which had been made up, he told Henry C. Wright, by 'a most select assemblage', including many 'affluent' Quakers. 'So much formality and selectness takes all the warmth out of me; and I felt as dull and flat as though I had neither perception nor instinct.' Douglass, too, he believed, had 'seemed to labour under embarrassment' though 'he did much better than myself'. Garrison had also been concerned Douglass's talk would 'disturb' the mayor and the 'cautious and considerate' John Estlin – 'the former by his severe remarks upon slaveholders as "vagabonds" and "villains"' … and the latter by his "indiscriminate" assault on the American churches and clergy'. The mayor, though, whatever his true feelings at 'such plain talk', had wound up the meeting with some 'commendatory remarks'. (He had earlier filled a glass of water for Douglass, leading the *Mercury* to declare in mock outrage: 'What! A white man – a mayor – a man in authority – hand a glass of water to a Negro! Incredible!') Estlin, too, 'took exception at nothing that was said' and indeed seemed 'very much pleased' with the results of the meeting. 'The more I see of him,' Garrison concluded, 'the more I am satisfied that he means to be a true friend of the cause, and that he is the main spoke in the anti-slavery wheel, in all this region.'[9]

After a drive out to the countryside in Estlin's phaeton, the two American abolitionists returned to his Park Street home that evening for another private gathering, the forty or so invited guests, Garrison noted, comprised in the main of 'ministers, lawyers and merchants'. The following day they were back on a public stage, speaking to a 1,000-strong audience of 'a more popular cast', the 6*d* cost of the tickets doing little to temper the eagerness of the crowd, many of whom were forced to stand in the aisles throughout to listen to the famous escaped slave – the 'lion of the occasion', as Garrison wrote to his wife, everywhere he went. A few weeks later, a similarly priced ticket would gain one entry into a talk by the Revd Joseph Wolff – the widely travelled Jewish Christian missionary known as 'the missionary to the world' – on his recent trip to Bukhara in modern-day Uzbekistan, part of the Bristol Athenaeum's autumn/winter series of lectures.[10]

Douglass's visit, Mary Estlin exulted to Chapman, had given 'fresh zeal' to the anti-slavery cause in the city. She expected a significant increase in the amount of material sent to that year's Boston Bazaar and described how, even thought their expectations had been high, Douglass still managed to exceed 'the picture we had formed' in terms of his 'outward graces', 'intellectual power', 'culture' and 'eloquence'. Her father was similarly impressed and felt certain a local branch of the new Anti-Slavery League would quickly be formed, a move he approved of, believing the British and Foreign Anti-Slavery Society 'superannuated'.

Mary Estlin also thought Garrison's impeccable behaviour and easy manners had 'dispelled many prejudices', opinions of him in the city having previously been clouded by the slurs and insinuations of rivals. Her father, however, was not so sure on this point, outlining to May how the editor's presence had brought undue attention to the divisions in the American anti-slavery circles, splits many ordinary Britons did not understand, a number of disgruntled members of the Bristol and Clifton Ladies' Anti-Slavery Society asking why they should not be allowed to give aid to the Joseph Sturge-supported American and Foreign Anti-Slavery Society as well as Garrison's organisation. Estlin also wrote that no really 'influential persons' had given their support to the new Anti-Slavery League yet, saying Thompson's name, no matter what Garrison and Douglass believed, carried 'little weight' in the country. 'An able man & excellent speaker, none deny him to be; but he is looked on as a sort of adventurer, trading by his wits in any cause open to him.' Estlin is harsh, but the core point had some merit, not that the two American abolitionists admitted as much as they continued their tour.[11]

'Theological Negroes'
From Bristol, Douglass and Garrison travelled south by train to the city of Exeter. Arriving on the evening of Thursday 27 August, they were taken immediately to the home of Revd Francis Bishop, a friend of the Estlins and another Unitarian link in the British anti-slavery chain, the Unitarians sense of themselves as a persecuted minority having long manifested itself in support for victims of oppression. Inspired by May, they had already sent a strong anti-slavery address across the Atlantic in the winter of 1843, urging their American brethren to do much more for the cause. The British Unitarians – some of whom only

half-jokingly referred to themselves as 'theological Negroes' – were also particularly sympathetic to Garrison, having been subjected to the same taunts of religious 'heresy' and 'infidelity' from evangelical denominations. Bishop, who had met Garrison at the World Anti-Slavery Convention in the summer of 1840, would even name his daughter born a few weeks after the editor's visit Caroline Garrison Bishop.[12]

As at Bristol, the two visiting abolitionists spent their first night in Exeter almost on display – fielding questions and queries from the friends of their host packed into the house. The following evening found them at the 'densely crowded' hall of the sumptuously decorated Subscription Rooms, Garrison taking the lead on this occasion and speaking at some length before Douglass finally took to the stage. According to the *Inquirer*, the voice of Unitarianism in England, Douglass carried the audience of almost 800 'completely along with him' in a speech that took in his own beatings, the Free Church controversy and the fact that even the American President James K. Polk owned slaves. A consummate performer, he also made a great show out of buttoning up his coat and twisting his countenance into a 'grave and canting aspect' before delivering his stock impression of a southern preacher sermonising to slaves. Scanning his eyes over the assembled crowd, he then concluded with an evocative description of how he had the 'glorious' scene before him – 'Daguerreotyped in my heart' – and wished 'all the slaves of America could peep in, could see us just as we are, and know as I know, the sympathies of this audience for their down-trodden spirits', the audience filing out into the night filled with pride – though not before passing a resolution establishing a branch of the Anti-Slavery League and purchasing copies of the escaped slave's *Narrative*, new editions of which were being published by the London firm of R. Yorke Clarke & Co.[13]

Garrison returned to London the next day, via Bath and a short visit with the legal academic Edward Strutt Abdy, who had made some connections with American abolitionists while touring American penal institutions in the 1830s. Douglass, however, remained in Exeter, delivering a second talk before travelling back up through the West Country, a journey that took in appearances on consecutive nights from 31 August to 3 September in Bridgwater, Taunton, Bristol (again) and Worcester. Built along the banks of the River Parrett in Somerset, Bridgwater actually had the distinction of being the first British town to send an anti-slavery petition to Parliament (though part of the reasoning behind that 1785 document seems to have been jealousy of the way involvement in the slave trade had seen Bristol overtake it in importance as a port). Douglass spent some time with the local Unitarian minister, Russell Lant Carpenter, a brother of Mary Carpenter whom he had met in Bristol and biographer of their late father, the much-esteemed Revd Lant Carpenter. He then entered the small Public Hall amidst the 'the most enthusiastic cheers' of the 400 people present, going on to praise 'free and brave England' as the 'paragon of Christian purity' amid a familiar catalogue of the iniquities of slavery. He also appealed to the women of the town to make 'useful and fancy articles' for the Boston Bazaar. 'Every stitch, every painting, embodied and shadowed forth a spirit of freedom and spoke of the power of English sympathy; and against that sympathy all opposition was fruitless.' The call was quickly heeded, with Lucy Browne, whose home he also visited, informing Chapman a few weeks later that the town was sending over seven boxes of contributions. Of Douglass, she added: 'He left behind him in our little circle, as I doubt not he has done in very many other circles in England, warm feelings of friendship and attachment to him personally and sincere sympathy and desires for his success in the noble cause which he so eloquently and ably advocates.'[14]

Reaching Taunton, a large town in Somerset, Douglass declared:

Let the press, the pulpit, the forum, and the nation, speak in tones that cannot be misunderstood by America. Tell them that public opinion in England – the moral feeling of this country – that pure and manly feeling which swept from your own colonies the damning degradation of slavery – is now being directed against the slavery of the United States.

An impressed Revd R. M. Montgomery urged all present to purchase copies of Douglass's *Narrative* while a Revd Henry Addiscott remarked that the 'large and attentive' audience at the city's Public Hall 'had heard pretty conclusive evidence that evening, that the colour of the skin had nothing to do with the power of the mind, and that a bright intellect could shine through a dark coat'. At the Broadmead Public Rooms in Bristol, a venue that held everything from scientific lectures to minstrel shows and magic shows, he spoke passionately of 'deeply-wronged Africa' while also facing accusations he had been too severe in his strictures on Methodists, a body who had played a significant role in the crusade to emancipate the West Indies slaves. In reply, Douglass asserted simply that, whatever their past efforts they now continued to hold 'fellowship' with the Methodist church in America, 'which church hugged to its communion men bloody with the guilt of slavery'.

Keeping to the same theme, he encouraged the audience at the Natural History Society at Foregate Street in Worcester 'to get the pulpit and the press to speak out, regardless of the revilings [*sic*] of the slaveholders, and to create in England such a horror of slavery and a slaveholding religion, that the members of Christian churches in England may be led to disclaim any denominational fellowship with the churches of those States in which slavery exists'.[15]

'The Beloved Bard of Negro Freedom'

Douglass reconnected with Garrison in Birmingham, their meeting on the evening of Saturday 5 September 'more fully attended than we had anticipated' given it was held at short notice and clashed with the Birmingham Music Festival, the charismatic young German composer Felix Mendelssohn (a favourite of Queen Victoria and Prince Albert) having premiered his oratorio

Elijah just a few days earlier. The Ethiopian Serenaders would also appear during the festival, a *Birmingham Journal* advertisement for their Town Hall concert promising songs with titles like 'Come, Darkies, Sing' together with a selection of 'Tales and Anecdotes of True Negro Life'. (They also performed 'Old Dan Tucker' and 'Buffalo Gals', less controversially themed works that remain staples of the American folk scene.) The Free Church controversy still simmering, the same issue of the *Journal* contained an advertisement for a new book, *The Free Church and Her Accusers in the Matter of American Slavery*, a defence of the Free Church by the Scottish journalist Andrew Cameron. Elsewhere in the paper, a public house called the Malt Shovel was to let, coal boats and coal carts were for sale and savings of 30 per cent were to be had at Cropper's Hats on New Street. 'Woodhouse's Aethereal [*sic*] Essence of Ginger', meanwhile, guaranteed immediate relief for 'Cholera, Indigestion, Spasms, Cramp and Bowel Complaints'.[16]

Like so many of the British cities Douglass would pass through, Birmingham had been deeply connected to the slave trade, the firm of Hiatt, for example, thriving for decades on the production of the 'Nigger collars' and leg shackles used to bind slaves together on the ships carrying them across the Atlantic. Members of the famous Birmingham Lunar Club, however, had matched their interest in inventions and scientific experiments with a strong commitment to the anti-slave trade movement, the eighteenth-century potter Josiah Wedgwood creating the iconic 'Am I Not A Man And A Brother' medallion that would become a potent symbol of allegiance to the anti-slavery cause in the era of William Wilberforce and Thomas Clarkson, used to illustrate snuffboxes, bracelets, brooches, coat-pins and much else. Lucy Townsend, meanwhile, would establish the first female anti-slavery society in Britain in the city in 1825. Birmingham was also home to Joseph Sturge, Garrison finding the mind of John Dymond, a local Quaker banker, 'tainted' towards him by 'the Broad Street Committee', the editor's shorthand name for the British and Foreign Anti-Slavery Society taken from the street in which their London headquarters were found.

Douglass (who actually got on reasonably well with Sturge), Garrison and Thompson would breakfast with the British and Foreign Anti-Slavery Society leader the morning after their talk, a tense two-hour affair that ended in stalemate. 'Coalition was impossible,' Thompson wrote to Richard D. Webb, 'both parties must pursue their own course.'[17]

From Birmingham, Douglass and Garrison had planned to go to the Lake District to visit the Ambleside home of Harriet Martineau, the writer and journalist whose three-volume work *Society in America*, based on a trip across the Atlantic in the mid-1830s, placed her firmly on the side of the abolitionists. Martineau, however, whose brother James, a well-known Unitarian minister, was also broadly sympathetic to the anti-slavery cause, had just embarked on an extensive tour of Egypt and the Near East that would result in the publication of *Eastern Life: Present and Past*, another work mixing travel with philosophical reflection. A close friend of Maria Weston Chapman (her literary executor and first biographer) from her time in America, the plump, voluble but almost completely deaf Martineau would assuredly have welcomed them with the same openness she bestowed upon the Hutchinson Family when they visited her 'picturesque cottage of rough stone' earlier in the year, arranging a boat trip on a lake and even an open-air concert in a nearby farmer's field, which she listened to with 'her trumpet to her ear' and later wrote up in the *People's Journal*.[18]

The trip to Ambleside abandoned, Douglass remained in Birmingham for a couple of days, most likely at the home of Arthur Naish, a Quaker whose father William had written several books and pamphlets on slavery and the slave trade. Douglass then travelled north to Carlisle, where he stayed with the family of Jonathan D. Carr, another Quaker and the founder of the famous biscuit-makers Carr's of Carlisle. Heavily involved in a number of reform movements, including the campaign against the Corn Laws, the Carrs had already played host to Douglass about a month earlier, when he had been travelling down from Scotland to meet Garrison in London. 'I recently got a little circle to work for the Bazaar in Boston, consisting of [a] few influential young ladies in Carlisle … They will send a box this autumn,' the escaped slave had written to Chapman shortly after that visit. 'Mr J. D. Carr of the same place will send you a valuable contribution to the refreshments consisting of a large box of fancy biscuits.'[19]

While Douglass was in Carlisle, Garrison made his way to Leeds, where he met the radical publisher Joseph Barker, examining his new steam-powered printing press and revelling in relaying his rags to (relative) riches story to his wife Helen – 'sprung up from a beggar boy to the position of a great, active and glorious-minded reformer'. He was also thrilled to recount how he had seen posters all over the city advertising the latest issue of the *People's Journal* and its 'Memoir, by Mary Howitt, of William Lloyd Garrison'. Carrying on to Sheffield, a city 'famous for its cutlery' and 'almost as populous as Boston', Garrison was welcomed to the home of Mary and Rebecca Brady, Quaker sisters in their fifties who ran a girls school at Leavy Greave. Garrison already knew the city quite well, having stayed with Mary Anne Rawson, long-time leader of the Sheffield Female Anti-Slavery Society, during a visit after the World Anti-Slavery Convention in 1840. Born into a wealthy family, Rawson, whose organisation had been the first in Britain to call for the immediate emancipation of the slaves in the West Indies, lived amidst the magnificent surrounds of (the long-since demolished) Wincobank Hall on the outskirts of the city. It was also here that Garrison first met James Montgomery, the poet and editor who as a young man had been heavily influenced by the French Revolution, serving time in prison in 1795 for a poem celebrating the fall of the Bastille. Well known for the long anti-slavery poem 'The West Indies', written in 1809 in the aftermath of the abolition of the slave trade, among many other popular works, the deeply spiritual Montgomery would go on to be described in the abolitionist press as 'the beloved bard of Negro freedom'.[20]

Situated just off Glossop Road on the west end of the city, the Brady sisters' Leavy Greave home was full of visitors and well-wishers when Garrison arrived. The septuagenarian

Montgomery, however, the writer of innumerable hymns as well as poems, was an absentee, sending a letter of apology from his nearby home at the stately, Ionic-columned terrace, The Mount. Though increasingly frail – 'too weak and low in spirit' – he nonetheless promised to be at the Quaker meeting house where Garrison was due to give a talk with Douglass the following evening – Friday 11 September. This was actually the first occasion such a venue had been opened to the American editor on this tour, Garrison blaming the 'poisonous influence' of Sturge and the Broad Street Committee for turning the Quakers so thoroughly against him.[21]

With Sheffield manufacturers having apparently stamped 'Death to Abolitionists' on Bowie knifes earlier in the year, possibly in response to Douglass's attacks on the Free Church, Garrison was surprised to find the 'spacious' meeting house in the Hartshead area of the city 'crowded to overflowing – the aisles deeply filled by persons standing from seven to nearly eleven o'clock – and hundreds [more] unable to gain admittance'. Although Douglass was slightly late, having travelled down from the town of South Shields near Newcastle where had gone to give a talk after Carlisle, 'everything went off well'.

Old age failing to blunt his political radicalism, the poet Montgomery (a statue of whom stands outside Sheffield Cathedral) nodded gravely throughout at the stories of bloodhounds chasing slaves and of male slaves being forced to whip their loved ones in front of their masters. The success of the Anti-Corn Law League still clear in the mind of the audience, the two Americans had also held it up as the example their new Anti-Slavery League would follow, the meeting finally coming to an end with Douglass selling a 'considerable number' of his *Narrative* to the 800-strong crowd.[22]

Douglass and Garrison visited Rawson at her 'Eden-like abode at Wincobank' the next day. Taking leave of Leavy Greave and the 'true reformers' Mary and Rebecca Brady they then travelled south, the American editor complaining about the high price of the first-class carriages on the trains. The second- and third-class carriages, meanwhile, on which he was usually forced 'for economy's sake' to ride, looked 'as if they were made for the transportation of convicts'. What America lacked in freedom, he half-joked to his wife, it made up for in the comfort of its public conveyances.[23]

'Confusion Worse Confounded'

After a brief sojourn in London that included a trip to Vauxhall Gardens as well as the large public meeting against the Evangelical Alliance on 14 September, Douglass was on the move again, travelling up to Scotland via Sunderland, where he gave a speech at the city's Athenaeum that was 'replete with thrilling statements, fervid denunciations and stirring and eloquent appeals'. Garrison had gone ahead, embarking on the evening of 18 September on an exhausting twenty-four-hour journey from London to Glasgow by coach and train that almost broke him. 'I left in the night train, and though travelling in the first class car, could get no sleep, the change in the weather had been so sudden, and the cold was so great,' he wrote to Henry C. Wright. Arriving at Newcastle at about nine o'clock the following morning, he was driven by coach to Berwick. 'I had to take an outside seat, and got thoroughly chilled through. Sixteen miles from Berwick, it began to rain steadily, and, having left my umbrella in London, I got considerably wet.' Another train brought him to Edinburgh, whereupon the passengers for Glasgow had to get out in the dark and walk with their luggage through 'mud and water' some distance. He boarded one train but was then shunted onto another, finally arriving in Glasgow in the midst of yet more 'drenching rain' at about ten o'clock in the evening. 'Such vexatious arrangements (or, rather, such want of arrangements) I have never before seen,' a deeply disgruntled Garrison continued, writing from the home of the Glasgow abolitionist Andrew Paton, who had met him in the wet at the train station. 'In fact, with all the boasted order and regularity which are said to prevail on this side of the Atlantic, in every department of life, I do maintain that nothing can be worse than the management of the railways.' He concluded with a quote from *Paradise Lost*: 'It is "confusion worse confounded."'[24]

Although deeply unimpressed by the British rail system, Garrison, like Douglass, had benefitted greatly from the surge in railway building, the 16,000 km of track laid down across the country (up from 3,200 km just four years earlier) enabling the abolitionists to spread their anti-slavery message far quicker than would have been possible before. With prospectuses for new lines filling the pages of newspapers and hundreds of bills for new railway schemes winding their way through Parliament (every new line requiring its own piece of legislation), railways had taken hold of the public imagination to a barely credible degree, Charles Dickens weaving the sights and sounds of this exhilarating new mode of transport into *Dombey and Son* – which would begin its serialisation around this time – and the septuagenarian painter J. M. W. Turner finding inspiration for his *Rain, Steam and Speed* (first exhibited at Royal Academy in 1844) during a journey from Bristol to London.

Many others, however, found the promises of instant returns and high dividends far more inspiring than any ethereal fusing together of steam and fog against a night sky. A Parliamentary report on the number of subscribers to the lines authorized in 1845 alone running to more than 500 pages.

'Amongst those names are to be recognised the leading nobility, the largest manufacturing firms and representatives of every branch of commerce, art, science and literature,' wrote one commentator. 'Peers and printers, vicars and vice-admirals, professors and cotton spinners' were all involved, as were 'barristers and butchers, Catholic priests and coachmen, bankers and butlers ... the lawyer madly risking his client's money; the chemist forsaking his laboratory in search of a new form of the philosopher's stone, the Jew, the Quaker, the saint and the sinner.' Even the Queen approved, revelling in the speed with which she could travel from Windsor to London and in the freedom the trains brought from the heat and dust of coach travel.[25]

Working on the novels that would make them famous in the Haworth parsonage they shared with their clergyman father in West Yorkshire, the three Brontë sisters, Charlotte, Emily and Anne, joined the frenzy, with Emily, in particular 'reading every paragraph & every advertisement in the newspapers that related to railroads' in the period before she started writing *Wuthering Heights*. Charlotte, the eldest sister whose *Jane Eyre* Isabel Jennings would praise to Chapman soon after it publication in 1847, was more wary, sensing the potential for malfeasance beneath the transformative lustre of the rails. She was right to be concerned, George Hudson, the 'railway king' in whose York and North Midland Railway Company the sisters had invested, eventually fleeing to France when his questionable financial practices – essentially elaborate Ponzi schemes – began to unravel. 'The real object of the concocters of railway schemes has not been to devise desirable and good lines of railway but to start a scheme ... in plain language, to rob and delude the public, by squandering and embezzling the deposit money,' the *Bankers' Magazine* had warned. 'Pettifogging attorneys and rejected engineers are the true authors ... of three-fourths of the railway schemes before the world at this moment.' *The Times*, too, had foreseen trouble, a series of articles unmasking the financial irresponsibility underlying the 'railway mania' losing it advertising revenue but proving prescient when the railway bubble, like every other bubble, eventually burst, bankrupting businesses and families and leading to a devastating number of suicides even as Douglass made his way on the rails through the country.[26]

'A Sisterly Welcome'

Douglass was reunited with Garrison in Glasgow, the two Americans walking the hills around nearby Bowling Bay with the Scottish abolitionist John Murray before proceeding to a hastily arranged meeting in a church in Greenock on the evening of Tuesday 22 September. 'Frederick opened the meeting, and, in the course of his speech, dealt very faithfully with the Free Church, which caused some hissing among the snakes belonging to that brood; but this was trifling, in comparison with the amount of applause bestowed,' Garrison informed Wright, the Free Church issue returning to the fore now that the pair were in Scotland. The meeting was successful and there was a vote to set up a branch of the Anti-Slavery League. Nevertheless, Garrison felt that more needed to be done in the shipbuilding town that was home to Robert Steele & Co., the company that constructed the *Cambria*. 'I am told that it is sadly lacking in intellectual activity and moral life.'[27]

After a night at the Temperance Hotel in Greenock, the abolitionists moved west to Paisley, Garrison exulting in one of the 'most crowded and enthusiastic' meetings he had seen 'on this side of the Atlantic' in a letter to the *Liberator*. 'Commend me to the weavers and other operatives in Paisley, for intelligence, sagacity, and appreciation of right sentiments!' he declared, the two Americans proceeding afterwards through Glasgow, Edinburgh, Dundee and Kilmarnock, the flu-wracked editor's spirits kept strong by the great receptions and the constant company of Scottish friends like the Murrays, Patons, Wighams and Smeals. Douglass, too, was fatigued, having already described how he felt 'almost overcome' by the incessant travel and public appearances. Weary or not, the tour continued, invitations to speak in 'all parts of the kingdom' reaching the abolitionists every day and Garrison in particular determined to make the most of what he believed could be his last visit to the British Isles, so much so that he soon decided to postpone his departure by a further two weeks, until the sailing of the *Acadia* out of Liverpool on 4 November.[28]

Douglass and Garrison left Scotland in early October, taking the steamer from Ardrossan to Belfast, a seven-hour journey through the night on choppy waters. They gave two talks that were well attended, in spite of the 'Infidel! Infidel' cry raised against Garrison in the local press and the reluctance of some anti-slavery supporters who had helped Douglass during previous visits to give aid to the editor of the *Liberator*. Garrison continued south alone, taking a coach from Portadown to Drogheda before boarding a train for the remainder of the journey to Dublin, where he would stay with Webb:

And, oh! the amount of human suffering, filth and destruction, which met my eye during every step of the journey. I was frequently melted to tears, and for the first time in my life saw human beings, especially women and children, in a situation that made me lament their existence! Yet I was assured that

I saw the best portion of the labouring poor in Ireland! Alas! for them, with the famine which is sorely pressing them, in consequence of the entire failure of the potato crop – the food on which they have subsisted from time immemorial. Multitudes, beyond a doubt, – in spite of all that the government can do to give relief, – will miserably perish for the want of the absolute necessaries of life. O, the poor women! O, the poor children! O, the poor babies! Heaven send them speedy succour.[29]

Heaven, however, did not send any succour. Nor did the British government, the new Prime Minister Lord John Russell, wedded to the dogma of *laissez-faire* economics, pulling back even from his predecessor Peel's limited relief measures – including the establishment of a Relief Commission to organise food depots and co-ordinate local relief committees – just as a second and much more extensive potato failure hit Ireland. Politically, Russell had been seen as a friend to Ireland, having worked closely with Daniel O'Connell in the 1830s. Nevertheless, it would be under his government that food shortage turned to famine, a devastating holocaust that in the course of six years killed at least one million people from starvation and related diseases.

Garrison left famine-stricken Ireland on the evening of Thursday 8 October, meeting up with Douglass – who had made his own way back across the Irish Sea – the following morning at Brown's Temperance Hotel in Liverpool, the American abolitionists ever-eager to give their custom to temperance-supporting businesses. Together with Thompson, they then made their first foray into Wales, travelling the short distance to Wrexham where they received 'a sisterly welcome' at the 25 King Street home of Sarah and Blanche Hilditch – the latter of whom was deaf and dumb – abolitionists who had been sending contributions to the Boston Bazaar for a number of years. Almost immediately, they held a meeting in the Town Hall that drew a fifth of Wrexham's 5,000 inhabitants; the stairs, hallways and aisles of the building all crowded to their limits. Already 'fired' up with 'zeal' by Douglass's *Narrative*, Sarah Hilditch would be just as impressed by the escaped slave's performance in person, describing him as 'a living example of the capabilities of the slave', proof they were more than 'mere chattels – with bodies formed for Herculean labour, but without minds, without souls'.[30]

Garrison, meanwhile, had been particularly moved by his time with Blanche Hilditch. 'Tell her, that though I was compelled to be mute in her presence, not knowing what signs to make to hold intelligent converse with her, I felt that our spirits needed no vocal utterance,' he wrote a few weeks later to Sarah. The editor had even referenced Blanche's disabilities in his speech at the Town Hall, when he noted that:

> There is before me a lady who has also given her mind to that [abolitionist] course. Year after year, and yet was deaf and dumb (cheers). She is known on the other side of the Atlantic for her benevolence, and with much eloquence is there pleading for the poor slaves. She knows that there are also in America three million of the human family who are also deaf and dumb, not by birth, or the providence of God ... and she says 'I will do what I can to enable them to speak.'

This image of a woman who could not speak, yet whose influence could reach across the Atlantic and give a voice to the voiceless slave, it has been suggested, was a powerful manifestation of the 'moral force' philosophy underpinning Garrisonian abolitionism.[31]

From Wrexham, the trio of abolitionists made their way to Manchester where they joined Wright at a large public meeting at the Free Trade Hall, the focus of which was a renewed attack on the Evangelical Alliance. They then split up, Douglass heading to Rochdale, Thompson to London, Wright to Dublin and Garrison to Darlington, where he met the Quaker Elizabeth Pease, a member of one of the wealthiest families in the nort of England and a long-time leader among British abolitionists whose health was regrettably poor around this time. The four anti-slavery speakers came together again for a large meeting in Liverpool on the evening of 19 October, an event that had originally been scheduled as a farewell soirée for Garrison.

'The Metropolis of Slavery'

Although a number of recent works have emphasised the strong undercurrent of anti-slavery feeling running through the city from the late 1700s, Liverpool was a worthy bearer of the title 'the metropolis of slavery', ships from its port dominating the British slave trade for much of the eighteenth century – carrying more than a million enslaved Africans to lives of bondage across the Atlantic – and a majority of its inhabitant's livelihoods – be they sail-makers, rope-makers, seamen, the proprietors of the shops supplying food for the long journeys or the owners of the alehouses in which workers drank their wages around the docks – linked in some way to the 'nefarious trade'. The connection remained strong even after abolition in 1807, Liverpool merchants and shipbuilders turning to the rapidly expanding slave economies of Cuba and Brazil with their sugar, coffee, cocoa and rum. Liverpool was also the port through which vast quantities of slave-grown cotton from the United States continued to enter Britain. Furthermore, the long-honed skills of its shipwrights were often surreptitiously put to work on illegal, foreign-flagged slave ships.[32]

Pro-slavery – or, at least, anti-abolitionist – sentiment was still present when Douglass and Garrison entered the city, the *Liverpool Courier* attacking them for 'heaping all sorts of abuse and vilification' on the leaders of the Evangelical Alliance. Garrison also posited the 'American influence' as the reason no local worthies (mayors or ministers) joined them on stage for their Concert Hall meeting. 'Well, we can get along without them, perhaps much better than with them,' he remarked to Pease, refusing to consider such dignitaries a loss. 'The heart of THE PEOPLE is sound, and they give us, in every instance, their hearty approbation.' The people certainly seemed supportive that night, the venue 'densely crowded' and Douglass giving a 'long and powerful speech' that was 'loudly applauded'.[33]

Originally conceived as a grand farewell soirée, Garrison's decision to postpone his trip home by a fortnight meant the Concert Hall meeting turned into the springboard from which he, Douglass and Thompson would launch one last, frantic dash through Scotland, the three abolitionists (together with

Thompson's wife and a London journalist William Farmer, who was close to Thompson) sailing from Fleetwood to Ardrossan before proceeding through Glasgow to Kirkcaldy, Dundee and Perth among other towns and cities, a steamer along the 'noble' River Tay the mode of transport used between the last two named stops. The Edinburgh Ladies' Anti-Slavery Society, still led by the Jane and Eliza Wigham, presented Garrison with an 'elegant tea service' in commemoration of his efforts, an action which, while well-intentioned, had unfortunate consequences back in Boston, the never-wealthy editor being forced to pay a hefty tax on the gift.[34]

The abolitionists were back in Liverpool for Garrison's departure for Boston on board the *Acadia* on the morning of Wednesday 4 November, friends and supporters from around the British Isles, including Webb from Dublin, Isabel Jennings from Cork, Andrew Paton from Glasgow and the Hilditch sisters from Wrexham, having gathered to see him off, others, like Naish in Birmingham, sending fond farewell letters. 'With a full heart and suffused eyes, I have watched the little steamer, conveying you and the other dear friends again to the shore, till it was lost in the distance,' he wrote to Sarah Hilditch from his cabin:

> I know not how to express my feelings, in view of such a demonstration of personal friendship, and sympathy and regard for the cause which I humbly advocate ... I desire to remain behind awhile, for a thousand reasons; but ten thousand demand my return home to the United States. My dear wife is waiting to embrace me with open arms – my children are shouting joyously in anticipation of my return – a thousand friends are waiting impatiently to greet me.[35]

Suffering dreadfully from seasickness once again as he traversed the Atlantic, Garrison found solace in thoughts of the 'numerous and dearly beloved friends' with whom he had spent the last three months in Britain and Ireland. He would have also had the satisfaction of feeling his sojourn had made a real difference, the establishment of the Anti-Slavery League creating an opportunity of wresting control of the British anti-slavery scene from the Sturge-dominated British and Foreign Anti-Slavery Society. The concerted tirades against the Evangelical Alliance, too, seemed to have had an effect, a meeting in Manchester in early November to set up its British branch resolving that no slaveholders would be allowed join its part of the organisation – though the group still gave itself room for manoeuvre by refusing to cast aspersions on the 'personal Christianity' of slaveholders and refusing to give any opinion with regard American slaveholders and the American branch of the Evangelical Alliance.[36]

The *Acadia* also carried an extra-large number of boxes of contributions for the forthcoming Boston Bazaar, which included a piece of lacework from a young girl named Sarah Ann White from Kingswood Infant School near Bristol. 'This small piece of lace was wrought by the little girl whose name it bears, in the following way,' an accompanying note read: 'She obtained from her mother a halfpenny, in lieu of one week's sugar. With this, she purchased two farthing balls of cotton, and from these produced the lace, an instance of self-denial worthy of imitation.' Another piece from Bristol, a miniature figure of a 'market woman', was 'peculiarly instructive to those who declaim so eloquently against anti-slavery effort, on the allegation that "the slaves are better off than the British peasantry"' because of the inscription it contained:

> I be a poor, hard-working body, 'tis true;
> I works hard and lives hard, I knows that I do;
> But I works hard for they as I loves to my heart,
> And if I dont do't, they 'ont make my back smart.
> We struggles together, my old man and I,
> To settle the young 'uns before we do die.
> What we gets is our own, as I says; and we're free,
> And happen what 'ool, tis a comfort to me,
> That nobody never can tear me from he!

There was also a contribution from the 'illustrious Italian exile' Giuseppe Garibaldi for the special issue of the *Liberty Bell* abolitionist magazine that was always published in conjunction with the Boston Bazaar together with daguerreotypes of anti-slavery friends like the Dubliners James Haughton and Richard Allen, which Garrison had picked up as he made his way through the British Isles, taking advantage of the then recently invented photographic process.[37]

At one point, Douglass, looking 'stately & majestic' as he bid Garrison farewell, had intended on returning to America on the same sailing of the *Acadia*. 'My Anna says "Come home" and I have now resolved upon going home,' he had written to a British friend in late August. 'I shall sail for America on the fourth November – and hope to meet the beloved one of my heart by the 20th of that month.' A few weeks later, though, he was informing Isabel Jennings in Cork of a change of plan:

> I am now about to tell you something which will make you think me the most fickle of men. I have decided to stay in this country six months longer … in consequence of the advice both of Mr Garrison and Mr Thompson. Both think the present a most favourable opportunity for remodelling the anti-slavery feeling of this country and bringing it to the aid of the true anti-slavery society in America, and each think it would be wrong for me to miss it.

Douglass was aware of the hurt this would cause his wife, having already written to Anna telling her to expect him home. 'Disappointment', however, 'is the common lot of us all', he continued resignedly, lurching as he had all summer and autumn from the thrilling highs of great platform speeches and the warm camaraderie of the long coach and train journeys with Garrison to deep pangs of sorrow at being so long removed from his family and his home.[38]

Foregoing his own opportunity to return to the United States, Douglass's sombre mood would not have been helped by saying goodbye to the friend and mentor by whose side he had waged a simultaneously exhilarating and exhausting three-month campaign all over the British Isles. Whatever ill feelings Douglass had towards Maria Weston Chapman and other white Boston abolitionists, they do not seem to have yet impacted on his relationship with Garrison, Douglass writing a warm letter to him around the time of his departure that called their tour one of the 'happiest' periods of his life.[39] The editor, for his part, does he seem to have indulged in any of the snide comments abolitionists like Webb made about Douglass. Nor does he seem to have betrayed any real sense of annoyance or envy, even in private letters to his wife, at being – to the broader public mind – the supporting cast member in their particular tour.

There were also moves afoot to make Douglass's remaining in Britain more than worthwhile.

7

'I AM A MAN'

On 5 December 1846, Hugh Auld, the forty-seven-year-old carpenter and shipbuilder who once chastised his wife Sophia for teaching the young Frederick Douglass to read, put his signature to a deed of manumission declaring 'my NEGRO MAN named FREDERICK BAILEY, otherwise called DOUGLASS ... to be henceforth free, manumitted, and discharged from all manner of servitude'. A week later, the transaction was complete, another flurry of signatures in a Baltimore attorney's office presaging the handing over of a bank draft for just over $700 to Auld and the filing of the appropriate papers in the Baltimore Chattel Records Office. Douglass was free, legally free; a human being, no longer a chattel.[1]

The process leading to this most pivotal of days in Douglass's life had begun with a forlorn glance across the North Sea from a beach near Newcastle a few months earlier, the deep waters stirring the escaped slave's emotions as always and perhaps reminding him of the Chesapeake and home. Travelling down from Edinburgh to meet Garrison in London in early August, he had stopped off in the shipbuilding and coalmining town in the north-east of England, delivering a few lectures and staying at the Summerhill Grove home the forty-year-old Quaker grocer Henry Richardson shared with his wife Anna. With Douglass's own wife, also Anna, having rejected the idea of moving to England, he was committed to returning to America, whatever his circumstances. In public, he was strong and assertive, stating to the editor of *Protestant Journal* in Belfast, in response to taunts he had abandoned his family and was hiding out abroad, that: 'No inducement could be offered strong enough to make me quit my hold upon America, as my home. Whether a slave or a freeman, America is my home, and there I mean to spend and be spent in the cause of my outraged fellow-countrymen.' Privately, however, his feelings were much more mixed, with one abolitionist paper, the *Pennsylvania Freeman*, quoting Hugh Auld as being determined to seize Douglass upon his return and 'cost what it may ... place him in the cotton fields of the South'. The statement does not seem to have had any real basis, abolitionist papers as prone to hyperbole as the rest of the press. Nevertheless, real dangers remained, with Douglass's highly publicised condemnations of the slave system across Britain and Ireland earning him the special ire of slaveholders on the other side of the Atlantic, the success of the tour making the target the publication of his *Narrative* put on him even larger.[2]

Standing close to Douglass during that outing to the seaside, Ellen Richardson, Henry's sister, sensed the sorrow in his demeanour, his downcast look across the water. 'Observing his sadness,' wrote the American social reformer Ida B. Wells, to whom Ellen recounted the events some years later, 'she suddenly asked him, "Frederick, would you like to go back to America?" Of course his reply was in the affirmative and like a flash the inspiration came to her, "Why not buy his freedom?"'[3] With Douglass's blessing, Ellen's sister-in-law Anna was soon writing to Hugh Auld to see if he was willing to sell the slave's manumission, and if so for what price. Auld replied relatively promptly, a letter of 6 October stating he would take £150 – a modest amount compared to what Douglass might have fetched at a slave market in New Orleans but plenty for a piece of property 3,000 miles out of reach. Auld's willingness to negotiate undermines the image Douglass and others created of him as a man bent on revenge. Instead, money seems to have been his main motivation for a not particularly well-off individual who had a growing family to support (a second son joining the young Tommy whom Douglass had known) and whose work may have been suffering in the aftermath of a huge storm that had wreaked terrible damage to Baltimore's wharves that autumn. He may also simply have wished to be free of the unwanted attention Douglass brought on the family.

As soon as Auld's positive response reached England, Anna and Ellen Richardson, together with Ellen's cousins, the Carlisle-based sisters Eliza Nicholson and Jane Carr, organised a series of public meetings, most notably in Edinburgh, to make their plans known. Henry, meanwhile, engaged Walter Lowrie, a former United States senator from Pennsylvania, to act as their agent in the deal, Lowrie in turn securing the services of Baltimore attorney J. Meredith. With the money raised astonishingly quickly – the Radical politician John Bright, at whose Rochdale home Douglass would soon stay, contributing a cheque for £50 – Lowrie was able to inform Auld that he had the bank draft on 24 November. This message set in train the final few phases of the deal that ended at ten o'clock on the morning of 12 December, when under the authority of an A. W. Bradford, clerk of the Baltimore Chattel Records Office, Douglass ceased to be a slave, the £150 converting to the $711.66 cost of freedom.[4]

'The Buying of Frederick'

A deeply religious and philanthropic couple who had first met as children at Ackworth, a leading Quaker school in Yorkshire, Henry and Anna Richardson were long-established members of the anti-slavery community in Britain, campaigning against slavery in the West Indies in the 1830s and opening their home to Douglass's friend Charles Lenox Remond during his tour in the early 1840s. They were also involved in the peace movement, with Henry serving as editor of the *Peace Advocate*, the journal of the Newcastle Peace Society, while Anna, a large-featured woman neatly dressed and wearing a Quaker bonnet in surviving portraits, edited the *Olive Leaf*, a peace magazine for children that spawned several 'Olive Leaf' circles. Anna, a friend of the prison reformer Elizabeth Fry, was also the undisputed head of the 'free produce' movement, an arm of the anti-slavery movement that encouraged Britons to refrain from the use of slave-grown cotton and which harked back to the earlier free sugar movement – which her own mother had strongly supported.[5]

On a more local level, Henry led the Newcastle Bible Society and helped found a so-called 'ragged school' for boys in the city, the common name for these charity schools coming from the uniformly worn-out, dirty and 'ragged' clothes worn by the poor pupils who attended them, half-starving and unable to afford even the paltry sum required to go to regular schools. First established around 1820, the rapid spread of these schools, most of which offered food and clothing as well as at least some modicum of education, was yet another sign of the debilitating poverty lurking beneath the industrial glories of Victorian Britain, Charles Dickens getting the inspiration for *A Christmas Carol* from a visit to London's Field Lane Ragged School in the early 1840s. Mary Carpenter, another abolitionist friend of Douglass's, meanwhile, would be involved in setting up of a number of ragged schools in the Bristol slums before turning her attention to pioneering work in the area of child penal reform, for which she received financial support from Lady Byron, widow of the famous poet and a long-time supporter of social causes who had attended the World Anti-Slavery Convention in 1840.

A headmistress at the Royal Jubilee School for Girls in Newcastle, Ellen Richardson shared her brother and sister-in-law's commitment to social justice, her 'commanding presence' and 'Friends bonnet' seared into the memory of generations of students, most of whom came from the poorer parts of town or surrounding colliery villages. Drawn in particular to the struggles of the penurious families of the small fishing village of Cullercoats on the north-east coast, an area she had visited regularly since childhood, she organised the construction and running of a 'crèche-school' where the youngest children could stay and play while their mothers sold fish in neighbouring towns and villages, an institution that developed quite naturally into a primary school for all the local children. 'Ellen Richardson's interest in these fisher-people was maintained to the end of her life, and in her old age she welcomed them to her house in Rye

Hill, enjoying their hymn-singing, and cheering them with her practical advice and sympathy,' noted a memorial soon after her death. Indeed, it seems likely it was on the sandy beach at Cullercoats Bay that she stood with Douglass the fateful day she determined to purchase his freedom.[6]

The Richardsons had no moral qualms about the purchase of Douglass; it was simply a practical measure they felt would benefit the anti-slavery cause, one they would repeat a few years later for another escaped slave-turned-orator William Wells Brown. Many radical Garrisonians, however, were deeply conflicted about the move – as Douglass knew well would be the case (for if not a matter of certain controversy, it would surely have been attempted before). 'I could not aid nor approve of the buying of Frederick as I thought it compromising of principle, & a recognition of the right of property in man,' wrote Catherine Paton from Glasgow to Maria Weston Chapman, Mary Welsh writing from Edinburgh in a similar vein the very same day. On the other side of the Atlantic, the Philadelphia Female Anti-Slavery Society likewise condemned the action as 'a deviation from anti-slavery principle', other commentators maliciously suggesting Douglass had 'cheapened himself ... before the slaveholders'.[7]

Writing directly to Douglass from Doncaster in the middle of December, Henry C. Wright was firmly in the group one of Douglass's biographers, William S. McFeely, has ably described as 'moralists bent on purity – someone else's purity'. Wright focused on the symbolic importance of Douglass's remaining a slave of the United States: 'Your appeal to mankind is not against the grovelling thief, Thomas Auld, but against the more daring, more impudent and potent thief – the Republic of the United States of America.' Douglass, however, preferred to be a free man working for the anti-slavery cause rather than a martyr. He also wanted to be able to return to his family without fear. William Lloyd Garrison, to the surprise of many, supported the 'ransoming' of Douglass. 'Already, an avalanche of anxiety and distrust has been removed from his heart. And how happy must be his wife and children to know that he is free!' he wrote, having performed some contortions in the *Liberator* to show he was not contradicting his own ideology. Nevertheless, the general tenor of the Garrisonian response served only to push Douglass further away from their organisation.[8]

'A Spirited Ode'

Douglass spent most of November and December, the period during which negotiations to secure his freedom played out, in Manchester, a city whose phenomenal growth into the economic powerhouse of the north was based largely on the slave-grown cotton feeding the spinning and weaving machines of its innumerable textiles factories, the vast, brick-like edifices that dominated the cityscape and the lives of its citizens. Nevertheless, perhaps because it felt at more of a remove from the trade in human beings than Liverpool, which had actually built the ships that carried enslaved Africans across the Atlantic, Manchester does not seem to have experienced the same angst about its role in the slave system as its north-west neighbour, playing a decisive role in the campaigns to abolish both the slave trade and slavery in the West Indies. Douglass, meanwhile, had already been cheered loud and long at a crowded meeting at the Free Trade Hall earlier in the year.[9]

Manchester was also the spiritual home of the Anti-Corn Law League leaders Richard Cobden and John Bright, both of whom Douglass admired. Taken by the contrasting nature of their physical appearance, personalities and political styles, he would later describe how:

Mr Cobden – for an Englishman – was lean, tall and slightly sallow, and might have been taken for an American or a Frenchman. Mr Bright was, in the broadest sense, an Englishman, abounding in all the physical perfections peculiar to his countrymen – full, round and ruddy. Cobden had dark eyes and hair, a well-formed head high above his shoulders, and, when sitting quiet, a look of sadness and fatigue. In the House of Commons he often sat with one hand supporting his head. Bright appeared the very opposite in this and other respects. His eyes were blue, his hair light, his head massive and firmly set upon his shoulders, suggesting immense energy and determination. In his oratory, Mr Cobden was cool, candid, deliberate, straightforward, yet at times slightly hesitating. Bright, on the other hand, was fervid, fluent, rapid – always ready in thought or word. Mr Cobden was full of facts and figures, dealing in statistics by the hour. Mr Bright was full of wit, knowledge and pathos, and possessed amazing power of expression. One spoke to the cold, calculating side of the British nation, which asks if the new idea will pay? The other spoke to the infinite side of human nature – the side which asks, first of all, 'Is it right? Is it just? Is it humane.'[10]

Douglass would become especially friendly with the whole Bright family, including John's brother Jacob, who would also go on to a career in politics, and his sister Priscilla, later Priscilla Bright McLaren, a noted activist in both the anti-slavery and women's rights movements. Whether they discussed the slave-grown nature of the cotton that underpinned the family wealth is unknown.

Taking lodgings at 22 St Ann's Square in the centre of the city for the winter, Douglass seems likely to have also spent some time with local abolitionists like Rebecca Moore, who had already hosted him at her rented home at Atoll Place, Higher Broughton earlier in the year. A daughter of Benjamin Clarke Fisher, at whose home Douglass had spent a number of happy weeks in Limerick in November 1845, Rebecca had been involved in the anti-slavery scene for many years, campaigning in the late 1830s against the efforts of Caribbean planters to bring 'white slaves' from Ireland across to the West Indies. She had ended up in Manchester through the work her Dublin-born husband, Robert Rowan Ross Moore, a barrister and reformer, did with the Anti-Corn Law League. Although abandoned by her husband, the resilient Rebecca, an 'incredibly tough, optimistic and intelligent woman' according to her descendant the writer Charlotte Moore, stayed on in the city, forging a career as an educator and journalist in the face of serious hardship. Heavily pregnant around the time of Douglass's sojourn in the city, she would also raise a son on her own, the distinguished doctor and medical historian Sir Norman Moore. In later years, Rebecca, still carrying a strong Irish accent but having moved away from the Quakerism of her youth, would even have her portrait painted by John Butler Yeats, father of the great Irish poet.[11]

While staying in Manchester, Douglass delivered lectures to promote the Anti-Slavery League in the city's Corn Exchange as well as surrounding towns like Rochdale, Oldham, Stockport and Ashton-under-Lynn. At Warrington, meanwhile, it is possible he spent a night at the home of the wealthy wire manufacturer Thomas Glazebrook Rylands (whose vast private library, including first editions of important texts from the 1500s, was later bequeathed to the University of Liverpool) after a speech at the local Mechanics' Institute. The reports from most of these talks were positive, with halls 'completely filled', new branches of the Anti-Slavery League set up and a Ladies' Anti-Slavery Society established in Rochdale for 'the purpose of getting up needlework' for the Boston Bazaar. Others, though, were 'thinly' or 'poorly' attended, leading to accusations that the British and Foreign Anti-Slavery Society was working in the shadows to undercut its nascent rival. It is also instructive to note the limited knowledge the denizens of these towns had of American slavery, an activist in Rochdale, for example, home to a major reformer like Bright and close to the slavery-steeped cities of Liverpool and Manchester, still describing the subject as 'almost new to the people'. John B. Estlin, too, would write of the 'entire ignorance & apathy respecting Slavery' in 'some of the central towns of England'. Douglass had made a big impression in major cities like London and Bristol (where a short novel about slavery, Charles Hooton's *A Tale of Louisiana*, was serialised in the *Mercury* throughout December, appearing on the same page as advertisements for the issue of the *People's Journal* containing Mary Howitt's profile of the escaped slave). Much work remained to be done, however, in the towns, villages and hamlets of provincial England, the great tide of anti-slavery feeling that had swept through the country in the lead-up to abolition in the West Indies now more than a decade in the past.[12]

Apart from the newspaper reports of these speeches, there are few surviving records from Douglass's two months living in Manchester. They may have been lost with the passage of time.

It is also possible he was taking time out of the spotlight and simply not corresponding much. Or it could have been a lonelier, more contemplative period, the escaped slave starting to process the possibility of freedom while wrestling with the manner with which it was being achieved, knowing the accusations that would come his way. Douglass was also ill around this time, postponing a meeting in Leeds for a week in the run-up to Christmas. He was still not well at the rescheduled meeting, a local newspaper describing how his 'strength failed him' midway through his speech, forcing him to take a break. Wright, too, was suffering at this time, being tended to by the Brady sisters in Sheffield. George Thompson, meanwhile, who would suffer the devastating loss of one of his young daughters just after Christmas, had earlier sent a letter of apology for not showing up at Douglass's talk in Stockport, citing 'impaired health, in consequence of his labours in the cause during the last two months'. Garrison, it seems, had run them all into the ground.[13]

Douglass was still unwell when he attended a grand soirée (preceded by a large sit-down meal with over 1,000 guests) at the Music Hall on Nelson Street in Newcastle on the evening of Monday 28 December, a convivial gathering to celebrate Douglass's manumission at which the local reformer and writer E. P. Hood's 'spirited ode' 'We'll Free the Slave' was first performed, sung to the air of Robert Burns's 'Ye Banks and Braes o' Bonny Doon' and beginning:

> How bright the sun of freedom burns,
> From mount to mount, from shore to shore!
> 'The slave departs, the man returns,'
> The reign of force and fraud is o'er:
> 'Tis Truth's own beam, from sea to sea,
> From vale to vale, from wave to wave;
> Her ministers this night are we,
> To free, to free, to free the slave!

John Joseph, an 'African Negro' who had been sold into slavery before somehow making a life in England, also spoke briefly at this event. (Interestingly, this seems to be the only occasion where Douglass shared the stage with another black person during his tour, a sign perhaps of a collective desire of black Britons to maintain a low public profile, leaving anti-slavery crusading to middle-class whites.) A day later, Douglass absented himself from a second anti-slavery meeting in Newcastle, sending a letter with some comments instead. He then summoned enough strength to see out the year with talks in nearby Sunderland and Hexham – where once again the question of American slavery was described as being 'new to the people'.[14]

'The Tyrant's Rod'

Although free to return to America, Douglass began the New Year apparently determined to continue promoting the Anti-Slavery League across England. 'Were I to consult my own case, or yield to my inclinations, I should at once quit the shores of England, and come home to my family and friends, and to my American field of labour,' he wrote to Garrison. 'But the times, and the exigencies of the cause, seem imperatively to demand my presence here. I have now acquired a position, from which I think I am able to do good service to the cause; and it would be wrong, in my judgement, to abandon it just now.' Stressing the interconnectedness of the two countries, he continued: 'All must confess the desirableness and importance of keeping up a strong anti-slavery sentiment in England. Anti-slavery in England is Anti-slavery in America – and labour expended in the cause here, is felt there.'

There were signs his continuing efforts were proving worthwhile, with a Free Church Anti-Slavery Society just formed – 'Their rallying-cry is, "*No quarter to slavery!*"' – and the United Secession and Relief Churches, two Scottish Presbyterian denominations, resolving to no longer hold 'communion with men-stealers'. Nevertheless, the task that lay ahead was far from smooth:

> The cause here is far from being what it ought to be. In nine out of ten of all the towns, where, a few years ago, there were active and powerful organisations, there is now no trace of one to be found … The spirit of liberty and of equal

justice, whose gigantic arm broke the tyrant's rod, and gave unconditional freedom to 800,000 souls in the West India islands, must be again summoned in the contest. Since the auspicious day, on which it smote the galling fetter from the slave, and, like a tornado, scattered the infernal altars of slavery in the Colonies, it seems to have grounded its weapons, left the conflict, retired from the field, drawn its curtains, and gone to sleep.

It was not, however, 'the sleep of death', Douglass continued more positively. 'The giant is still alive. A few shrill blasts of the trump of freedom will startle him into activity, and open his piercing eye again upon our common foe.'[15]

Douglass began this stage of his tour at Carlisle and South Shields before alighting at Darlington, home of the forty-year-old Elizabeth Pease, scion of a tremendously wealthy Quaker family and much-admired leading light of the British anti-slavery scene after whom Garrison had named his recently born daughter. 'Much had I longed to see this remarkable man, and highly raised were my expectations; but they were more than realised,' Pease recounted in a letter to Garrison, going on to describe Douglass as a 'living contradiction' to 'that base opinion, which is so abhorrent to every humane and Christian feeling, that the blacks are an inferior race'. Though too ill to attend, his meeting at the town's Assembly Rooms, she understood, had been 'crowded' and 'most enthusiastic', even if disturbed towards the end by a local minister speaking up in support of the Evangelical Alliance. Some Quakers, she also admitted, believed Douglass 'too unsparing in his condemnations of slaveholders', consigning them 'one and all to eternal perdition'. Pease, however, was firmly on his side. Indeed, her disaffection with elements of Quaker thinking would see her leave its fold in later years.[16]

Giving the lie to the chides of abolitionists like Richard D. Webb and John B. Estlin that he might not have the stomach for the 'uphill work' needed to build an organisation, so used had he become to 'sailing on the tide of popularity' in the metropolises of Britain, Douglass continued from Darlington through a litany of far from glamorous northern and midlands towns like Kirkstall, Wakefield and Leicester (where he had been invited to speak by the outspoken Baptist minister J. P. Mursell).[17] The start of February found him in Coventry, home at one point to the famous African-American actor Ira Aldridge, who had delivered a few anti-slavery addresses while managing the city's theatre in 1828. Douglass delivered his own anti-slavery address in Coventry to a crowded St Mary's Hall, staying afterwards with the family of John and Joseph Cash (perhaps at John's magnificent Sherborne House abode), Quaker brothers who had just established their famous silk-weaving business and who like their Birmingham cousins the Cadburys would take a deep philanthropic interest in the education and living conditions of their workers. A month later he was further south in the Essex town of Colchester, whose Ladies' Anti-Slavery Society had been one of the most prominent in the campaign to end slavery in the West Indies before gradually drifting into abeyance. Speaking at Northampton, meanwhile, Douglass found himself not far from the grandeur of the Montagu family's Boughton House, where an escaped slave named Ignatius Sancho had once worked as butler before going on to become a renowned man-of-letters in Georgian London and the first known black Briton to vote in an election. There were also a few forays into London, including for a series of Anti-Slavery League meetings at the Mansion House Chapel in Camberwell, which was then little more than a village on the outskirts of the great city.

Douglass's correspondence from this period indicates he believed the furtherance of the Anti-Slavery League was a 'mission' worth pursuing, a letter to Pease, for example, stating his desire to give another talk in Darlington in order to make the town more acquainted with 'the merits of our great enterprise'. Nevertheless, there may have been another factor in his decision to remain in England through the early months of 1847, supporters led by the Richardsons having started a new fundraising campaign to provide him with an independent income once he returned home, thus enabling him to devote more time to anti-slavery work. Douglass, however, suggested using the money to purchase a steam printing press so he could start a newspaper. He already had ample evidence of the power of his written words, his *Narrative* making its way into the homes and souls of people all over the British Isles and his missives to the *Liberator* capturing the attention of Horace Greeley who asked him to write a column for the *New York Tribune*. The Belfast-based Revd Isaac Nelson, indeed, had hailed Douglass as 'an intellectual phenomenon ... in the republic of letters'. A career in the press also carried the chance of a more sedentary life, a far from inconsequential factor for a young man with a young family who had essentially been on one long speaking tour for six years, ever since he joined forces with Garrison. A well-run black newspaper, he further argued, would elevate African-Americans' conceptions of themselves at the same time as dealing a heavy blow to pro-slavery stereotypes of their intellectual inferiority, especially at a time when he claimed there were no black-run newspapers in the entire United States. Having charted his own course successfully through England, Scotland, Ireland and Wales for well over a year, it is possible, too, Douglass was motivated by a desire to chart his own abolitionist course once returned to America, the thought of being again a mere agent of the American Anti-Slavery Society, an underling of not just Garrison but also the abrasive Maria Weston Chapman, surely chafing. If, as seems possible, he knew of the Richardsons' plan from the time of his week-long stay in Newcastle just after Christmas, it would put a somewhat different complexion on his decision to remain in England. Was he more interested in the 'testimonial' or the Anti-Slavery League?[18]

'The Great Black Man'

Although originally scheduled to stay in England until the summer, Douglass decided to return to America early, purchasing a first-class ticket in London on 4 March for a sailing of the *Cambria* (still under the watch of Captain Charles Judkins) from Liverpool a month later. Perhaps he was suddenly eager to get home to his family and country – as a free man no less. He may also have sensed that the Anti-Slavery League was failing to gain the momentum he had hoped for, despite the generally warm reception he met with at speeches across the country. If thinking more selfishly, it is possible, too, that he chose to leave as soon as he was confident the fundraising campaign being undertaken in his name was going to reach the amount needed to purchase a printing press. Whatever the reason, Douglass was given a tremendous send-off at the London Tavern in Bishopsgate on the evening of Tuesday 30 March, his speech on the occasion quickly turned into a pamphlet, priced *6d* and printed by R. Yorke Clarke & Co., the same London company that had just published the latest edition of his *Narrative*, the total sales of which would reach around 13,000 over the course of the tour of Britain and Ireland.

A select gathering of about 600 'persons of great respectability', including prominent clergymen, public officials, journalists and a 'very many elegantly dressed ladies' as well as friends like the Ashursts, Howitts and Estlins, the soirée began just after six o'clock with light refreshments accompanied by music from the acclaimed English vocalist Henry Russell in the grand Corinthian-columned dining room of the Tavern that had previously hosted radicals and intellectuals like John Wilkes, Thomas Paine and Joseph Priestley. Letters of apology from some of the invited guests unable to attend were then read out, including from Douglass Jerrold of *Punch* and Viscount Morpeth, the latter the type of establishment figure John B. Estlin believed the Anti-Slavery League needed at its head, but who would never associate with it on account of Garrison's social radicalism. Charles Dickens, recently returned from the Continent and still working on *Dombey and Son*, which was in the midst of serialisation, likewise sent his regrets to one of the event's organisers:

Devonshire Terrace, 25th March, 1847.
Sir – I beg to acknowledge receipt of your obliging letter, and to express my regret that a particular engagement will prevent my attending the Soirée in honour of Mr Douglass, on Tuesday the 30th.

I esteem the invitation of the Committee as an honour; and I trust I need hardly say that I feel a warm interest in any occasion designed as a denunciation of slavery, and a mark of sympathy with anyone who has escaped from its tremendous wrongs and horrors.

Begging to thank you, and through you the Committee,
I am, Sir, your faithful Servant,
Charles Dickens.

Taking charge of proceedings, Thompson offered up an appreciation of Douglass as an abolitionist and as a man. John B. Estlin, William Howitt and others followed suit, Douglass thanking them all warmly before, towards the end of his own often emotional two-hour speech, he addressed the deep impact the nineteen-month tour had made on him. 'I have known what it was for the first time in my life to enjoy freedom in this country,' he told the audience, recalling how he had arrived upon their shore 'a degraded being, lying under the load of odium heaped upon my race by the American press, pulpit and people', and how in even the supposedly free northern states he had been kicked out of trains, omnibuses and churches and denied entry into theatres, lyceums, zoos and other public attractions of all kinds. 'I was mobbed, I was beaten, I was driven, dragged ... outraged in all directions,' he continued, with every white man, 'no matter how black his heart', able to insult him with impunity.

I came to this land – how great the change! The moment I stepped upon the soil at Liverpool, I saw people as white as any I ever saw in the United States ... and instead of seeing the curled lip of scorn, the fire of hate kindled in the eye of the Englishman, all was respect and kindness. I looked around in vain for the insult; I looked, for I hardly believed my eyes; I searched to see if I could see in an Englishman any look of disapprobation of me on account of my complexion – not one ... I have visited your Coliseum, your museum, your gallery of paintings; I have even had the pleasure of going into your House of Commons, and still more, into the House of Lords ... In none of these places did I receive one word of scorn ... When I return to the United States I will try to impress them with these facts, and to shame them into a sense of decency upon this subject ... Why ... the Americans do not know that

I am a man; they think the Negro is something between the man and the monkey. The very dogs here … know that I am a man. I was at a public meeting in Bromley the other day, and while I was speaking, a great Newfoundland dog came and put his paws on the platform, and gazed up at me with such interest, that I could tell, by the very expression of his eye, that he recognised my humanity. The Americans would do well to learn wisdom upon this subject from the very dogs of Old England.

'I came a slave; I go back a free man,' Douglass concluded simply and powerfully, his heart 'overborne' with the remembrance of the countless kindnesses bestowed on him during his tour and the large audience rising as one to give three loud cheers, then lining up by the platform to 'shake hands with the great black man before his departure from England'.[19]

From London, Douglass travelled up through Bristol (from whose anti-slavery activists he had recently received a silver inkstand) to Liverpool, where, the great cheers and applause from his farewell soirée till echoing through his mind, he was suddenly stopped short, brought face-to-face with the hard realities of life as a black man in America. The 'curled lip of scorn' returned with a vengeance in this city so wound up with the slave economy of the American South, Charles MacIver, a partner in the Cunard Line with offices near the docks, refusing him entry to the first-class cabin for which he had a ticket. Douglass protested, stating that the London agent of the Cunard Line had assured him the policy that forced him into steerage on the journey over had been rescinded. MacIver, however, was immovable, insisting the London agent had acted 'without authority', the racist sentiments of the company's American passengers still prioritised over any morality, the 'dominion of slavery', in Douglass's words, extending its reach from 'the star-spangled banner' to a British port 3,000 miles away. Into the breach came Judkins, who had accompanied Douglass to MacIver's office, offering to give up his own commodious quarters to the former slave. MacIver relented, but only after extracting promises from Douglass that he would not enter the saloon room or engage in any public talks on board the ship.

The next day, Douglass, a mixture of seething and subdued, took leave of the many friends and supporters who had gathered to see him off, telling them he felt as if he were 'going *from home* to a land of oppression and slavery – a land of man-stealers'. He had already penned a dispatch for the press from Brown's Temperance Hotel detailing the situation with regard to the Cunard Line and fulminating that 'it was not until I turned my face towards America that I met anything like proscription on account of my colour'. Published in the behemoth that was *The Times*, which followed it up with an article expressing its 'disapprobation and disgust at a proceeding wholly repugnant to our English notions of justice and humanity', Douglass's letter was quickly reprinted in papers across the British Isles, from the *Tyrone Constitution* to the *Bradford Observer* and from the *Dundee Courier* to the *Northampton Mercury*, all of whom denounced the manner of his treatment, the ensuing controversy so great Samuel Cunard was forced to issue a public apology. Douglass did not know this, however, as the *Cambria* made its wind-buffeted way across the Atlantic, the abolitionist taking his meals on his own and describing how 'the lash of proscription, to a man accustomed to equal social position, even for a time, as I was, has a sting for the soul hardly less severe than that which bites the flesh and draws the blood from the back of the plantation slave'.

Douglass's dark mood lifted with the approach to America, the former slave leaping onto the wharf in Boston on the late afternoon of Tuesday 20 April a celebrity and icon of international standing, his name ringing through the press on both sides of the Atlantic, his *Narrative* on its way to 30,000 sales and German and French editions about to be published. More than that, however, he was a man returning to his family, rushing for the short train ride to Lynn with barely a nod towards the admirers gathered to greet him. 'When within fifty yards of our house, I was met by my two bright-eyed boys, Lewis and Frederick, running and dancing with joy to meet me. Taking one in my arm and the other by the hand, I hastened to my house.'[20]

'The Slave's Cause'

Encouraged and applauded almost every step of the way, Douglass would always consider his time in Britain and Ireland a transformative experience, a milestone in his personal and political development that went beyond the mere gaining of legal freedom. Away from the dictates and demands of the American Anti-Slavery Society, he had grown much more confident, more cosmopolitan, begun to follow his own path, the clearest manifestation of this new independence of mind – hints of which had been seen from his first months in Ireland and fallings out with the arch-Garrisonian Webb – coming in the decision to move his family farther from the Garrisonian enclave of Boston to the town of Rochester in upstate New York a few months after his return to America. With funds from the testimonial raised in his name by supporters across the British Isles, he established a newspaper there, much to the chagrin of Garrison and other abolitionist leaders with whom he soon irrevocably split, the title of the paper, the *North Star*, a reference to the directions ('Follow the North Star') given to runaway slaves trying to reach the northern states and Canada.

'I have already bought an excellent and elegant press, and nearly all the necessary printing materials,' Douglass wrote to J. D. Carr in November 1847, the transfer of the money having been placed in the Carlisle biscuit manufacturer's capable hands – the £445 17s 6d gathered together converting to $2,175.

> I am solemnly impressed with the importance of the enterprise; and I shall enter on my duties with a full sense of my accountability to God, to the slave, and to the dear friends who have aided me in the undertaking. In the publication of the paper, I shall be under no party or society, but shall advocate the slave's cause in that way which in my judgement, will be the best suited to the advancement of the cause.

The break with Garrison had been personally painful, but for Douglass it had to be made, the former slave becoming in effect his own movement as soon as he returned from the British Isles, no longer in need of being 'accredited' by the American Anti-Slavery Society as he had in the summer of 1845.[21]

Inspired by the Irish leader Daniel O'Connell and deeply affected by the scenes of poverty that shadowed him all over the British Isles, the changes wrought went further still, for it was during this tour that the great humanitarian Douglass was born. Where previously his focus had been purely on anti-slavery, he increasingly turned his attention to the 'wrongs and sufferings' of the 'great family of man', speaking out, for example, in support of Europe's oppressed masses during the 'Year of Revolutions' in 1848 – a continent-wide conflagration to which only Britain seemed immune, a great Chartist demonstration failing to spark rebellion and an Irish rising quickly put down.[22] Douglass also attended the world's first Women's Rights Convention in Seneca Falls, New York, that year, remaining a dedicated suffragist all his life. Subsequent years would see him lend his weighty voice and influence to campaigns for free public education, prison reform and the abolition of capital punishment – 'Murder is no cure for murder'. Late in life, Douglass would devote a lot of time and energy to Haiti, a country that, as the first black Republic in the world following a successful slave uprising against Napoleonic rule, had always carried a special significance for African-Americans.

Douglass may have been transformed by his time in Britain and Ireland, but what impact did he have on the countries he visited? The tour was certainly a success, the hundreds of speeches delivered and thousands of copies of the *Narrative* sold raising great awareness of the anti-slavery cause among all classes of society, from weavers and teachers to a multitude of mayors, religious ministers and aristocrats. He was eulogised in radical papers like the *People's Journal* and even found favour in establishment icons like *The Times*. He also talked anti-slavery long into the night with an array of influential artists and writers and stayed in the homes of leading politicians like Thompson and Bright. Douglass was the catalyst for the formation of new anti-slavery groups and the inspiration for others to refocus their energies. The campaign against the American Churches also paid some dividends, with Belfast Baptists and Independents among other groups sending anti-slavery addresses to their co-religionists in America after hearing him speak. The Free Church of Scotland, meanwhile, had to contend with the formation of a Free Church Anti-Slavery Society as well as uncomfortable questioning at their General Assembly and a storm of public opprobrium. Perhaps most importantly, the transatlantic dimension to the anti-slavery movement seemed to have been strengthened – just as Garrison had hoped when first hatching the plan to send Douglass abroad.

A particularly tangible measure of Douglass's success was an increase in donations for the Boston Bazaar. 'There can be no doubt that much of the sweep of the Bazaar this year may be attributed to him – for from all I can learn the contributions from this side of the Atlantic will be finer than ever,' a still-embittered Webb was forced to admit in late 1846, praising Bristol in particular, whose colourful array of contributions had even been put on display prior to passage across the ocean, a reporter from a local paper noting especially the 'neat specimens of basket work' made by the students of the Blind Asylum.

The *Liberator* was certainly impressed with the quantity and quality of the donations – 'freedom's gifts' – from across the Atlantic, making special mention of the 'exquisite' paintings, ornaments and ladies' clothes. There were also 'Scotch clan tartan shawls', Tunbridge ware envelope cases and card trays, ring stands, silk tablecloths, children's bonnets and an 'astonishing variety' of 'linen-knitted toilette cushions, sofa cushions, carriage cushions and elbow cushions' together with a tapestry depicting Queen Victoria's coronation, sabre-shaped letter openers made from a piece of Mossgiel Thorn that had once grown at the home of Robert Burns, a large collection of watercolour drawings donated by Lady Byron and a silver-mounted jewel box made from a piece of oak from Carlisle Castle, where, the paper noted, Mary, Queen of Scots had once been imprisoned. A 'Toy Table', meanwhile, held innumerable dolls, puzzles, games, kites and illustrated storybooks that could be purchased as Christmas presents, the paper then going on to attempt to list – over the course of several tightly packed columns of the paper – the names of all the transatlantic donors, from the abolitionist stalwarts like the Jenningses and Hilditches to lesser known figures like the dressmaker Mrs Pickering on the Isle of Wight.[23]

Despite these apparent gains, the thousands-strong meetings across Britain and Ireland did not turn the anti-slavery campaign into a broader mass movement, the new Anti-Slavery League dissipating quickly after Douglass's departure, its first annual convention, held in the summer of 1847, turning out to be its last. John B. Estlin had foreseen trouble from an early stage, stating he did not know of 'a single influential person *anywhere*' who had joined the new organisation and blaming Garrison's getting '*unnecessarily*' mixed up with 'vexed English questions' like Chartism, which put off potential middle-class support. (Estlin clearly discounted the involvement of Radical politicians like John Bowring, who had chaired the Anti-Slavery League's convention.) For Anna Richardson and others, the Anti-Slavery League's avowed position as an adjunct of the American Anti-Slavery Society was a problem, placing undue pressure on British activists to choose sides among the American factions, when she believed they should be able interact freely with all friends of the cause that side of the Atlantic. More generally, Catherine Clarkson, commenting shortly before her venerated husband's death, suggested that while there was no pro-slavery party in the country, 'too many seem to think that having paid 22,000,000 [pounds] to redeem our own slaves England has nothing more to do'.[24]

In Scotland, the Free Church held on to its 'blood-stained' money, riding out the admonitions until they eventually quietened, the main dissident voices within the church moving to ministries in Canada by 1850. The controversy certainly failed to impinge on the personal popularity of Chalmers, who was buried with 'kingly honours' in Edinburgh amidst a crowd of almost 100,000 having died quietly in his sleep, of heart failure, in May 1847, a few weeks after Douglass's departure.[25] The Evangelical Alliance, too, showed resilience, overcoming divisions and dissensions and continuing to exist to this day in the guise of the World Evangelical Alliance.

A devastating backdrop of famine, meanwhile, saw the anti-slavery movement in Ireland fall away sharply. As early as October 1846, when donations for the Boston Bazaar from other major cities were reaching record proportions, Webb was lamenting how Dublin's contribution 'cut a wretched figure', the distress caused by the famine diverting attention away from the cause, the spiky publisher himself joining the Central Relief Committee of the Society of Friends, the body established by Joseph Bewley (the tea and coffee merchant whose name still adorns several well-known cafés in Dublin) to raise funds, organise relief measures and distribute supplies. It was a similar story in Cork, even if one activist there believed it a 'testament' to Douglass's impact that contributions from the city were not even less. A year on and Webb did not even bother to circulate appeals for the Boston Bazaar outside his immediate circle, so 'frightful' was the extent of 'poverty and pauperism' all around. 'I tell you, it's a miserable country for a man to be in, and I would be heartily glad to be well out of it,' he wrote Chapman. Two years later, the famine still strangling the populace, he derided the idea of holding an anti-slavery bazaar in Ireland. It would be looked on as a piece of 'philanthropic knight errantry' and should be abandoned.[26]

Drawn more to the charismatic Douglass than the anti-slavery movement *per se*, the contributions to the Bazaar from the rest of the British Isles also fell away after his departure. Lucy Browne in Bridgwater had signalled as much early on, telling Chapman in April 1847, just a few days after Douglass had left Liverpool on the *Cambria*, that she feared 'we shall have much less to send you than we had last time,' the previous year's contributions having been made 'in the midst of the enthusiasm' excited by his visit to the town. 'Now although he has inspired not a few with an interest in the cause which will not pass away,' Browne continued more reassuringly, counting herself among that number, 'yet I do not know how far it will be permanent in many [others] who shared it strongly at the time.' In the event, Bridgwater combined with some other towns like Evesham in Worcestershire to send a box of contributions to the Bazaar that November, including some dried flowers from the banks of 'Shakespeare's Avon'. Browne also wrote warmly of how if 'a wish could carry us across the Atlantic' there would be 'a good many English visitors at the Bazaar'. More telling, however, is the fact that communications – and therefore contributions – between Browne and Chapman seemed to cease after that year, the people of Bridgwater, like those of the British Isles entire, failing to live up to the promise they showed while Douglass travelled the land.[27]

Abolitionists – black and white, male and female, slave and free – continued to tour Britain and Ireland in the years after Douglass. Wider interest in the cause also flared up occasionally, for instance after the publication of Douglass's friend Harriet Beecher Stowe's famous anti-slavery novel *Uncle Tom's Cabin*. Nevertheless, by the time of his hastily arranged second journey across the Atlantic in late 1859, a fraught dash away from capture after being implicated in an attempted slave rebellion, the anti-slavery scene in the British Isles was still centred on the same small coterie of families – the Allens, Webbs, Haughtons, Smeals, Patons, Estlins, Wighams and Richardsons – the famous first tour, it seems, having had far greater impact on Douglass than the celebrated ex-slave had on the countries he visited.

8

'CRACKS IN THE ANTI-SLAVERY WALL'

Frederick Douglass was speaking before a large audience at the National Hall in Philadelphia on the evening of Tuesday, 18 October 1859 when word filtered through that a wiry, stern-faced white abolitionist named John Brown, together with a band of about twenty accomplices, had taken hold of a federal army arsenal in Harpers Ferry, a picturesque town on the banks of the Potomac in what is now West Virginia. Rumours of the raid – which Brown hoped would prove the prelude to a wider slave revolt – had been circulating all day. Their confirmation, however, still had a 'startling effect', Douglass wrote, the famous former slave repairing quickly to the home of a friend in the city.

The following morning, Douglass learned of the capture of a badly wounded fifty-nine-year-old Brown by a company of United States Marines led by Col Robert E. Lee, the already much-decorated scion of a prominent southern family, ten members of Brown's force, including two of his sons, having died in the fighting. A number of Brown's letters were also secured, implicating Douglass and several other well-known abolitionists in the raid. Douglass had known Brown for many years, the two men staying at each other's homes. He was also familiar with the plans for the attack on Harpers Ferry, if not the precise details, attending a secret meeting a few weeks earlier where he had been urged to join the enterprise. Douglass refused, believing Brown's scheme doomed to bloody failure. Nevertheless, the sheer fact of his closeness to Brown – a man who had shown few qualms about violence when killing three men during the series of armed clashes between pro- and anti-slavery groups in the Kansas Territory in the 1850s that would become known as 'Bleeding Kansas' – shows how far Douglass had travelled from the non-violent doctrines of William Lloyd Garrison and the American Anti-Slavery Society. In part, this was his true personality coming through, non-resistance never really seeming to sit well on a man whose speeches were full of bellicose language and who was used to fighting back when attacked, whether it be by the cruel farmer Edward Covey, dockers in Baltimore or pro-slavery mobs in the North. However, it was also a consequence of the desperation Douglass and many other abolitionists felt in the aftermath of the Supreme Court's infamous 1857 'Dred Scott' decision, which denied citizenship to all Americans of African origin. 'Slavery seemed to be at the very top of its power,' Douglass wrote of this period, the entire apparatus of the state caving in to slaveholders' demands.

Anxious to apprehend all those connected with an attack that had electrified the entire country, a message was sent from Washington directing the sheriff of Philadelphia County to arrest the still strongly built forty-one-year-old Douglass. Luckily, the telegraph operator who took down the message was sympathetic to the anti-slavery cause. Delaying delivery of the message, he hurried instead to Douglass's lodgings, imploring him to leave the city as soon as possible. Heeding the advice, Douglass headed for the wharf and a steamer that would take him to New York. Pacing anxiously across the deck and expecting arrest any minute, it is easy to imagine his mind wandering back to his original escape from slavery twenty-one years earlier. Eventually, the welcome cry of 'All ashore' rang out and those not travelling returned to the wharf. The paddles of the steamer began to turn and Douglass was in New York by nightfall, making his way to the home of another friend and sending a coded telegraph to his eldest son Lewis to 'secure' any documents in his Rochester office relating to Brown.

Despite fears that the authorities would be lying in wait, Douglass made his way back to Rochester, albeit by a more circuitous route than normal. He did not stay long, however, having being advised that the governor of New York was certain to comply with any requisition order – in essence an extradition request – issued by the furious, slavery-supporting Governor Henry A. Wise of Virginia. In the mistaken belief that Douglass was in Michigan, Wise (a future Confederate Army general) would send just such an order to that state, charging the abolitionist leader with 'murder, robbery and inciting servile insurrection'. And so Douglass was escorted by his close friends Amy and Isaac Post, two former Quakers who were about twenty years older than him and who had long been involved in the abolition movement, down to the wharf near the mouth of the Genesee, the river that flowed through Rochester to Lake Ontario, from where he would catch a ferry to Canada. It was a path he had helped many escaped slaves take, Douglass having long matched his soaring oratory and strident writings with practical help for fugitive slaves, the hillside home he and Anna had made a couple miles outside of Rochester becoming an important stop on the Underground Railroad. In Canada, he stayed at a 'low Dutch Tavern' for a while, keeping out of sight before boarding the Allen Line paddle steamer *Nova Scotian* in Quebec. Once again he was a fugitive leaving behind a wife and family with no clear idea of when he would return, that family having increased by one with the birth a daughter, Annie, a decade earlier. Once again he would find sanctuary in Britain, the *Nova Scotian* landing in Liverpool on 24 November after a twelve-day voyage that was 'cold, dark and stormy', much like the mood of the country from which he was fleeing.[1]

'Jezebel'

Although the John Brown affair gave it extra impetus, Douglass had been planning a trip across the Atlantic for several months, most of the connections made during his first tour of Britain and Ireland having held strong in the intervening years and many contributions previously destined for the Boston Bazaar now redirected to a similar event in Rochester. The acrimonious split with the American Anti-Slavery Society had cost him the support of important activists like the Estlins in Bristol and Wighams in Edinburgh. Nevertheless, it was largely allies from the British Isles who kept the *North Star* afloat during its precarious first few years of existence, as Douglass struggled to marry the constant need for money-making lecture tours with the time necessary to learn the craft and graft of running a newspaper. The *British Banner*, for example, a religious newspaper edited by the Independent minister Dr John Campbell, a man who had hailed Douglass at his London speeches, at one point urged a thousand of its readers to donate £1 each to ensure its survival. Transatlantic allies had also helped establish the *North Star*'s successor, *Frederick Douglass's Paper*, in whose pages the eponymous editor would relentlessly attack slavery during the tumultuous 1850s – the era of the controversial Fugitive Slave Act (which placed a stern legal onus on all federal and state officials to work to return runaways to the South) as well as 'Bleeding Kansas' and 'Dred Scott' – becoming in the process the most formidable black leader in a country that by the end of the decade held almost 4 million slaves, the phenomenal profitability of 'King Cotton' showing no signs of abating and the number of slaves increasing exponentially to meet the demand.

Julia Griffiths, an English woman about seven years Douglass's senior, was particularly vital to the eventual success of his newspaper projects. Introduced to each other towards the end of his first tour, they had quickly struck up a close friendship. Douglass, indeed, seems to have befriended the whole family, Griffiths reminiscing fondly of how her younger sister Eliza had pinned a 'white camellia' to his coat the night of his farewell soirée in London – an event her brother Thomas Powis Griffiths, a member of the British and Foreign Anti-Slavery Society, had helped organise – only to see a restless Douglass knock off all the 'beautiful' petals with his nervous fidgeting. Griffiths, who seems to have lived in and around London for most of her life to this point and whose mother was said to have been a friend of William Wilberforce, had also gathered together a collection of books and pamphlets for Douglass around this time, which would form the basis of his soon-to-be-extensive personal library. Later, she sent over copies of *The Times* and the *Illustrated London News* before travelling across the Atlantic with Eliza in the late 1840s. Originally intended as a six-month tour to improve their understanding of the abolition movement as well as of the lives of black communities (including many runaway slaves) in Canada West, she ending up staying in Rochester, even living at Douglass's home for an extended period of time. Eliza went with her, soon marrying the *North Star*'s printer John Dick and moving to Philadelphia.[2]

Perhaps because her father had been involved in the print trade, working as a bookseller and publisher at various points in his somewhat erratic working life, Griffiths immediately brought a greater sense of stability and purpose to Douglass's then-flailing *North Star*, acting as his chief business manager, editor, publicist and fundraiser. She helped double the paper's circulation and pay off its debts, all the while contributing a literary column and other pieces. The African-American physician James McCune Smith – who would author the introduction to Douglass's second autobiography, *My Bondage and My Freedom*, a book on which Griffiths did substantial rewriting – noted the 'high literary abilities' that went along with her book-keeping prowess. Griffiths also got involved with local anti-slavery organisations as well as other reform groups in the rapidly expanding city, which was not far from Niagara Falls. More surreptitiously, she assisted in the ferrying of fugitive slaves across the border to Canada, an enterprise in which the whole Douglass family was engaged, Anna often awoken in the middle of the night to 'prepare supper for a hungry lot of fleeing humanity' while her sons lit fires in the rooms in which they were being hidden, Douglass constantly adding rooms to their house in order to accommodate the ceaseless trail of runaways wending their way along the Underground Railroad.[3]

Douglass's connection with Griffiths was not appreciated by all, the pair drawing vile taunts from passers-by as they walked the streets of Rochester or New York – America at large still deeply discomfited by the sight of black men and white women together in public. On a more personal level, Isabel Jennings in Cork became much more guarded in her communications, convinced the self-appointed gatekeeper was reading all his letters before passing them on. Rumours of an affair were also widespread, Jennings writing caustically to a friend: 'I am sure he thinks anti-slavery zeal is the strongest emotion she is capable of.' Resenting the role they believed she played in his leaving their fold (and overlooking the manner in which their own patronising behaviour had helped push him away), the Boston abolitionists, full of the self-righteousness that came with believing theirs was the only true abolitionist path, were particularly callous, labelling Griffiths, by now in her early forties, a 'Jezebel' in print as part of a concerted bid to discredit Douglass. (They had earlier attempted to dissuade British and Irish activists like Mary Howitt from aiding the *North Star*, which they characterised as a vanity project and certain to fail.) Even Garrison lowered himself to hinting at marital strife and writing of Douglass as a 'fallen Samson … slumbering in the lap of a prejudiced, sectarian Delilah', the latter a phrase that combined an insinuation of infidelity on the black abolitionist's part with a dig at Griffiths's past associations with the British and Foreign Anti-Slavery Society.[4]

Douglass castigated Garrison for invading 'the sacredness of my home' and dragging his family into what had been a dispute between rival abolitionist factions about tactics, centred at this time on the former slave's growing connection with Gerrit Smith's Liberty Party. Douglass also defended Griffiths, the woman who had helped rescue the *North Star* at a time when he really feared for its failure – a failure he felt certain would be used to deride the ability of black people more generally to run any form of business – as someone with 'a just claim upon my gratitude, respect and friendship'. Anna Murray, meanwhile, put her signature to a letter to the *Liberator* stating: 'It is not true that the presence of a certain person in the office of Frederick Douglass causes unhappiness in his family.' Garrison, however, saw evasiveness in the missive, in particular in the deliberate-seeming mention of Douglass's 'office' rather than 'home'– for by this stage Griffiths had left the Douglasses abode for lodgings with an English family in the centre of Rochester. There were certainly second-hand accounts of Anna saying, 'I *don't* care anything about her being in the *Office* – but I won't have her in my house' and it is not hard to imagine feelings of discomfort at sharing her home with a white woman so obviously devoted to her husband, especially when so much of their contact revolved around the books and newspapers Anna could not read, the world of words Anna's illiteracy did not let her enter, even if, as her loving daughter Rosetta recalled, she always took great pride in her husband's periodicals, with each publication a day of rejoicing in the home, every weekly issue 'another arrow sent on its way to do the work of puncturing the veil that shrouded a whole race in gloom'. As a further complication, Griffiths had also arrived on the Rochester scene at a time when Anna was still struggling to adjust to her new life in upstate New York, after the move away from the close circle of friends she had in Lynn, the African-American women who had supported her so much during her husband's first prolonged absence in Britain and Ireland, a move Rosetta characterised as perhaps her 'greatest trial'.[5]

Despite the constant innuendos, there are signs relations between the two women were not necessarily (or at least not entirely) fraught, Griffiths writing in later years, soon after the birth of Rosetta's first child, the Douglasses first grandchild, of how she would 'give a great deal to see [Anna] & Rose nursing baby & to have a good cup of tea with her & a nice "Maryland biscuit"'. It was a warm, heartfelt line, one that fits well with the recollections of Rochester neighbours who, unlike the Boston abolitionists, saw her daily, remembering a friendly, outgoing woman who would 'talk about anything at any time and as long as anybody will hear her'. Furthermore, Anna was well used to her home being full of lodgers, the Douglasses seeming to conceive of their places of residence as essentially open homes for family, friends or fugitive slaves. In Lynn, a young woman named Ruth Cox, an escaped slave Douglass had met on one of his lecture tours, was informally adopted by the family, a far from irregular occurrence among African-American families of the time, living with them under the alias Harriet Bailey (Douglass's mother's name) for a number of years before getting married. In Rochester, her place was filled by Anna's sister Charlotte, as well as a revolving array of young black apprentices who worked on the *North Star*. John Dick, the Griffiths sisters and others, too, stayed for various periods of time. Rosetta Douglass also made a significant virtue out of her mother's ability to correctly discern the 'character of those who came around her'. If this was the case, would she really have let Griffiths stay in her home for the best part of three years if concerned about her motivations toward her husband?[6]

While it is impossible to know Anna's true feeling about Douglass's closeness to Griffiths, the tawdry rumours do a disservice to his deep affection for his wife, the 'beloved one of my heart' as he once wrote to Anna Richardson. Nor are they a fair reflection of a marriage that was much more a relationship of equals than the mere union of the 'great man' and meek 'helpmeet'. The Douglasses may have had quarrels and difficulties, but it would not be wise to take the pulse of their relationship from the bitter admonitions of rivals like Garrison and Maria Weston Chapman.[7]

'Our Meeting Was a Joyous One'

Although clearly strong-willed and resilient, the constant barbs about her intimacy with Douglass may have been a factor in Griffiths returning to England in the summer of 1855. Not that the move severed their ties, Griffiths touring cities across the north of England and Scotland establishing new (non-Garrisonian) anti-slavery societies and collecting money for Douglass's many projects, including the new periodical *Douglass's Monthly* and organisations formed to aid fugitive slaves. 'They like to have letters, giving Anti-Slavery information, to read at their meetings,' Griffiths wrote to Douglass of the societies with which she was involved, constantly cajoling him into prompter replies to his transatlantic donors. Letters recounting escapes to freedom were especially popular, as they gave British and Irish activists a real sense that their efforts were having an effect on the struggle in America. Douglass got the message, writing to one group: 'I wish your society could have seen the twenty fugitives we have helped on their way to Canada during the past week ... Every example leaves the system weaker ... and ... slavery must soon fall in the Border States.' Griffiths also kept Douglass's name in the broader public consciousness, getting extracts from his letters published in the *Leeds Mercury*, one of the most important provincial papers of the era.[8]

The by-now forty-seven-year-old Griffiths curtailed her speech-making and cross-country travels after her March 1859 marriage to Revd Henry O. Crofts, a widowed Methodist minister in Yorkshire who had previously worked in Canada and was described as 'an excellent anti-slavery man' in Douglass's paper on account of his work among escaped slaves there. Nevertheless, she remained the major conduit through which communications made their way to Douglass and was a natural first stop when he returned to Britain's shores that winter. 'You may well suppose that our meeting was a joyous one,' he wrote to a friend, finding Julia, now a stepmother to three young girls, the 'same zealous, active and untiring worker that she ever was' and emphasising how her husband, too, was glad to meet and receive him. While making the Crofts' Huddersfield home his main base, Douglass also spent a number of nights with the Unitarian Revd Russell Lant Carpenter and his wife Mary, a couple whom he had first met in Bridgwater in Somerset thirteen years earlier but who now lived at the Salem Parsonage in Halifax a few miles north of the Crofts. In Leeds, meanwhile, he stayed with the Forsters, 'a family of much intelligence, wealth and refinement', the forty-one-year-old former Quaker William Edward Forster a rising Liberal Party politician and Jane Martha, the 'Lady of the House', the eldest daughter of the 'celebrated' Dr Thomas Arnold, educationalist and former headmaster at Rugby School. Douglass got to know the Radical Halifax MP and future Cabinet minister James Stansfeld, too, who was married to Caroline Ashurst, daughter of the literary family the former slave had spent many happy evenings with in London during his first tour. His Newcastle hosts, of course, were the Richardsons.[9]

Ensconced in Huddersfield or Halifax and perhaps enjoying the serialisation of Charles Dickens's latest work, *A Tale of Two Cities*, Douglass also took the time to correspond with a number of other old friends and supporters. 'I have not at all forgotten that I was once the guest of your dear home in Coventry,' he wrote to a Mrs Cash in December, 'nor that you and your dear household have kindly stood by me in my anti-slavery labours during the last dozen years.' In particular, he wished to be remembered to Cash's daughter Eleanor, who, like so many other female anti-slavery activists, was increasingly involved in the women's rights movement. 'Tell her I am as much like the picture she took of me as the wear and tear of thirteen years will permit me to be.' To Maria Webb in Ireland, meanwhile, he explained somewhat melodramatically how he could never have taken the chance of being taken into custody in America, for even if the courts of Virginia failed to convict and 'kill' him for anything connected with 'Dear Old Brown', they would have certainly done so for the simple fact of 'my being Frederick Douglass'.[10]

Such fears receding now that he was out of the United States, Douglass adopted a lighter tone in his letters, describing to Amy Post how while the talk in the houses in which he stayed was occasionally a 'trifle more reserved than I like', he was so 'amiable' people generally allowed him a 'little more freedom' than they would others. 'I sometimes make even the dignified Quakers ... laugh and feel funny ... which you know is very unfavourable to stiffness,' he continued to the erstwhile Quaker Post, before recounting how he had also gone shooting with William Edward Forster. 'He is a capital shot and is prepared to defend his country from the French – and from anybody else who may be disposed to make an attack,' Douglass joked, the reference to France no doubt connected to a recent war scare involving the two countries.

Nevertheless, there remained some difficulties, with money tight and Douglass asking his American correspondents – like the impeccably moral Post who, as an aside, asked him to 'give my love' to Griffiths Crofts, which she would not have done had she harboured serious reservations about their earlier closeness – to send 'double postage' so he would not have to cover the costs of letters home. There was also the important work of spreading the anti-slavery word, Douglass embarking on a lecture tour that at times matched the frantic pace of his first transatlantic sojourn, filling halls in towns and cities like Liverpool, Sheffield, Leeds, Bradford, Dundee, Falkirk and Arbroath throughout the winter of 1859–60 and receiving once again great praise for his glowing oratory in the local press.[11]

'Brave and True'

'Upon reaching Liverpool I learned that England was nearly as much alive to what had happened at Harpers Ferry as was the United States, and I was immediately called upon in different parts of the country to speak on the subject of slavery,' Douglass recalled many years later of the start of his second tour, news of John Brown's attack having being carried swiftly across the ocean by the newly laid transatlantic telegraph cable – the first communications through which had been a set of congratulatory messages between Queen Victoria and President James Buchanan. Douglass's own role in the affair, naturally, was the subject of much interest. For some, it was cause of concern, Douglass having to reassure the secretary of the Sheffield Anti-Slavery Association, a body formed just a couple of years previously under the auspices of Griffiths Crofts, that his 'mission' was 'wholly peaceful' and unconnected to any 'plan or purpose involving a resort to arms' for the 'liberation of my Brothers & Sisters' in slavery. 'I neither took part in that transaction nor counselled it,' he wrote of Harpers Ferry, fully aware of the manner in which nearly all British abolitionists, raised on the moral force doctrines of their great heroes William Wilberforce and Thomas Clarkson, looked askance at violent insurrection. Despite this, he pointedly refused to disown the 'brave and true' Brown or condemn the use of violence, telling an audience at the Mechanics' Institute in Wakefield in west Yorkshire in the middle of January 1860 that while he was not there to advocate 'forcible emancipation', nor could he support any 'theory of peace' that left the slaves 'helpless' in the hands of their masters. 'Slavery was itself an insurrection,' he declared, 'and the slaveholders were a band of insurgents armed against the rights and liberties of their fellow men – for there was no time when the blood of the Negro was not being shed.'[12]

By this stage, news of Brown's execution after a summary trial had reached Britain, 'the Virginia hyenas', as Douglass's eldest daughter Rosetta described them, hanging him in early December, his dignified bearing and evocative prison writings seeing him eulogised by Ralph Waldo Emerson, who pronounced him a 'new saint' readying to 'make the gallows glorious like the cross'. In Britain, even staunch moral force Quakers like Eliza Wigham in Edinburgh were moved to write of the 'the murder of this man whom all must admire & whose bearing throughout had been worthy of a martyr'. Nevertheless, other British abolitionists gave Douglass the 'cold-shoulder' because of his supposed involvement in the affair. Leading politicians and powerful organs like *The Times*, too, stayed firm in their condemnations of Brown, British fears of violent insurrection having being recently reawakened by the 'Indian Mutiny'.[13]

Douglass returned to the topic of Brown at a crowded meeting at Queen Street Hall in Edinburgh in late January, his first speech of this tour in the Scottish capital he still called the most beautiful city in the world. Interrupted by loud cheers and applause on more than thirty occasions during the course of the two-hour speech, Douglass described how Harpers Ferry had 'stirred a fever in America such as never before existed'. He then exalted his old friend Brown as a 'noble, heroic and Christian martyr' and insisted that 'when a man had been reduced to slavery he had a right to get his freedom – peaceably if he could, forcibly if he must'. To those who argued Brown's actions had achieved nothing, Douglass countered they could yet prove 'the brick knocked down at the end of the row by which all the rest were laid prostrate', the meeting ending with the Revd G. D. Cullen, an eminent missionary and friend of the Scottish explorer Dr David Livingstone (who at this time was in the midst of a five-year exploration of the Zambezi river in Mozambique), calling for a motion, 'which was enthusiastically carried', thanking the speaker for his 'eloquent and stirring address'.[14]

Although an issue of great interest and immediacy, Douglass did not confine his speeches to Brown and Harpers Ferry, delivering, for example, an early incarnation of his famous 'Self-Made Man' lecture – a talk he would deliver regularly over the course of the next thirty-five years, reshaping it with great care for each new generation of listeners – at the highly appropriate setting of the Mechanics' Institute in Halifax, with its class rooms, technical drawing rooms and large library of almost 4,000 books all available for the edification of the city's working class. He also discussed the forthcoming American presidential election on a number of occasions, stating his clear preference for the recently formed Republican Party's candidate, who at this stage seemed likely to be the (moderately) anti-slavery William Henry Seward, Douglass's increased engagement with party politics and elections through the 1850s another result of his move away from Garrison. There were the usual flashes of humour, too, Douglass, in Scotland, comparing in an exaggeratedly self-deprecating fashion his 'poor little anti-slavery speeches' with the 'tremendous outburst of eloquence' of the Free Church minister Revd Candlish at a recent, unrelated anti-slavery event. 'Why, it almost atoned for a great many other things,' he intoned sarcastically, the audience all in on the joke about Douglass's old adversary from the 'Send Back the Money' campaign. Recalling a speech in the same hall in Wakefield more than a decade earlier, meanwhile, Douglass also took great pleasure in observing how there had been 'no declension in anti-slavery spirit' in that city.[15]

This was not the case throughout the country entire.

'Pro-Slavery Poison'

On the afternoon of Thursday, 28 August 1856, a nondescript platform in King's Cross railway station in London played host to a slightly surreptitious meeting between Queen Victoria and Harriet Beecher Stowe, the lithe, forty-five-year-old American author of the famous anti-slavery novel *Uncle Tom's Cabin*. Published four years earlier, *Uncle Tom's Cabin* had been an immediate sensation on both sides of the Atlantic, with toy characters, playing cards, jigsaws, wallpaper and even crockery and cutlery inspired by the book selling out in shops across Britain. Making use of her new-found celebrity, Stowe had sent a copy to Prince Albert in the hope he would show the 'simple story' to the Queen, believing it might 'win from her compassionate nature, pitying thoughts for those multitudes of poor outcasts' – by which Stowe meant fugitive slaves – 'who have fled for shelter to the shadow of her throne'. The ploy worked, the royal couple becoming avid fans of the novel that would go on to become the best-selling book in nineteenth-century Britain after the Bible. Victoria, indeed, was so enamoured with

Stowe's book she ensured that her private secretary arranged the 'accidental' meeting at King's Cross when the author visited London on a publicity tour for a subsequent novel. The unusual venue allowed the Queen (who is also thought to have sat for the African-American photographer James Presley Ball around this time) to circumvent the diplomatic difficulties that may have stemmed from any official meeting with such a prominent abolitionist. It also lent a breezy informality to the meeting, with Victoria and Albert, who were on their way to their Scottish home at Balmoral, able to talk freely about their admiration for the book while the four royal children present 'stared their big blue eyes almost out of looking at the little authoress of *Uncle Tom's Cabin*'.[16]

Although Stowe's image of 'multitudes' of fugitive slaves crowding Britain's shores is an exaggeration, they certainly existed. There was John Joseph, the 'African Negro' who had attended one of Douglass's talks in Newcastle in late 1846. The more famous Ellen and William Craft, a married couple, had made their home in London for more than twenty years after escaping slavery in Georgia in the most remarkable of ways, the fair-complexioned Ellen disguising herself as a male plantation owner while William posed as her slave during a nerve-jangling four-day journey north aboard trains and steamers. Many free blacks, too, had sought refuge from American racism in British cities, including the scholar William G. Allen, the first African-American employed as a professor at a white college, who was forced into exile after violent opposition to his marriage to one of his white students. William P. Powell, the owner of several boarding houses for sailors along the east coast, was another, moving his family from New York to Liverpool in 1851 and securing work with the British Customs Service. 'I came to this country a poor despised outcast,' Powell wrote some years later, 'driven from my native country for no "colour of crime" but for the "crime of colour."'[17]

With visiting abolitionists like the mercurial Henry 'Box' Brown – who earned his nickname because of the ingenious way he had literally mailed himself to freedom in a large wooden crate – continuing to attract large audiences, Britain's anti-slavery resolve appeared firm on the eve of Douglass's winter 1859 arrival.

Closer inspection, however, reveals 'cracks in the anti-slavery wall', the transitory applause greeting abolitionists like Brown and the Crafts disguising the essentially moribund state of much of the British anti-slavery scene in the 1850s, the British and Foreign Anti-Slavery Society failing to gain anything like the same traction of the anti-slavery movements of the 1790s and 1830s in the pursuit of its stated goal of 'universal emancipation' and many of its branches existing in name only. Touring Britain just a few months before Douglass, the Garrisonian abolitionist Samuel J. May had been struck by the manner in which most of the country thought slavery was 'none of their business'. Similar views had been cropping up in correspondence between Garrisonians for some time, leading to suggestions for a new and 'stronger' Anti-Slavery League. ('You doubtless remember that this was tried, some fifteen years ago,' Samuel May Jr, cousin of the Samuel J. May mentioned above, wrote to Richard D. Webb in Dublin. 'I recollect becoming a member of it, and making a small subscription at the time.') The establishment of a network of 'Anti-Slavery Libraries' was also mooted, the change in temper so clear Douglass made it the focus of one of the first speeches of his tour.[18]

Sharing the stage with the Revd Crofts and numerous other dignitaries including the local MP James Stansfeld, Douglass had begun his speech at the Mechanics' Institute in Halifax on the evening of 7 December 1859 with an evocative description of how the right to freedom was 'inscribed on every human soul'. Recalling the immense personal impact of his first tour of the British Isles, he then described to loud cheers how he had returned to America 'almost forgetting that he was a black man' or that he had a 'woolly' head. Nevertheless, while grateful for again being so warmly welcomed, Douglass also expressed his disappointment to his 1,000-strong audience at finding – barely two weeks into his tour – that opposition to slavery no longer garnered the same level of emotional investment or political attention as before, one of the most essential components of the great anti-slavery wall with which he wanted to surround the slaveholding South collapsing as a new 'doctrine' of 'non-intervention' with regard to American slavery took hold in Britain. Slavery, Douglass insisted, was not some 'tariff' or 'postal regulation' that countries should legislate themselves but a 'vile system of blood' that outraged 'all the great principles of justice, liberty and humanity'. It was not an 'American question' or an 'English question' but a 'great human question', he continued, asserting that Britain's 'glory' in striking the shackles off 800,000 slaves in the West Indies gave it the 'purer moral sentiment' necessary to purge the evil of slavery, an evil so powerful it paralysed all connected to it in America, from the government and judiciary to religious ministers and members of the press. Returning to this theme of the necessity of aid from outside forces before another audience, he reached for the biblical image of the 'Redeemer' stretching his hand down from above, suggesting how as the power that 'reformed the dram shop' came from the 'regions of sobriety', so the power that would 'overturn slavery' had to come from a 'country uncontaminated by slavery'.[19]

Among the reasons Douglass ascribed for waning anti-slavery sentiment was the simple fact that its most ardent advocates were getting older, acknowledging in one of his Halifax speeches that he was now speaking to an almost entirely new generation, one whose moral compass had not been forged in the crucible of West Indies emancipation. He also blamed the insidious influence of pro-slavery travellers from America who accentuated the humanity and kindness of slaveholders, reserving his harshest criticisms for the pro-slavery religious ministers whose words carried so much weight in Britain. Douglass was also concerned about the skewed view of slavery British travellers to the South brought back with them, emphasising the care with which slaveholders – and indeed southern society as a whole – hid the worst excesses of slavery from white visitors they wished to impress. This was an important point to get across, for it was often those same Britons who had been shown around slave plantations by well-dressed, Bible-quoting slave-owners and their decorous wives who were the most vociferous in public debates about slavery once returned home, insisting in a myriad letters to local papers that slaves were not abused and comparing unfavourably the anarchy of the North – with its class struggles, penurious immigrants and free blacks – with the well-ordered, civilised way of life in the South, where good manners were sacrosanct, tradition prevailed and the various ranks of society all knew their place.[20]

Douglass's diagnosis was correct – at least partially – other factors including the way in which the Crimean War, which Douglass referenced in at least one of his speeches, had diverted the energies of many of the country's anti-slavery activists to the Peace Society. Joseph Sturge, for example, the leader of the British and Foreign Anti-Slavery Society who would die a few months before Douglass's return to Britain, even travelled to St Petersburg to meet Tsar Nicholas I in a Quaker-led effort to avert conflict. More recently, the Franco-Austrian War of early 1859 (also known as the Second War of Italian Independence) had drawn Britons back to the cause of Italian unification, a movement that for many decades had powerful sympathisers in Britain and which would soon be accomplished under the leadership of the figures like Giuseppe Garibaldi – though its final form would not please the weary arch-Republican Giuseppe Mazzini, the Italian patriot Douglass had met in London in the summer of 1846.

Somewhat ironically, the anti-slavery movement in Britain was also seen a victim of its own success, younger reform-minded men and women taking anti-slavery sentiment for granted as a fundamental tenet of British life and investing their energies instead in other, more pressing-seeming political and social concerns. Writing in the *Edinburgh Review* in 1858, Harriet Martineau was more abrupt, stating simply the new generation found anti-slavery 'old and tiresome'.[21]

More insidiously, racism was also on the rise, Douglass contrasting before an audience at the Nelson Street Lecture Room in Newcastle in late February 1860 the manner in which he had heard hardly any negative words about 'the colour with which God had clothed him' during his first trip through Britain with the fact that 'American prejudice' could now be found in nearly all its large 'commercial towns'. Douglass blamed the United States for despoiling his beloved Britain – the very phrase 'American prejudice' implying racism was a distinctly American ill – accusing the 40,000 Americans who visited the country annually of pouring 'the "leprous distilment" of their pro-slavery poison into the ears and hearts of the British people'. The 'Ethiopian minstrels' who came over from the United States were a particular source of contempt, their shows – lapped up by tens if not hundreds of thousands of paying British spectators – having grown inordinately more callous and cruel in their depictions of African-Americans, especially the 'happy' slaves singing their way dim-wittedly through life on the southern plantations.[22]

Blinded by his Anglophilia, Douglass failed to discern how the problem ran deeper; British attitudes toward race – often wrapped up with the related issues of labour and class – having undergone a slow but significant evolution since the West Indies emancipation, the controversial Scottish critic Thomas Carlyle's *Occasional Discourse on the Nigger Question* finally bringing the issue to the fore of public debate in the early 1850s. Focusing on the precipitous economic decline of the West Indies since the abolition of slavery, Carlyle (ignoring the profound effects of the abolition of sugar duties and essentially blaming the newly emancipated slaves for not being able to undo in a decade the unquantifiable damage wrought over the course of two centuries to both their collective psyche and to the soil of the sugar islands) portrayed the freed people – or 'pumpkin-eating Quashees' – as inherently lazy and intellectually inferior, with all black people characterised as little more than 'two-legged cattle'. Assailed in some quarters, his vicious words nevertheless created the space in which respectable authors like Anthony Trollope could write of the 'Negro's idea of emancipation' being the freedom to 'lie in the sun and eat breadfruit and yams' all day, and where letter writers to local papers felt emboldened to describe slaveholders in the American South as being 'burdened with the care and control of four millions of an inferior race'. Passages, too, of Charles Darwin's epochal *On the Origin of Species*, published the very day Douglass arrived in Liverpool on board the *Nova Scotian*, would be selectively co-opted by pro-slavery apologists and so-called 'scientific racists' both sides of the Atlantic, much to the chagrin of the author, a staunch anti-slavery man who as the grandson of Josiah Wedgwood had been immersed in the abolitionist scene from childhood.[23]

'*War of Extermination*'

The incessant infighting between the various anti-slavery groups –
the British and Foreign Anti-Slavery Society, the American and
Foreign Anti-Slavery Society and the Liberty Party on one
side and the American Anti-Slavery Society on the other with
Douglass and his followers floating somewhere in between – was
also extremely off-putting to the wider British public, the depths
of animosity clear in the extreme language used against each
other, Mary Estlin urging a 'war of extermination' against the
anti-Garrisonians at one point in the early 1850s, shortly before
engineering the formal breakaway of the Bristol and Clifton
Ladies' Anti-Slavery Society from Sturge's organisation. A few
years on, the last letter her father John B. Estlin ever sent was one
of resignation from the British and Foreign Anti-Slavery Society,
the elder Estlin hearing 'the voice which summoned him from his
work on earth to his reward in heaven' just days later, during –
appropriately enough – a specially convened anti-slavery meeting
at his elegant Park Street home.[24]

Unsurprisingly, Douglass's decision to tour Britain was met with
immediate suspicion among Garrisonians. 'He will do mischief,'
Samuel May Jr observed, asserting that although Douglass might not
attack the Garrisonians in public, 'in private his malice will have full
swing'. Mary Estlin, previously so enamoured of Douglass, wrote in
a similarly harsh tone of how she was certain he would succeed in
promoting his 'own interests' rather than those of 'the cause's true
friends'. Once Douglass arrived, however, some Garrisonians felt
they should attend his talks, with Joseph Lupton, for example, a
wealthy and well-connected Leeds woollen manufacturer in his forties
(whose descendants include Catherine Middleton, the Duchess of
Cambridge) believing the former slave, whatever his faults, 'cannot
but do some good by stirring up anti-slavery feeling in this country'.[25]

'We have had no communication with him,' Eliza Wigham
wrote from Edinburgh of Douglass, the man she had once housed
so happily, which must surely have felt somewhat sad and strange
for the softly featured and delicately built thirty-nine-year-old
Quaker. Nevertheless, she too thought he might 'do some good',
considering the moribund state of anti-slavery feeling in the

country, and although she does not seem to have attended any of his talks in the city, she was at least able to soothe Garrisonian concerns, reporting that he had not said 'anything hostile to the American Anti-Slavery Society in his speeches'. In Glasgow, meanwhile, where Douglass definitely did question Garrisonian policies, the Smeals and Patons also seem to have kept their distance, not that this stopped thousands of others filling the City Halls and other venues for talks by the famous American visitor, most of which cost about a shilling to attend.[26]

There was some interaction between the rival groups, Douglass sharing a stage with the Garrisonian Sarah Remond, sister of his old (and now largely estranged) friend Charles Lenox Remond as well as an important activist in her own right. 'You would have smiled if you had been in Leeds a few evenings ago,' he wrote to Amy Post around Christmas 1859, 'when Sarah Remond ... and myself appeared upon the same anti-slavery platform. I think it must have been embarrassing to Miss Sarah – though she did not rebel. We both spoke. She with her <u>accustomed</u> calmness, and I – whatever you please. The audience was much pleased with the two blacks from America.'[27]

At one point, it also looked like Douglass and George Thompson, much feebler than heretofore having been through several spells of serious ill-health since losing his seat at the 1852 General Election, would enjoy a reunion, the American writing to the former MP in February after being assured by Ellen Richardson he 'would not object to getting a line' from him. 'Don't hold me as an enemy,' Douglass had signed off, looking forward to their meeting, a meeting that never materialised, the two abolitionists finding themselves instead on opposite sides of a debate about whether the American Constitution was a pro- or anti-slavery document, delivering a series of lectures in response to each other's charges all through the spring, the *Scottish Banner* expressing regret at the 'feud' between the two men who fifteen years earlier had 'passed from platform to platform' rousing 'the country into enthusiasm upon the subject of man-selling'. During his first tour, Douglass had heartily assumed the American Anti-Slavery Society position that the Constitution was explicitly pro-slavery, a 'covenant with death and an agreement with hell' in Garrison's memorable words. A decade's worth of deep thought, though, had changed his mind, his speech at the Queen's Rooms in Glasgow on the evening of 26 March an erudite and concise distillation of the ways in which far from being guaranteed by the Constitution, slavery was a violation of it. A piece of work to make any constitutional lawyer proud, even Garrison admitted it was 'infernally able'. The arguments involved, however, were too obtuse to stir popular sentiment – no 'Send Back the Money' clarion call here – the fact that the entire affair ended in something of a pamphlet war between Douglass and Thompson only adding to the impression the abolitionists were wasting their energies in incessant in-fighting.[28]

'Light and Life'

By the start of April, Douglass had spent four months touring the north of England and Scotland, delivering lectures that seemed successful in terms of the attendances and publicity they garnered even if there remained the strong sense many came just to see the famous American figure in their midst rather than from a real desire to immerse themselves in his cause. Letters to friends and supporters around Britain and Ireland suggest he planned on going to London and Dublin. He certainly intended visiting France, arranging a passport through the French Embassy in London after being rebuffed by the American ambassador. A devastating family tragedy, however, put an end to these plans: Douglass's youngest daughter Annie died on 13 March, just nine days before her eleventh birthday, from what the local papers termed 'brain congestion' – a catch-all nineteenth-century diagnosis for any condition, such as meningitis, that inflamed the brain tissue.

The news of Annie's death would have been totally unexpected for Douglass, who had just been sent a letter from his Rochester friend Amy Post informing him his family 'seem to be all well'. A short time earlier, indeed, he had received a note from Annie in her own hand, at the end of a letter from his older daughter Rosetta. 'Annie attends school regularly,' Rosetta had written. 'She writes daily in her English writing book and intends to astonish you with her advance in penmanship.' Annie's note itself was an endearing mix of stories from school – 'I am proceeding in my German very well for my teacher says so … I expect that you will have a German letter from me in a very short time' – with her thoughts on the news that 'Poor Mr Brown is dead', the young girl having often played with the executed abolitionist when he stayed with the Douglasses. There was also a simple anti-slavery poem she planned to recite in class that went:

> O he is not the man for me
> Who buys or sells a slave
> Nor he who will not let him free
> But send him to his grave.
> But he whose noble heart beats warm
> For all men's life and liberty
> Who loves alike each human form
> O that's the man for me.

'We heard from dear father last week,' Rosetta would write to a friend soon after Annie's death, taking up the task of communications on behalf of her mother, 'and his grief was great.' Douglass's impressively mature twenty-year-old daughter hoped his next letter would 'evince more composure of mind'. Composure, however, was the furthest emotion from the deeply distressed abolitionist's mind, the pure sorrow of grief no doubt mixed with guilt at being so far from home at so vital a time. Determined to return to America 'regardless of the peril', Douglass boarded a ship for Portland, Maine, travelling back to Rochester surreptitiously via Canada and keeping a low profile for a few months. The house he returned to was shorn of its 'light and life'. The country was on the brink of civil war.[29]

9

'YOUR SECOND HOME'

On the evening of Tuesday, 14 September 1886, a remarkably robust sixty-eight-year-old Frederick Douglass stepped onto the deck of the luxury ocean liner the *City of Rome*, his dramatic shock of white hair and full white beard marking him out almost as much as the colour of his skin. Travelling with his new wife Helen Pitts Douglass, his first wife Anna having died four years earlier, he was embarking from New York on a year-long tour of Europe and Africa, a tour that would allow him 'look into the faces and hear the voices' of the 'many friends' he wanted to see in Britain and Ireland once more, those 'who, when I was a stranger, took me in; when I was an exile, sheltered me; when I was poor, helped me; and when I was a slave, ransomed me'. The tour was something of a delayed honeymoon for the couple. It also offered respite from the controversy that surrounded their marriage, for not only was Helen twenty years younger than her by now far-famed husband, she was white, the daughter of a staunchly abolitionist family (descended from the original *Mayflower* pilgrims no less) who had all but disowned her, many white abolitionists of the era supporting marriage between the races more in theory than practice.[1]

As befitted his status as a writer and orator of world renown, Douglass had been seen off with a banquet at Revere House attended by scores of city dignitaries and friends, including the frail seventy-nine-year-old James Buffum who had been by his side for that tumultuous first journey across the Atlantic on board the *Cambria*. The *City of Rome*'s crossing was far more civilised, relaxing and calm, Douglass reposing in their well-appointed stateroom and reading Ralph Waldo Emerson's *English Traits* while Helen mixed with the other passengers and marvelled at the ocean. Invited to give a talk, Douglass was greeted with warm applause instead of threats to throw him overboard.

The journey was also much quicker, the powerful *City of Rome* coming in sight of the coast of Ireland after just eight days at sea. A day later it docked in Liverpool, Douglass stepping onto British soil for the first time since his grief-induced rush home twenty-six years earlier.[2]

'Here Comes My Friend Douglass'

Returning to America in the spring of 1860, Douglass had feared arrest on account of his links to Harpers Ferry, particularly as he had been directly implicated in testimony given before a Senate inquiry into the affair. John Brown's execution, however, had dramatically altered the public mood in the North, the senators shelving their inquiry for fear of creating any more martyrs and the relatively unheralded Illinois lawyer and former congressman Abraham Lincoln – a man who had long railed against the power of the slave-owning states – stealing a march on his more established rival William H. Seward in the battle to be the recently established Republican Party's nominee for that year's presidential election, especially after the latter gave a supine Senate speech full of concessions to the South. 'John Brown frightened Seward into making his last great speech,' Douglass would write not entirely hyperbolically. 'In that speech he stooped quite too low ... and lost the prize that tempted the stoop.'[3]

Although the Republicans were far from truly abolitionist, focused instead on curtailing the spread of slavery into the new states like Kansas coming into existence in the West, the increasingly politically pragmatic Douglass saluted Lincoln's election as President that November, a victory he sensed presaged conflict between the North and the South. When the Civil War finally erupted in April 1861, instigated by the secession of South Carolina from the Union, followed closely by ten more slave-owning states, Douglass supported it wholeheartedly, touring and writing relentlessly and becoming an all-out propagandist for the North – even if frustrated at the initial reluctance to make it a war explicitly about slavery. He also urged the admission of African-American soldiers into the North's ranks, a move that came to pass in February 1863 with the formation of the 54th Massachusetts Infantry Regiment, the fated regiment two of his young sons joined instantaneously. The announcement of the Emancipation Proclamation, meanwhile, on 22 September 1862 (coming into effect on 1 January 1863) was simply the happiest moment of his life.

Douglass met Lincoln in August 1863; the former fugitive – as first an escaped slave and then a suspect in an attempted slave insurrection – invited to the White House for a discussion about the discrimination faced by African-American soldiers in the Union army, leaving impressed with the 'solid gravity' of the President's character. He was back a year later, Lincoln soliciting his advice in advance of the upcoming presidential election, an election the President feared he might lose given the stalemated state of the conflict and disgust among many in the still deeply racist North that it had been turned into a war about abolition. They met for the final time at Lincoln's second inauguration on 4 March 1865, the President, 'like a mountain pine high above all others', ambling up with a hearty 'Here comes my friend Douglass' when informed that the most famous black man in America had been stopped from entering the White House for the inaugural ball by two policeman, the curse of prejudice lingering on despite emancipation and imminent victory in the Civil War. Lincoln's death just over a month later, assassinated by John Wilkes Booth – a talented Maryland-born actor who, fascinated by the theatricality of Brown's public martyrdom, had attended the abolitionist's execution – was, Douglass lamented, a 'personal as well as a national calamity'.[4]

After the war, Douglass continued to lecture and write, tracing the sorrowful vicissitudes of the African-American experience as slavery gave way to segregation rather than real freedom in the South and the early hopes of Emancipation Day were lost in the emergence of lynch mobs and the Ku Klux Klan. He ran another newspaper, the *New National Era*, and became a Republican Party stalwart, an establishment figure, to some degree, campaigning for presidents from Ulysses S. Grant to Rutherford B. Hayes and James Garfield and growing wealthy from lecture tours and comfortable government posts like the Marshall of the District of Columbia and Recorder of Deeds for the District of Columbia, positions that saw him move from Rochester to Cedar Hill, the large and beautiful house perched high on a hilltop with a sweeping view of Washington, DC, that would be his final home.

Douglass also clung close to the near-sacred memory of Lincoln, delivering an address at the unveiling of the Freedmen's Memorial Monument to Abraham Lincoln (also known as the Emancipation Memorial) in Washington on 14 April 1876 that recalled how 'under his wise and beneficent rule we [African-Americans] saw ourselves ... lifted from the depths of slavery to the heights of liberty and manhood'. His audience that day, the eleventh anniversary of Lincoln's death, included President Grant and an illustrious array of politicians, diplomats and judges. Later years and later speeches saw Lincoln proclaimed the 'greatest statesman that ever presided over the destinies of this Republic' and the 'great and good man' with a 'godlike nature' who 'went up before his Maker with four millions of broken fetters in his arms as evidence of a life well spent'.[5]

'The Pen is Your Weapon'
Douglass's rise to prominence during the Civil War was followed avidly across the Atlantic, newspapers all over the British Isles reprinting his major speeches during the conflict, including 'The Slave's Appeal to Great Britain', in which in typically elaborate but cutting prose – 'Have no fellowship, I pray you, with these merciless menstealers, but rather with whips of scorpions scourge them beyond the beneficent range of national brotherhood' – he urged the country to refrain from recognising the independence of 'the so-called Confederate States of America'. Although Britain held firm to its policy of neutrality and never recognised the South as an independent country, the fact Douglass felt compelled to

make such an appeal shows that despite broad revulsion for the 'peculiar institution' of slavery, there was a significant degree of support for the southern states in the country. The Prime Minister Lord Palmerston, for one, once lauded by the British and Foreign Anti-Slavery Society, was instinctively drawn to the South, his 'fear of democracy' outweighing his 'distaste for slavery'. Commercial considerations were also at play for the Prime Minister – 85 per cent of the raw cotton arriving in Lancashire (then the world's largest manufacturer of cotton fabrics in the world) coming from the South and almost five million people in Britain dependent upon this industry and its subsidiary trades; as was a sense – aided and abetted by early victories on the battlefield – that the southern states would eventually break away and that it behoved the government to maintain good relations with them. His Chancellor of the Exchequer, William Gladstone, also spoke warmly and incredibly impoliticly in public of 'Jeff Davis' – Jefferson Davis, the President of the Confederacy – having 'made a nation'.[6]

The Times, the most powerful paper of the era, was almost outrageously pro-South, sacking its famous war correspondent William Howard Russell when its editor John Delane felt his reports were too favourable to the North. (Towards the end of the war, John Wodehouse – later first Earl of Kimberley – a future Foreign Secretary, would record in his diary having met '"Delane" of *The Times*' at a party, the editor 'big with the "melancholy" news of a fresh Confederate defeat'.) Elsewhere, commentators utterly opposed to slavery still found reasons to decry or distrust the North. 'The North hates the Negro,' Charles Dickens, who had just published *Great Expectations*, stated bluntly, denying there was any humanitarian or anti-slavery impulse behind the Union's prosecution of the war. Earlier, the introduction of the Morrill Tariff, setting a stunningly prohibitive 40 per cent tariff on foreign imports – including British manufactured goods – had seen the *Economist* flirt with support for the Confederacy and Harriet Martineau rage that while the sin of the South was slavery, the sin of the North was protectionism. Nor did the North's rabble-rousing press or Anglophobic politicians do much to soothe relations, constantly calling on the Lincoln administration to seize Canada and make war on Britain.[7]

At one point, during the winter of 1861/2, the two countries did come close to war, after a British mail ship, the *Trent*, sailing from Cuba, was forcibly stopped at sea by a northern warship. James Mason and John Slidell, two prominent southern representatives travelling to Britain to make the case for formal recognition, were discovered and taken to prison in Boston. 'Outrage on the British flag – the Southern Commissioners Forcibly Removed from a British Mail Steamer,' proclaimed *The Times*, Palmerston, too, quite aggressive at first, threatening 'to read a lesson to the United States which will not soon be forgotten' and dispatching thousands of extra soldiers to Canada. But if public indignation was one thing, genuine appetite for war was quite another. Palmerston realized this and with the aid of his Foreign Secretary Lord John (now Earl) Russell and Prince Albert, came up with a form of wording in the official correspondence that enabled the Lincoln administration to release the men without losing face.[8]

Despite these difficulties, the majority of the British public, whatever their conflicted thoughts about the North, leaned strongly toward support of the Union cause, a remarkable act of solidarity seeing struggling Lancashire cotton workers – their workplaces closed and wages decimated on account of the Union blockade that stopped cotton from the South from reaching the country – hold a public meeting at the Free Trade Hall in Manchester on New Year's Eve 1862, the day before the Emancipation Proclamation came into effect, that called on Lincoln to keep fighting until 'chattel slavery' – 'that foul blot on civilisation and Christianity' – was wholly defeated. Lincoln, deeply moved, replied: 'I cannot but regard your decisive utterances ... as an instance of sublime Christian heroism which has not been surpassed in any age or in any country' – words inscribed on the base of the statue of the President located in the city's Lincoln Square. He also sent over aid supplies to the stricken region, the *George Griswold* docking in Liverpool in early February 1863 with 15,000 barrels of flour alongside supplies of bacon, bread, rice and corn. Douglass's old friend John Bright, meanwhile, was so strongly pro-Union he was labelled the 'Member for America' in Parliament; Lincoln, indeed, carrying a copy of Bright's speech urging his re-election in his pocket the night he was killed watching *Our American Cousin* – a comedy built around Anglo-American mutual misunderstandings – at Ford's Theatre in Washington, DC.[9]

Wrapped up in the war effort, Douglass still managed to correspond with his British supporters, Julia Griffiths Crofts at one point pleading with him not to enlist when he was giving serious consideration to joining the Union army: 'Never fight with the SWORD, the pen is your weapon,' she entreated. The end of the war then saw 'warm congratulations' sent across the Atlantic to Douglass, as well as promises to collect clothes and money to help the newly freed people. British Garrisonians, too, celebrated the North's victory, even though they had struggled somewhat at the start of the fighting, not readily computing the volte face that saw the American Anti-Slavery Society – dedicated hitherto to nonviolence and to the dissolution of the Union – support an armed conflict aimed at preserving the Union. A couple of summers later, Mary Carpenter, with whom Douglass had stayed in Halifax in 1860, asked him over to her new home in Bridport in Devon on the south coast of the country, certain he had earned himself a 'holiday': 'We are living in a very pretty … district, with fair open sea & pleasantly hilly & undulating country … I should like to take you [on] some of our favourite walks & to introduce you to some of our kind friends.' Little did she realise she would have to wait twenty years for the invitation to be taken up.[10]

'To Shake Thee by the Hand'

'Everything about the Docks much the same as forty years ago … no sign of decay anywhere … the people full of life and activity', wrote Douglass of his arrival in Liverpool on 23 September 1886, the vibrant port city still accounting for much of trade in and out of a country at the zenith of its imperial power, Queen Victoria approaching her fiftieth year on the throne and Lord Salisbury, the dominant new force among the Tories, having recently supplanted the septuagenarian Liberal Gladstone as Prime Minister. The *Liverpool Mercury* that day carried news of trouble in Ireland as well as a rising in Spain and the murder of Christian converts in Uganda. It also advertised the serialisation of *The Golden Hope, A Romance of the Deep* by W. Clark Russell – 'the most popular sea story writer of the day'. (Hermann Melville was an admirer, dedicating his *John Marr and Other Sailors* to Clark.) Earlier in the year, Robert Louis Stevenson's *Jekyll and Hyde* had been a bestseller on both sides of the Atlantic.

The Douglasses stayed in Liverpool for almost a week, taking in museums and galleries as well as making a trip to nearby Chester to see its cathedral and Roman ruins. Douglass marvelled at the crush of 'omnibuses, carts, carriages and people' moving through the never-still streets of a city once so synonymous with the slave trade, one of the few cities to give him a less than fulsome welcome during his first tour forty years earlier. 'One sees in this moving mass the immense energy there is in this English nation,' he opined. And yet he was also struck by the short stature and wretched appearance of many of the 'working people' once he looked at them individually rather than as just part of the heaving crowd; men, boys and girls hurrying along 'in scarcely any clothing at all, barefooted and bareheaded' while beggar-women sang in 'mournfully heartbroken and heart breaking strains' to feed their children.

'They afford few of what is called the typical Englishman,' Douglass concluded of the crowds of Liverpudlian workers. His view of the 'typical Englishman', however, much like his view of Britain as a whole, was hopelessly idealised, the fact that he had encountered desperate scenes of poverty all across the British Isles decades earlier failing to dent his belief that all English people should have a bit of 'John Bull' about them, broad-backed and ruddy-cheeked. Similarly, the British government's behaviour during the American Civil War had done little to quell his confidence in the country's inherent might and beneficence. Indeed, as recently as the summer of 1885 he had delivered a lecture in America entitled 'Great Britain's Example is High, Noble and Grand', a panegyric not just of the British abolitionists like Wilberforce and Clarkson but of an entire country that was 'great' not just in name but 'great in her knowledge, great in her industry, great in her civil and social order, great in her wealth, her power, her progress and her prestige'.[11]

From Liverpool, the Douglasses travelled south by train – Helen getting her first real feel for the 'beautiful landscape' of rural England, its well-tended hedgerows criss-crossing the lush green fields – to St Neots, a 'quaint' little town 'of 4,000 inhabitants and no newspaper' on the banks of the Great Ouse not far from Cambridge. Here they were met with 'open arms' by Julia Griffiths Crofts, the formidable woman who had berated waiters for refusing to serve Douglass in New York restaurants now a seventy-five-year-old widow struggling to make her way through life and the running of a girls' day and boarding school, her husband's death six years previously having left her with little in the way of security for old age. Douglass, who had kept in touch with Crofts through the years, did not record his feelings at the reunion with the woman who had once been so central to his life, perhaps wary of the emotions such an act would wrench up. Helen, however, who was about thirty years younger than Crofts, paints a warm picture of the 'trio' enjoying long morning walks, sightseeing excursions and 'everlasting eating' at the 'cheerful' cottage Crofts shared with at least one of her now-adult stepdaughters. Douglass gave a talk at Crofts's school and the local Corn Exchange as well as being taken out on the Great Ouse on a neighbour's yacht. A 'pilgrimage' to Cambridge, meanwhile, made a strong impression on Helen. The 'trio' then journeyed to London for a day to view the many wonders of the Colonial and Indian Exhibition, a grand attraction that brought more than five million visitors to its specially built pavilions in South Kensington during its six-month duration. The Douglasses also fitted in a trip to the Unitarian Revd Russell Lant Carpenter and his wife Mary in Bridport, the famous abolitionist finally making good on his promise to visit and delivering a speech at the Town Hall on 15 October before departing for the continent. There would be no meeting, however, with Carpenter's sister, another Mary, the reformer Douglass had known in Bristol and who had died in 1877, her pioneering work in the fields of women's education and juvenile incarceration having earned her an audience with Queen Victoria.[12]

Dining with Helen and Julia in a Cannon Street hotel in London during a break from the Colonial and Indian Exhibition, discussing, perhaps, the Jaipur Gate they had just seen (and which can now be found at the entrance to the Hove Museum near Brighton), Douglass had been approached by an enterprising journalist from the *Daily News*. Agreeing to an interview, the 'gifted and heroic' man whom Lincoln had 'distinguished with his friendship' expounded on the unhappy state of affairs for African-Americans in the United States, pointing out (incorrectly) how while Russian serfs had been given land upon their own emancipation in 1861, the slaves in the South had been 'turned out destitute to the open sky'. Another reporter to inveigle their way into the famous former slave's company around this time was impressed with how Douglass, 'a heroic specimen of the coloured man', still stood 'straight and stalwart' even though he was near seventy years old and talked proudly of 'feeling neither ache nor stiffness'. Douglass, the writer continued, loved Britain 'with an unquenchable affection' and thought the Colonial and Indian Exhibition epitomised 'the glory and the power and the genius of the British Empire'.[13]

With Douglass's intention to come back to Britain in the spring made known in both interviews, he started to receive letters inviting him to visit towns and cities across the country upon his return; Ethel Leach, for example, a young woman deeply involved in the women's rights movement, asking him to stay at her Great Yarmouth home. They had met in Washington a few years earlier, she reminded him, when she had travelled there with the aged Chartist George Jacob Holyoake and his daughter Emily. Leach, later Great Yarmouth's first female mayor, would publish a short book on her time in America, a thrillingly positive account that described her visit to the abolitionist tourist spot that was 'John Brown's Fort' in Harpers Ferry, the fact that

Americans continued to use Dickens as their first reference point for all matters British evidenced in the manner in which a Boston paper directed its readers to the opening scenes of *David Copperfield* – set in Great Yarmouth – when discussing Leach's home town.[14]

Paul Moyneaux, the young African-American actor who was also the brother of Frederick Douglass Jr's wife Virginia, was another interesting correspondent hoping to meet up in the spring. Like the great tragedian Ira Aldridge more than half a century earlier, Molyneaux had travelled to Britain in the hope of gaining the recognition his colour denied him on the still deeply racist American stage. (He had previously toured the country with Taylor's Jubilee Singers, an offshoot from or rival to the more famous Fisk Jubilee Singers, the first group to bring 'Negro spirituals' like 'Swing Low Sweet Chariot' to worldwide audiences.) Learning of Douglass's being in Britain from an article in the *Christian Age*, he wrote of his plans to get more involved in politics when he went back to America, having enjoyed 'equal rights' in England for too long to 'tamely yield to the whims and prejudices of our white countrymen at home'.

There were mentions, too, of important theatrical personalities like Henry Irving and Wilson Barrett and the promise of work with a small touring company in the not-too-distant future. Nevertheless, Molyneaux's career in Britain does not seem to have gone anywhere close to planned, for although he does not directly ask Douglass for money, it seems implied in the picture of poverty – 'the gaunt wolf close at my heels' – he gives the wealthy abolitionist, hardly eating for weeks at a time and having to walk from Reading to London and back for the want of coach or train fare. Unfortunately, Molyneaux's career would never take off, the actor who once won favourable reviews for his *Othello* returning to America in the late 1880s, dying shortly thereafter, unheralded and unfulfilled.[15]

Douglass was also contacted by Zadel Barnes Gustafson, an American poet and journalist living in London who could be something of a nuisance, once pestering Mark Twain for a loan of a substantial amount of money after an interview. A note

The Hutchinson Family. Ardent anti-slavery activists and one of the most popular musical groups of the period, the Hutchinsons travelled across the Atlantic with Douglass in 1845. (Library of Congress)

Sheet music cover for the Hutchinson Family's 'The Fugitive's Song', which was inspired by Douglass's escape from slavery. (Library of Congress)

William Lloyd Garrison, *c.* 1851. Editor of the radical abolitionist newspaper the *Liberator*, Garrison joined Douglass for part of his tour of Britain and Ireland. ('Wendell Phillips, William Lloyd Garrison and George Thompson', Cab.G.3.24, Southworth & Hawes, Print Department, Boston Public Library)

Henry C. Wright, *c.* 1847, the American abolitionist who toured Scotland with Douglass during the 'Send Back the Money' campaign. ('Henry Clarke Wright', Cab.G.3.91, Antoine Claudet, Print Department, Boston Public Library)

Maria Weston Chapman, *c.* 1846, the Boston abolitionist with whom Douglass had a fractious relationship. ('Maria Weston Chapman', Cab.G.3.29, unknown photographer, Print Department, Boston Public Library)

Right: Richard D. Webb, the Irish Quaker and anti-slavery activist who hosted Douglass in Dublin. (Quaker Historical Library, Dublin)

Below left: Richard Allen, an influential Quaker and founding member of the Hibernian Anti-Slavery Society. (Special Collections, University College Cork)

Below right: James Haughton. The quintessential 'anti-everythingarian', Haughton campaigned against war, slavery, alcohol and capital punishment. (Wikimedia Commons)

Eliza Wigham, Mary Estlin and Jane Wigham, the Bristol- and Edinburgh-based abolitionists who worked closely with Douglass during his first tour of the British Isles. ('Eliza Wigham, Mary A. Estlin and Jane Wigham', Cab.G.3.118, unknown photographer, Print Department, Boston Public Library)

Daniel O'Connell. Although best known as an Irish nationalist, 'The Liberator' was also one of the most forceful anti-slavery voices of the nineteenth-century world. (Library of Congress)

John Bright, the MP who combined work with the Anti-Corn Law League with support for the anti-slavery movement. Douglass stayed at Bright's home in Rochdale and kept in touch with members of the Bright family throughout his life. (Library of Congress)

George Thompson, c. 1851, MP for Tower Hamlets and the leading Garrisonian abolitionist in Britain. Douglass shared many anti-slavery stages with Thompson and also stayed at his house in London. ('George Thompson', Cab.G.3.25, unknown photographer, Print Department, Boston Public Library)

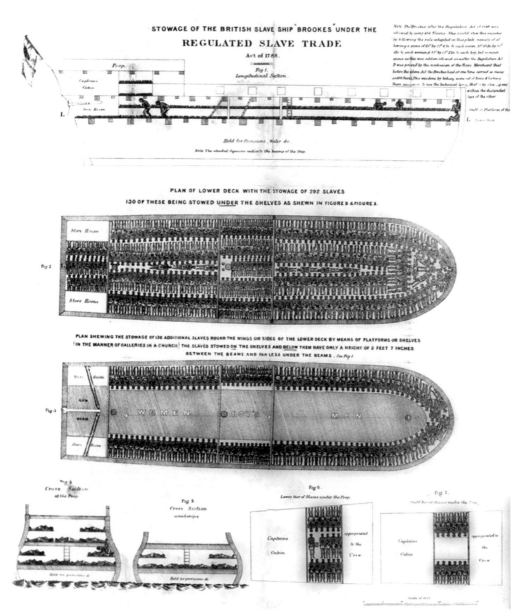

This famous poster of the slave ship *Brookes* was one of the most powerful propagandistic tools for early abolitionists like William Wilberforce and Thomas Clarkson. (Library of Congress)

The iconic 'Am I Not a Man And A Brother?' image, shown here above John Greenleaf Whittier's 1837 anti-slavery poem, 'Our Countrymen in Chains!' (Library of Congress)

Frederick
Douglass in a
daguerrotype
from *c.* 1855.
(Metropolitan
Museum of Art)

Robert Burns, the
Scottish poet whose
work Douglass greatly
admired and whose
birthplace he visited
in the spring of 1846.
(Library of Congress)

Above left: Portrait of the young Queen Victoria on sheet music cover of Charles D'Albert's 'The Queen's Waltzes'. Although careful in her public comments, Victoria was considered a friend of the anti-slavery cause. (Library of Congress)

Above right: Prince Albert's first public speech in Britain came at an anti-slavery meeting in London in the summer of 1840. (Library of Congress)

'Charles Dickens in his study at Gadshill.' Dickens admired Douglass's writing and gave a copy of *Narrative* as a present to his friend, the famous Shakespearean actor William Macready. Dickens's opposition to slavery was made clear in his 1840 travel book *American Notes*. (Library of Congress)

Above left: Hans Christian Andersen. Douglass spent time with the Swedish author at the London home of the writers William and Mary Howitt. (Library of Congress)

Above right: A favourite of Queen Victoria's, 'General Tom Thumb' drew crowds of thousands across Britain in 1846. (Library of Congress)

Right: The Ethiopian Serenaders, the popular blackface minstrel group who toured Britain around the same time as Douglass. (Library of Congress)

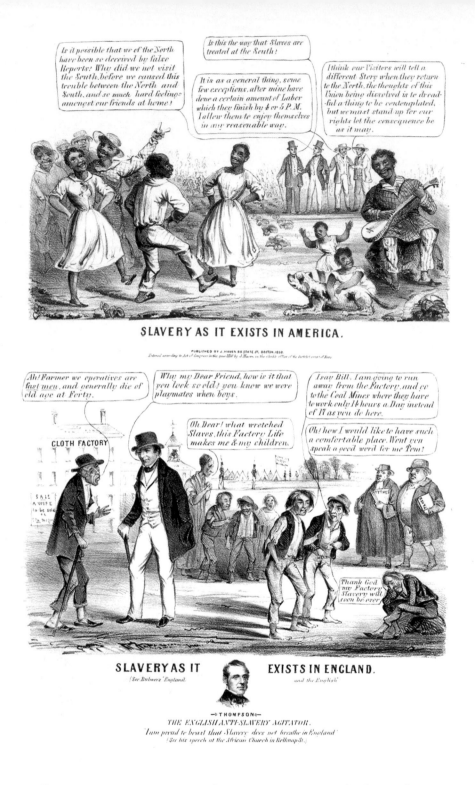

'Slavery As It Exists In America. Slavery As It Exists In England.' Pro-slavery political cartoon contrasting the lives of well-fed, dancing slaves in the plantations of the South with the shrivelled and starving wage slaves of Victorian Britain. (Library of Congress)

'The Last Moments of John Brown.' Print showing John Brown, under heavy guard, kissing an African-American child as he leaves jail on his way to the gallows. (Library of Congress)

Frederick Douglass, c. 1862. (Library of Congress)

'John Bull Makes a Discovery.' Political cartoon reflecting fears in the North that Britain would put cotton and economic self-interest ahead of support for emancipation of the slaves. (Library of Congress)

'Frederick Douglass appealing to President Lincoln and his cabinet to enlist Negroes,' mural by William Edouard Scott, at the Recorder of Deeds building, Washington, DC, built in 1943. Photographer: Carol M. Highsmith. (Library of Congress)

Anna M. Douglass. (National Park Service, Frederick Douglass National Historic Site, FRDO 246)

Douglass with his second wife Helen Pitts Douglass, *c.* 1885. Helen's sister Jennie (centre) was the only member of the Pitts family to support the marriage. (National Park Service, Frederick Douglass National Historic Site, FRDO 3912)

'Heroes of the Coloured Race.' (Library of Congress)

'A Champion of the Negro.' Portrait and obituary of Douglass in the 2 March 1895 issue of the illustrated London weekly the *Graphic*.

NARRATIVE OF THE LIFE

OF

FREDERICK DOUGLASS.

WRITTEN BY HIMSELF.

THIRD ENGLISH EDITION.

12mo., 3s. 6d.

" FREDERICK DOUGLASS.—We observe that this self-emancipated man has lately sent forth from the press a sketch of his life. Every body should read it. It is an exceedingly interesting as well as an ably written work. While lately in a part of Maryland, we were unexpectedly called upon by at least a dozen colored persons, some of them slaves, and others freemen, who had heard that we knew Frederick at the North, and who wished to hear news from their old friend. They knew him by his assumed as well as by his real name, and related to us many interesting incidents about their former companion."—*Philadelphia Elevator.*

" Narrative of Frederick Douglass—This admirable little volume is just out. It will doubtless prove a valuable auxiliary to the cause of abolition. Frederick is a strong man, and will not fail to arouse the sympathies of his readers in behalf of the oppressed. May he long live with his burning eloquence, to pour truth on the naked conscience of this wicked nation."—*Practical Christian,* (*U.S.*)

" This is a very remarkable little volume. It is remarkable as being the production of a slave, and one of that people whom it has always been the cue of slaveholders and slavery advocates to represent as incapable of intellectual vigour and ability. The narrative is written with singular ability, and, as a story of real life, is at once simply related, and one of the most thrilling and absorbing imaginable."—*London Atlas.*

" I regard the narrative of Frederick Douglass as a literary wonder. The incidents of his life are of such a kind as to hold the reader spell-bound, while they are related in a style simple, perspicuous and eloquent. I looked forward with much interest and some incredulity to a meeting with the author of this unique piece of autobiography, doubting whether any man reared a slave, and so recently escaped from bonds, could, under the circumstances, produce such a work. My meeting with Frederick Douglass dispelled my doubts; he is indeed an extraordinary man—the type of a class—such an intellectual phenomenon as only appears at times in the republic of letters."—*Rev. Isaac Nelson, Belfast.*

R. YORKE CLARKE & CO., 55, GRACECHURCH STREET.

BRITISH TESTIMONIAL OF ESTEEM

FOR

FREDERICK DOUGLASS,

AND OF SYMPATHY FOR

THE AMERICAN SLAVE.

A subscription is in progress for the purpose of presenting Mr. FREDERICK DOUGLASS with a Steam Printing Press. To those who are anxious to hasten the destruction of the giant crime of Slavery, it will be evident that the Press is the great weapon to be wielded in accomplishing it.

The recent disgraceful conduct of the agents of the Cunard Company of American Packets, in refusing to admit to the saloon of the Cambria, a gentleman of whom we dare assert that he was immensely superior in refinement and intellect, to any one of the passengers whose disgusting prejudice caused his exclusion, has illustrated in him the wrongs of his race and drawn universal attention to one, who may be termed the champion of the rights of the Negro.

He is the man who, of all others, is peculiarly fitted to engage in the editorship of a paper, the contributors to which shall exclusively be of his own race.

SUBSCRIPTIONS ARE RECEIVED BY

J. D. CARR, Esq., *Treasurer*, Carlisle.
R. YORKE CLARKE & CO., 55, Gracechurch-street.
AYLOTT & JONES, 8, Paternoster-row.
JOHN F. SHAW, 27, Southampton-row.
WILLIAM & MARY HOWITT, Howitt's Journal Office, 171, Strand.
JOHN L. LAWFORD, 34, Cambridge street, Hyde-park.
ROBERT K. PHILP, People's Journal Office, 69, Fleet-street.
CHARLES ZIEGLER, 17, South-bridge-street, Edinburgh.
J. B. ESTLIN, Park-street, Bristol.
ALEXANDER MORRIS, St. Ann's-square, Manchester.
JOSEPH SHEWELL, Colchester.
WILLIAM SPARKES, High-street, Worcester.
JOHN M. SPARKES, Darlington.
JACOB BRIGHT, jun., Rochdale.
THOMAS BAILEY, Proprietor of the "Nottingham Mercury," Nottingham.
JOSEPH LUPTON, 1, Blenheim-square, Leeds.
THOMAS HARVEY, 13, Briggate, Leeds.
MARY BRADY, Leavy Greave, Sheffield.
WILLIAM NAISH, Colemore-row, Birmingham.
JOHN DYMOND, Cathedral-yard, Exeter.
HENRY RICHARDSON, Summerhill-grove, Newcastle-on-Tyne.

Above left: An advertisement for Douglass's *Narrative.* (*Report of Proceedings at the Soirée Given to Frederick Douglass, London Tavern, March 30, 1847*)

Above right: An advertisement for the Douglass Testimonial. (*Report of Proceedings at the Soirée Given to Frederick Douglass, London Tavern, March 30, 1847*)

A modern mural to Frederick Douglass in Washington, DC. (Library of Congress)

from Arthur John Naish would have carried more emotional resonance for the abolitionist. 'My dear old friend of forty years ago,' the elderly Birmingham Quaker had written, longing to talk once more of all the friends they had survived. Naish, indeed, who had taken to re-reading all his letters following the death of his wife, had recently come across some from Douglass in 1846 – an example of the way Douglass's transformative first tour found ways to remain present in the lives of those it touched.[16]

A letter from Edinburgh, meanwhile, carried signs of rapprochement with another activist to whom Douglass had once been close, Eliza Wigham inviting him to stay at her 5 Grey Street home when he returned from the continent, though not before alluding to the fact that 'circumstances [were] decidedly different to those we have known in times past' – the emancipation of the American slaves, it seems, having put an end to the need to maintain a careful Garrisonian distance from Douglass, as she had done so scrupulously when he was in Scotland in 1861. 'We shall be glad to see thee once again ... to shake thee by the hand and to confer on the past, the present and the future and to be introduced to thy wife,' Wigham promised, the distinctive Quaker idiom a second language that had surrounded the former slave his whole adult life. Her once-redoubtable stepmother Jane was also 'still here', Wigham continued, though at eighty-four somewhat felled by old age, quite 'feeble' and losing her memory. This was an eventuality Douglass had prepared for, aware from the outset of his journey across the Atlantic that the realisation of the desire to revisit old friends of forty years standing would have 'a sad side as well as a cheerful one'.[17]

'Warm and Hearty Welcome'

Fulfilling a lifetime's ambition, Douglass arrived in Paris with his wife Helen on Wednesday 20 October, the former runaway slave delighting in everything the fabled city had to offer – everything except the blackface groups he came across, 'who disfigure and distort the features of the Negro and burlesque his language and manners in a way to make him appear ... more akin to apes than to men', the 'leprous distilment of American prejudice' continuing to infect minds all over the world.[18] There followed seven months of leisurely peregrinations through Europe – a 'grand tour' taking in the Cheateau d'If made famous in Alexandre Dumas's *The Count of Monte Cristo*, a gondola ride in Florence and a walk through Pompeii among numerous other sights and cities. The centrepiece of the tour was a spirit-salving return to the ancestral home of Africa, via a boat trip across the Mediterranean to Egypt and its pyramids, Douglass recalling how an old image of an Egyptian pharaoh always reminded him of his mother's face.

Returning to Britain in late May 1887, Helen received a telegraph calling her home to her ill mother in America. Douglass, who was not welcome in the Pitts household, stayed behind, beginning a final two-month tour through the lives of old friends with dinner at the London home of Margaret Bright Lucas, the women's rights leader and sister of the politician John Bright. Douglass does not seem to have met up with Bright himself, who was still alive but in poor health. He did, however, make his way to Bright's eldest daughter, Helen Bright Clark, in the small town of Street in Somerset (or Somersetshire as she called it), where her husband William Stephens Clark (the eldest son of one it founders) ran the famous shoe company Clarks. The women's rights campaigner, who would have been just seven years old when Douglass stayed at her childhood home in Rochdale, had written to him earlier in the year, describing how his name and the causes he espoused had always been close to her heart, Clark heavily involved, for example, in the British branch of the Freedman's Aid Society, which raised funds to provide former slaves with good-quality homes following the Civil War. His recently published autobiography *The Life and Times of Frederick Douglass*, she added, was a favourite in their house –and not just because the preface to the British edition had been written by her father.[19]

While still in London, Thomas Burt, the trade unionist son of a coal miner from the north of England who was one of the first working-class MPs to enter Parliament after the 1867 Reform Act, arranged another visit for the abolitionist to the House of

Commons, Douglass revelling in watching Gladstone – whom he had long admired despite his father's slaveholding past – assail his Tory opponents over the issue of Home Rule for Ireland, the dominant political question of the day, one great orator appreciating the efforts of another. Charles Spurgeon, the Baptist 'Prince of Preachers' he saw in action one Sunday morning and continued to correspond with after leaving the capital, was another new acquaintance. Older London friends, however, like William Ashurst, were mostly dead or, like the eighty-seven-year-old Mary Howitt, living abroad for their health. Douglass also seems to have been contacted by Charles H. Allen of the British and Foreign Anti-Slavery Society around this time, the aggressive imperialist intrusion of Britain and other European powers into the heart of Africa having seen that body's focus turn to the internal slave trade in that continent in the years since the Civil War.[20]

Having taken in Westminster Abbey and the Tower of London, Douglass, who gave no public talks during this last stay in Britain, seems to have made his way across to Birmingham where Naish had promised meetings with Joseph Sturge's son as well as the niece and nephew of the author Harriet Martineau, who had died in Ambleside a decade earlier. He then moved north to his great supporters in Newcastle, the Richardsons, the women who had secured his freedom. He also spent time with Elizabeth Mawson, co-owner of one the city's best-known shops, a landmark building that stayed open for more than a century. 'No words can express the deep pleasure and gratification that it was to me to clasp your hand again,' she wrote to the former slave she had first met as a young woman forty years earlier, at a time when her now-deceased husband John, too, was involved in the anti-slavery cause, organising talks and corresponding with William Lloyd Garrison and George Thompson.[21]

Carrying a note from Anna Richardson (whose husband Henry had died in 1885) that contained the words of a sacred poem called 'A Little While', Douglass next proceeded to Scotland and the long-awaited reunion with the 'angelic' Eliza Wigham and her stepmother (Eliza just called her 'mother') Jane in Edinburgh.

A letter from the renowned Scottish mathematician William Jack, meanwhile, indicates Douglass had dinner with Elizabeth Pease Nichol in the grounds of the University of Glasgow, where her husband Dr John Pringle Nichol had been the Regius Professor of Astronomy for a number of years before his death. Ten years older than Douglass, Pease Nichol, who had had to leave the Quakers after marrying Nichol in 1853, still had a great deal of vivacity about her. 'Certainly age does not wither her,' wrote another correspondent about this time of the grand dame of British abolition who, alongside Eliza Wigham and other Scottish activists, would still be petitioning the American government about the treatment of African-Americans in the mid-1890s, signing off as one who 'from 1830 worked for colonial and American abolition'.[22]

William Smeal and Andrew Paton, former guiding lights of the Glasgow Emancipation Society, were both dead by the time Douglass made it to the city on the Clyde for the final occasion, and so there is no way of knowing if they would have followed their fellow Garrisonian Wigham's lead in reconnecting with Douglass. Smeal, indeed, had died just a few weeks after Garrison's own final visit to the British Isles in 1877. The journey had been made just in time, a variety of ailments soon laying low the pioneering editor behind the *Liberator*. He died two years later, in the early summer of 1879, Douglass speaking warmly of his old anti-slavery mentor at a memorial service in Washington, DC, the two great abolitionists having repaired their relationship somewhat in the years after the Civil War. Thompson, meanwhile, the foremost British Garrisonian of the age, had preceded his American friend to the grave by just a few months, buried in Leeds on a wet and windy morning in October 1878 after years of ill-health, obituaries recalling his work as the 'well-known friend of the Negro slave' and noting how he too, like Douglass, had met Lincoln during the Civil War.[23]

Addresses in Douglass's diary and correspondence including a series of letters of introduction from Alexander Williamson, a Scotsman who had tutored Lincoln's children before joining the civil service in Washington, DC, suggest Douglass travelled further afield than Edinburgh and Glasgow while in Scotland. By the end of June, however, he was firmly south of the border again, getting the rest Ellen Richardson suggested his tiring body needed at the Carlisle home of her cousin Eliza Barlow (*née* Nicholson), whose sister Jane had been married to the recently deceased biscuit maker J. D. Carr. 'All the places I have visited, Newcastle, Edinburgh, Glasgow and now Carlisle, have given me warm and hearty welcome, making me as happy as I can be without you to help me,' he wrote to Helen, whose mother's health, he was glad to hear, was improving. 'The quiet of this Quaker cottage is something wonderfully tranquilising and wholly unlike the outside world,' he continued of the 'delightful' Murrell Hill Cottage Barlow shared with her son John Henry – later a prominent peace activist during the First World War – and daughter Mary, the family having moved from Edinburgh to be near relatives following the death of the *paterfamilias*, the veterinary surgeon John Barlow. Douglass could only stay a couple days, however, still needing to return to London before travelling to Bridport, Street, Bristol and Dublin prior to boarding the *City of Rome* again in Liverpool at the start of August for his journey home. Of Queen Victoria's Golden Jubilee, meanwhile, Douglass informed his wife that he had seen nothing, having deliberately avoided the capital during the 'august occasion' that took place that month on account of the large crowds, the celebrations including a royal banquet at Buckingham Palace attended by Kings and Queens from around the world, a grand procession through the streets of London and a night of fireworks which the ageing Queen watched in her wheelchair. (It was during these Golden Jubilee celebrations that Victoria met the young Indian waiter Abdul Karim, their close relationship the subject of a recent film starring Judi Dench.) Douglass also seemed to be putting off a trip to St Neots, where Julia Griffiths Crofts's stepdaughter Elizabeth was gravely ill, not wishing to be a distraction in a house during a time of sickness.[24]

Back in London at the start of July, Douglass, bearing up well 'under the strain of travel and constant visiting', wrote home to his son Lewis, describing how he was 'flying about' seeing 'old friends whom I shall never see again, some to whom I am indebted for many acts of friendship through long goneby [*sic*] years'. Rebecca Moore, the Irish-born abolitionist at whose home he had once stayed in Manchester, was one such old friend. Now living in the capital to be closer to her son Norman, she gave him directions to her home at the newly built apartment building Wedderburn House in Hampstead, the pair meeting up on Sunday 3 July. 'There is an omnibus to Hampstead from the Oxford St end of the Tottenham Court Road which would put you down at Lyndhurst Road on which the first turn to the left is Lyndhurst Gardens, that lead to Wedderburn Rd & House.' Alternatively, he could take the Underground to Swiss Cottage Station, then the northern terminus of the Metropolitan Railway, which had been the world's first underground railway when it opened in 1863. Earlier, Moore had asked Douglass to call in on her son at work at St Bartholomew's Hospital. He could also see her grandchildren there, she suggested, keen to make the most of this final opportunity for her family to meet a figure of such world renown.[25]

His last stay in London complete, Douglass went briefly to St Neots – where 'poor Lizzie' was 'almost skeletal' – before travelling south for another visit with the Carpenters, the 'tedious' six-hour journey from Paddington to Bridport (he had had to return to London to change trains) made up for by the warm reception of his hosts. The area was 'even more parched than in St Neots', he informed Crofts, a hot summer having taken its toll on the verdant land all across the south of England. To his wife Helen, meanwhile, he wrote: 'My friends here have not yet tired of me and I think would not if I stayed in England a year longer – but I am too long independent in spirit to live on my friends even when they desire me to do so.' More prosaically, he noted he needed to buy a new leather trunk to bring home Helen's Parisian dress as well as the gifts he had been receiving from his friends, including, from the Barlows, a leather frame for photographs of the Douglasses taken in Rome.[26]

The land around Street, too, was 'dried up' and not 'nearly so pleasant as usual', Helen Bright Clarke wrote shortly before welcoming Douglass to her Somerset home, where they talked politics and past times. While staying in Street, Douglass was also introduced to Clarke's neighbour and fellow Quaker Catherine Impey. 'Awakened' to the 'colour question' during a trip to America in 1878 and drawing inspiration from young activists like Booker T. Washington as well as Douglass, Impey would go on to found *Anti-Caste*, Britain's first explicitly anti-racist journal, the deceptively determined, slightly built Quaker who would later support conscientious objectors during the First World War attempting to bring down a worldwide injustice from the rooms of a modest stone farmhouse outside a small town in the west of England. In later years, she would arrange a British lecture tour for Ida B. Wells, like Washington one of the best-known of the new generation of African-American leaders, talented and resilient men and women who would spend their lives fighting the segregation laws that had slowly but surely spread through the South in the aftermath of the Civil War and would not be eradicated until the era of Martin Luther King, Douglass's true heir in the struggle for African-American rights and freedom.[27]

'Poor, Barefooted Ireland!'

'Poor, barefooted Ireland!' Douglass had exclaimed to Helen, gazing sadly upon the shore he had first set foot on four decades earlier when the *City of Rome* docked briefly in Queenstown (Cobh) in Cork on its way to Liverpool in September 1886. The country had never strayed far from his mind – albeit not always for positive reasons – his sympathy for the plight of the hundreds of thousands of Irish people forced to leave the country during the Famine giving way to anger as he watched them turn upon African-Americans as soon as they landed in Boston or New York, quickly adopting the racist tendencies of northern whites. Tensions between Irish-Americans and African-Americans reached a murderous nadir during the New York draft riots of 1863, Irish mobs attacking innocent black people on the streets. 'There is perhaps no darker chapter in the whole history of the war than this cowardly and bloody uprising, in July, 1863,' Douglass wrote.

For three days and nights New York was in the hands of a ferocious mob, and there was not sufficient power in the government of the country or of the city itself to stay the hand of violence and the effusion of blood. Though this mob was nominally against the draft which had been ordered, it poured out its fiercest wrath upon the coloured people and their friends. It spared neither age nor sex; it hanged Negroes simply because they were Negroes; it murdered women in their homes, and burnt their homes over their heads; it dashed out the brains of young children against the lampposts; it burned the coloured orphan asylum ... and forced coloured men, women and children to seek concealment in cellars or garrets or wheresoever else it could be found, until this high carnival of crime and reign of terror should pass away.

Douglass's account was exaggerated – but only just. And yet he never fully lost faith in Ireland and the Irish, making a number of speeches in favour of Home Rule in the 1880s.[28]

Much more important than any political speeches were the letters that had kept Douglass in touch with friends from Ireland, those exchanged with Isabel Jennings, in particular, full of warmth and honesty, 'My love to all at Brown Street' the regular refrain. Douglass was also in regular contact with Richard D. Webb, albeit largely on account of new editions of *Narrative* rather than any mutual regard. The two men, in fact, were still bickering over the portrait used for the second Dublin edition of the book – published in 1846 – as late as 1864. Nevertheless, the publisher was able to admit some of Douglass's good aspects, including his honesty about money. Douglass was also among the recipients of a letter Webb sent to friends in America after the death of his wife Hannah in 1862. Douglass, for his part, would be very welcoming to Webb's son Richard Jr when he visited America in 1859, apologising, indeed, for some harsh words he had recently written about Webb in his newspaper. Alfred Webb, another son, would be just as warmly received when he travelled across the Atlantic in the early 1870s. Douglass would continue to open his door to an array of Irish visitors in the years that followed, from Maria Webb's son Richard (yet another Richard Webb) to Lydia Shackleton, a well-known painter and member of the famous Ballitore Quaker dynasty.[29]

Douglass's most intimate Irish correspondence in later years was with Richard Allen, who still had a drapery business in Dublin. Allen had travelled to America with his second wife, Mary Ann Savage, in 1883, his first wife, Ann, having died in 1868. A month spent in the South made an especially deep impression on the old anti-slavery campaigner. He spoke at schools, attended African-American churches and looked over cotton fields in visits arranged by fellow Quakers. 'My heart did feel stirred at seeing such a number of coloured people *all free*,' wrote Allen, by now in his eighties, after attending morning prayers at a school in Memphis, Tennessee. At Fisk University in Nashville, meanwhile, Allen's wife noticed a print of Benjamin Haydon's painting of the World Anti-Slavery Convention hanging up in a room, bringing their host's attention to the fact that her husband was one of the figures depicted. They met Douglass in Washington, where he was Recorder of Deeds for the District of Columbia, the post where he first really got to know Helen Pitts who worked as one of his secretaries alongside his daughter Rosetta, the New York native having previously worked as a teacher, most notably of freed slaves during the Civil War. 'My Dear Richard Allen: Can it be that you are still alive and, more wonderful still, in America? I could hardly believe my own eyes when I read your note this morning,' Douglass wrote, the pair going on to spend hours talking about old friends and the chequered progress of African-Americans since Emancipation.[30]

The renewal of this friendship of some forty years' standing was followed by a flow of letters across the Atlantic. 'My Dear Friend,' Douglass wrote, 'I am obliged for your letter … It brought Brooklawn quite near me, and I could see yourself and Mrs Allen comfortably seated at your warm fireside. What a blessing this mail service between friendly souls is! How good that we can speak to each other over the wide waste of waters!' Allen, always happy to relive memories of his 'American ramble', responded, congratulating Douglass in one letter on his marriage to Helen. Douglass appreciated Allen's warm words when so many others, including his daughter Rosetta, had been harsh. 'My marriage has brought to me clouds and darkness and strong criticism for offending popular prejudice, but there is peace and happiness within. I was unwilling to allow the world to select a wife for me, but preferred to select for myself, and the world is deplored with my independence.'[31]

Douglass also raised the possibility of a visit to Ireland. 'It has long been my desire to look once more upon Ireland and to see some of the warm-hearted and generous friends who greeted me there forty years ago.' He worried, however, that any such trip would bring more sadness than joy, the majority of his friends from his first visit having passed away. Webb and Haughton, for example, had died within a year of each other, in July 1872 and March 1873 respectively. Allen, too, was in poor health, admitting that at eighty-three years of age he could look for nothing beyond 'temporary improvement'. He died a few months after writing this letter, in January 1886. A note on his death found in Douglass's private papers described how Allen was still talking about the old anti-slavery days to visitors while confined to his bed.[32]

Despite these reservations, Douglass did visit Ireland again, stopping off in Dublin for about a week in late July 1887, having concluded his English travels with a journey from Street to Bristol – where he may have been reunited with Mary Estlin who was still close to the Carpenters, visiting them in Bridport soon after Douglass – and a final stay at St Neots. The Irish leg of his year-long tour was a slightly strange but nonetheless fulfilling experience, Douglass surrounded for the most part by the children of his old friends rather than the friends themselves. He stayed with Maria Webb's daughter, Wilhelmina, in Killiney, County Dublin, one of her letters giving him the days on which the Bristol steamer crossed directly to Dublin and also the times of the trains from the city to her house. Wilhelmina had actually been corresponding with Douglass for a couple of years. 'Although this is the first time that I have addressed you by letter, my name may not be unfamiliar to you as the daughter of William and Maria Webb,' she had written in January 1885, adding that she had a 'very distinct remembrance' of him from when he had visited their house in Belfast. She had hoped Douglass would write a few words about her recently deceased mother for a memorial her sister Anna was putting together. Douglass happily obliged.[33]

In another letter, Wilhelmina told Douglass how her husband, John Webb, had been working as an apprentice in Limerick in 1845 and had met him several times at Benjamin Clarke Fisher's home. She also described how happy Richard Allen had been to read over some of the letters Douglass had sent her just before he died. Wilhelmina and Douglass continued to write to each other after he returned to America. Douglass sent press cuttings with little notes; Wilhelmina wrote mainly about family matters, the endless cycle of births, marriages and deaths, as well as that age-old Irish obsession – the weather. She also sent a photograph of herself and her husband as a Christmas present in 1887.

Deborah Webb, the publisher's daughter, on the other hand, would write thanking Douglass for a photograph he sent back of himself, everyone taking advantage of the advances in photographic technology – the first Kodak camera having just come onto the market around this time.[34]

Douglass also spent some time with Wilhelmina's sister, Anna Webb Shackleton, during his stay in Dublin, remembering the lines she had written as a precocious twelve-year-old just as he was about to leave Belfast: 'Oh then depart if it will spread the cause/Of justice, liberty and righteous laws.' Henry and Hannah Wigham, Wilhelmina's close neighbours in Killiney and members of the well-known Quaker clan Douglass had had many fond dealings with, were another family to see a good deal of the famous visitor. Hannah was a writer and Douglass had been impressed with her recently published biography of Richard Allen. She promised him a signed copy, together with a book on John Woolman, the eighteenth-century American Quaker and anti-slavery campaigner, with a few particularly 'prophetic' passages underlined. Lydia Shackleton, the artist, meanwhile, would send him a painting of Bray Head after he went home, together with a 'handful' of heather and furze from Howth Head so that Douglass would always have a bit of Ireland.[35]

While appreciative of the kindness and hospitality of Wilhelmina Webb and her friends, it is not hard to imagine Douglass's reunion with Susanna Fisher, the sister to whom he had been closest in Limerick, carrying a much deeper emotional resonance. She had married a man named Webb in the 1850s and now lived in Dublin. 'Sometimes it seems more like a dream than reality that you have been here – and we have really and truly seen you again – and not so very much changed at all,' she wrote the summer after seeing him again. 'The hair white certainly and the figure stouter and less active but the same spirit of the man.' She, too, had been writing to thank him for a photograph he had sent over, which we can assume took pride of place on the mantelpiece or wall of her tidy Rathmines home.[36]

Douglass did not make it out of Dublin on his final visit to Ireland. Nevertheless, his brief sojourn in the city was the signal for renewed contact with Isabel Jennings in Cork. There was still a great deal of affection in the letters, even if Isabel's news was not particularly happy. 'But you may not know that only three of the large family in Brown Street now remain in this region, called "The World,"' she wrote, giving the dates for the deaths of her parents and siblings. She had had problems with cataracts but was now 'wonderfully recovered'. Nevertheless, at seventy-four, she said she looked on death as a 'dear friend', although to 'the dear, loving Father I leave the time'. Douglass, too, was increasingly aware of his own mortality. Writing to Richard Allen a few years earlier on the possibility of returning to Ireland he had suggested that while there were a good many people whose hand he would like to shake again, it did not matter if he did it in this world or the next – 'It will not be long before we all meet on the other shore.'[37]

'America's Loss'

'May the winds and waves deal gently with you, and take you safely to your home on the other side of the water,' the Radical MP Burt wrote to Douglass as the famed orator prepared to board the *City of Rome* in Liverpool on Wednesday, 3 August 1887, Ellen Richardson bidding him adieu with a note aptly describing the 'soil of England' as 'your second home'. Douglass was certainly eager to extol its virtues in a series of talks he gave soon after his return to the United States (he in turn being the subject of talks in St Ives in Cornwall and Driffield near Hull). 'There is something about her landscapes so soft, so tranquil and restful, that the eye never tires of them. There is in them a quality of sweetness and peace. You look upon them as upon the finest pictures,' Douglass told an audience in Washington, going on to praise Britain's engineering prowess, economic strength and moral might. 'No man can travel within the borders of England without seeing that she is Great Britain, great at home and powerful abroad.'[38]

Douglass's final years saw him combine efforts to combat segregation and lynching in the South with work on behalf of benighted Haiti, the island nation where he had been appointed Consul General by President Benjamin Harrison. He also continued to support temperance and women's rights groups, including those in Britain, opening a correspondence, for instance, with the philanthropist Lady Isabella Somerset and the outspoken Baptist preacher Charles Aked, who, rather wonderfully, recounted in one letter how the earliest memory of his Unitarian friend the Revd R. A. Armstrong was of being 'nursed on your knee' during the then escaped slave's visit to the Armstrong home in Bristol in 1846, his father, the Revd George Armstrong, a close friend of the Estlins. Douglass kept in contact with his older friends across the Atlantic as well, though increasingly the letters assume a maudlin feel, with each year seeming to bring a new death and letters of commiseration being sent to mark the passing of Jane Wigham, Eliza Barlow, Russell Lant Carpenter, Anna Richardson and Mary Carpenter.[39]

Douglass joined them 'on the other shore' on the evening of 20 February 1895, dying of a heart attack at Cedar Hill having just returned home from a women's rights rally in the nearby capital. He was seventy-seven years old, even if his gravestone added a year, the uncertainty sown by slavery taking physical form. The elderly John W. Hutchinson, one of his fellow travellers on that first great trip to Britain and Ireland, sang over the grave; Rebecca Moore, another of the last surviving links to that first tour, expressing her sadness to Helen at 'your loss, of the coloured people's loss, of women's loss, of America's loss'. The eighty-three-year-old Griffiths Crofts, struggling financially and physically in St Neots – 'I have not the least idea what will become of me,' she lamented in one of her last letters to her old friend – and only three months away from her own death, would also have felt the loss very deeply.[40]

With a Reuters telegram carrying news of Douglass's death quickly across the Atlantic, papers all over Britain and Ireland printed long obituaries for the 'venerable ... champion of the freedom of the slave' alongside excerpts from his speeches. They also took pride in his myriad connections with the British Isles, noting especially how it had been British funds that purchased his freedom.

The report in the *Banbury Beacon* in Oxfordshire, however, showed racist attitudes towards people of African descent remained prevalent, the headline 'A Remarkable Mulatto' leading on to an article that stressed it was to the white blood in Douglass's veins that he owed 'the intellectual fibre that distinguished him'.[41]

Douglass's passing was also the spur for a raft of anecdotes and recollections, the former slave still looming large in the lives and memories of all those who he had met fifty years earlier, 'the impression his crusade created ... too deep to be soon forgot'. Sir Andrew Fairbairn, for example, the former Liberal MP who had worked in Newcastle as a young man, recounted to a journalist how he had seen Douglass speak there before meeting him again years later quite by chance on a boat on one of America's Great Lakes. Fairbairn introduced himself and they talked contentedly until separated by the dinner bell, 'coloured people' still not allowed to sit at the same table as 'white gentlemen'. 'Sir Andrew said he had received Mr Douglass at his own table in England and he did not know that the dining room of ... an American lake steamer was any more sacred than his own home in England.' The captain unmoved, the former wheelwright who went on to be knighted by Queen Victoria took his dinner with Douglass and the ship's African-American cook in the kitchen. 'How vividly we remember, as a mere boy, hearing him when, to stir up Great Britain to a sense of the evils of American slavery, he travelled [all] over the land,' another correspondent recalled. 'To hear his story, even as it then was told in conversation or in the newspapers, in mere threads and snatches, was enough to make the heart beat, and in listening to him to make one feel the full force of the words of Tennyson – "Man is man, and master of his fate."'[42]

Approaching the bicentenary of his birth, Douglass continues to make his presence felt across Britain and Ireland, his grand leonine visage staring down from a giant mural on Belfast's Solidarity Wall, his words illuminating the Irish novelist Colum McCann's *TransAtlantic*, his perfectly tailored clothing the inspiration for the Zanzibar-born but British-based Turner Prize-winning artist Lubaina Himid's *Frederick Douglass Lapels*. His transformative first tour, meanwhile, is commemorated in plaques from London to Cork and points between – with another planned for the Richardson's Summerhill Grove residence in Newcastle, the city on the Tyne where the escaped slave first learned of his freedom.

APPENDIX

POEMS AND SONGS

'Stranger from a Distant Nation'

Stranger from a distant nation,
We welcome thee with acclamation,
And, as a brother, warmly greet thee –
Rejoiced in Erin's Isle to meet thee.

Then *Céad Míle Fáilte* to the stranger,
Free from bondage, chains and danger.

Who could have heard thy hapless story,
Of tyrants – canting, base and gory;
Whose heart throbbed not with deep pulsation
For the trampled slaves emancipation.

Then *Céad Míle Fáilte* to the stranger,
Free from bondage, chains and danger.

Oh! why should different hue or feature
Prevent the sacred laws of Nature,
And every tie of feeling sever? –
The voice of Nature thunders 'Never!'

Then *Céad Míle Fáilte* to the stranger,
Free from bondage, chains and danger.

Then borne o'er the Atlantic waters
The cry of Erin's sons and daughters
For freedom shall henceforth be blended
Till Slavery's hellish reign be ended.

Then *Céad Míle Fáilte* to the stranger,
Free from bondage, chains and danger.

Daniel Casey, Cork 1845
(LCDP, 'Casey, Daniel', n.d.)

'The Land of the Slave'
(Suggested by a Passage in the Life of Fred. Douglass)

The boy made his rest where, for ages, waved on
One tree of a forest, whose thousands were gone;
But the soft Summer airs through its foliage still played,
And the wild birds rejoiced in the depth of its shade.
Oh! broad was the river, and lovely the scene,
That spread where the wilds of that forest had been;
The noon lay in splendour, on field and on wave,
But the boy knew it shone on the Land of the Slave.

And well might he cast his young limbs on the soil;
Their grace was for fetters, their strength was for toil;
For the current that blent with his life stream was one,
That burst, in far time, by the fount of the sun.
Oh! dark was the midnight that shadowed its course,
But his eye was still lit by the fire of that source;
For the changeless old charter, that liberty gave,
Hath a record still left in the Land of the Slave.

But, where might that weary eye rest, when it sought
Some spot where the brand of his memory was not;
He turned from the fields, with their Summer wealth filled,
For he knew in what terror their furrows were tilled;
He looked on the river, and thought of the day
Its water had wafted his kindred away.
And the tears of the young that had blent with its wave;
But, alas! for bright youth in the Land of the Slave.

He saw the far sky, like an ocean of blue,
And thought of the mother his infancy knew –
Of the love that through toil and through bondage she bore,
And the night-coming step that might seek him no more.
Oh! faint was the faith of his future, and dim
The hope that soul-masters had granted to him;
But they said that the grass had grown green on her grave,
And he wished her not back to the Land of the Slave.

Yet, ever the birds, in the branches above,
Sang on in the joy of their freedom and love –
Their freedom, that sceptre or sword never cleft;
Their love on which tyrants no footprints had left:
And oh! for their lot, where a shadow ne'er crossed
The light of the Summers his childhood had lost,
For their song that burst forth, like a stream from its cave,
And their wings that could waft from the Land of the Slave.

Young lover of freedom, that prayer was not vain,
Though far was the moment that shivered thy chain;
But woe for the heart that can find in the clime
Of its early remembrance but deserts of time!
Our isle hath her sorrows; the page of her years
Is dark with the memory of discord and tears;
But she still owns the heart and the hand that would save,
And we welcome thy steps from the Land of the Slave.

Frances Brown ('The Blind Poetess of Ulster'), Donegal 1846
(*Northern Whig*, 10 January 1846)

'To Frederick Douglass'

Amerigo Vespucci! well was given
Thy name to you, vast continent of lies;
The new-found world, whence sacred truth is driven,
Where men religion love, and God despise.

Vain, boastful Florentine! what though thy name
Is stamped upon the world Columbus found?
Thine is the falsehood, his the rightful fame,
If fame may spring from such accursed ground.

Dark was the day on which the vessel sailed,
Which bore thy name, chaste mother of our Lord!
Oh, how have lust and cruelty prevailed!
What hecatombs have fleshed the tyrant's sword,

Since holy Mary's barque first touched the shore,
Till then unknown to these, our Eastern climes!
America, go write thy name in gore,
No other ink will suit thy demon crimes.

Land of the bended knee, the vengeful arm!
Land of the crosier and the knotted thong!
Where bondsmen till the low-born freeman's farm;
Where men the weak oppress, and help the strong.

What though thy name is new in history's page?
A fungus nation, offspring of a night!
Thy deeds are worthy of a bygone age,
When crimes of shame were rife, which shunned the light.

Pizarro! Cortez! ye whose names supply
A byword to the world that loathes your deeds,
Hide your mean heads, to those whom you outvie
In acts at which the stoutest nature bleeds.

Thrice happy those, whom Spain's remorseless hand
Consigned to death, to cold oblivion's power!
Oh blest, thrice blest, that slain, that countless band,
Who rest forgotten, like you withering flower.

Another race is heir to all your woes,
A race transported from their native soil,
To one through which no steam of kindness flows,
To cheer the pathway of unceasing toil.

Oh, what a day was that for Afric's race,
When Spain sent out the restless Genoese,
Commissioned to reclaim redeeming grace
To lands encircled by the Western seas!

Redeeming grace! oh, mockery profane!
Spain plants the crop, but plants it deep in blood;
Nought fills her bosom but the love of gain –
'Tis sordid gold she seeks, not India's good.

Baptised, and ground to death, the Indian lies,
His name forgotten, and his race destroyed;
His people gone, another race supplies
The broken ranks, fills up the deadly void.

Age after age has slowly rolled away,
O'ercharged with Afric's groans and bitter tears;
Her sons the constant, unprotected prey
Of one whose galling yoke in woe she bears.

Rise, Afric, rise! oh, break the tyrant's band!
Each generous voice will cheer thee to thy right;
Stand up erect – the craven ne'er will stand
Before thine arm in Nature's rightful fight.

Douglass, we welcome thee to England's shore,
A brother-freeman, once a tyrant's thrall;

The planter's chain shall shackle thee no more,
Thy frame ne'er tremble at the driver's call.

Thy tongue, thine arm, thy foot, thy voice, is free –
Free as the air, the light, the mountain stream;
Thrice welcome to this land of liberty –
Look back on bondage as a bygone dream!

Thy tongue is loosened – loosened be the ties
Which held thy brethren in the Western shores;
Proclaim their wrongs, denounce the nation's lies,
Where man his brother hates, his God adores.

L. Sabine, Wales 1846
(*Liberator*, 27 November 1846)

'Frederick Douglass'

I'll be free! I'll be free! and none shall confine,
With fetters and chains, this free heart of mine;
From my youth I have learned on my God to rely,
And, despite my oppressor, gain freedom or die.

Though my back is all torn by the merciless rod,
Yet firm is my trust in the right arm of God;
In his strength I'll go forth, and forever will be
'Mong the hills of the North, where the bondman is free.

Let me go, let me go, to the land of the brave,
Where the shackles must fall from the limbs of the slave;
Where Freedom's proud eagle screams wild through the sky,
And the sweet mountain birds in glad notes reply.

I'll fly to New-England, where the fugitive finds
A home mid her mountains and deep forest winds;
And her hill-tops shall ring with the wrongs done to me,
Till responsive they sing, 'Let the bondman go free!'

New-England! New-England! thrice blessed and free,
The poor hunted slave finds a shelter in thee;
Where should blood-thirsty hounds ever dare on his track,
At thy strong voice, New-England, the monsters fall back.

Go back, then, ye blood-hounds, that howl on my path!
In the land of New-England, I'm free from your wrath;
And the sons of the Pilgrims my deep scars shall see,
Till they cry with one voice, 'Let the bondman go free!'

Great God! hasten on the glad jubilee,
When our brethren in bonds shall arise and be free,
And our blotted escutcheon be washed from its stains,
Now the scorn of the world, with three millions in chains.

O, then shall Columbia's bright flag be unfurled,
The glory of freemen, the pride of the world;
While earth's struggling millions point hither in glee,
To the land of New-England, the home of the free.

'An Ipswich Lady', Ipswich 1846
(*Liberator*, 4 December 1846)

'We'll Free the Slave'
(Air – 'Ye banks and braes of bonny Doon')

How bright the sun of freedom burns,
From mount to mount, from shore to shore!
"The slave departs, the man returns,"
The reign of force and fraud is o'er:
'Tis Truth's own beam, from sea to sea,
From vale to vale, from wave to wave;
Her ministers this night are we,
To free, to free, to free the slave!

We'll free the slave of every clime,
Whate'er the chain that binds his soul;
And publish forth this truth sublime,
From farthest Indus to the Pole,
That man, how proud soe'er he be,
Is but a poor and paltry knave,
Who joins not now with you and me,
To free, to free, to free the slave!

We'll free the slave, the poisoned bowl
Has fettered to low crime and care;
We'll bid him burst its harsh control,
And break its fetters of despair.
We'll free the slave of Mammon's power;
And War's poor darling, called the brave;
And Tyrants! yes, from this blest hour,
We'll free, we'll free, we'll free the slave!

Poor Afric's son, though slaves they be,
Shall spring to freedom and to light;
And what they shall be, you may see –
One of those sons is here to-night!
And Asia from her sleep supine,
And Europe from her feudal grave,
Yes, e'en America shall join,
To free, to free, to free the slave!

You laugh! but, ah! you do not know
How great a power the truth can wield;
Thought always aims the surest blow,
And wisdom is the safest shield.
The spirits of six thousand years
Are round us, and they make us brave;
Come, brother, quell ignoble fears,
And free, and free, and free the slave!

E. P. Hood, Newcastle 1846
(*Liberator*, 5 February 1847)

'Farewell Song of Frederick Douglass, on Leaving England'

What if the Negro's despised and degraded,
And scorn and reproach are heap'd on his head?
Perish the thought that would leave him unaided!
American soil shall be that which I tread.

Farewell to the land of the free!
Farewell to the land of the brave!
Alas! that my country should be
America, land of the Slave!

What if I've drunk of the cup that awaits me
One bitter foretaste already; shall I
Glean from the prospect no thought that elates me,
If in freedom's great cause counted worthy to die?

Farewell to the land of the free!
Farewell to the land of the brave!
Alas! that my country should be
America, land of the Slave!

Am I not wanted where warfare is waging?
Shall I, like a coward, not join in the fight?
Shrink from the onslaught when battle is raging,
Scared by the enemy's tyrannous might?

Farewell to the land of the free!
Farewell to the land of the brave!
Alas! that my country should be
America, land of the Slave!

Give me, then, Friends! the weapon that's wielded
Best in the cause I have sworn to uphold,
And I will fight on till the foe shall have yielded,
Or the years of sojourn on earth have been told.

Farewell to the land of the free!
Farewell to the land of the brave!
Alas! that my country should be
America, land of the Slave!

Julia Griffiths (music) and Thomas Powis Griffiths (words),
London 1847
(*Leicestershire Mercury*, 17 July 1847)

NOTES

List of Abbreviations

BPL – Boston Public Library, Anti-Slavery Collection

FDP – Blassingame, John W. (ed.), *The Frederick Douglass Papers*, series 1, 5 vols (New Haven, CT: Yale University Press, 1979–92)

LCDP – Library of Congress, Washington, DC, Frederick Douglass Papers

LWFD – Foner, Philip S. (ed.), *The Life and Writings of Frederick Douglass*, 5 vols (New York, NY: International Publishers, 1950–75)

QHL – Quaker Historical Library, Dublin

URFDP – University of Rochester Frederick Douglass Project

WLG – Merrill, Walter M. and Ruchames, Louis (eds), *The Letters of William Lloyd Garrison*, 6 vols (Cambridge, MA: Harvard University Press, 1971–81)

Introduction: 'The Traffic of Men-Body'

1 For the scene at Boston Harbour, see *Liberator*, 22 Aug. 1845 and Cockrell, D. (ed.), *Excelsior: Journals of the Hutchinson Family Singers, 1842–1846* (Stuyvesant, NY: Pendragon Press, 1989), p. 315.

2 Blassingame, John W. (ed.), *The Frederick Douglass Papers*, series 1, 5 vols [FDP] (New Haven, CT: Yale University Press, 1979–92), 1, p. 261.

3 After generations of indifference and obfuscation, the dramatic impact of slavery and the slave trade on all aspects of British society has finally started being brought to light by ground-breaking publications like Devine, T. M. (ed.), *Recovering Scotland's Slavery Past: The Caribbean Connection* (Edinburgh: Edinburgh University Press, 2015) and Olusoga, David, *Black and British: A Forgotten History* (London: Macmillan, 2016) as well as

projects such as University College London's 'Legacies of British Slave-Ownership'. Much of the information for this paragraph has been taken from these sources, together with articles from the BBC's 'Abolition' website, set up to commemorate of the bicentenary of the abolition of the slave trade in 2007.

4 Olusoga, *Black and British*, p. 230 shows how the £20 million set aside to compensate the 46,000 slave-owners affected by abolition represented 40 per cent of all government spending for the year 1833 and is the equivalent to around £17 billion today.

5 Sluiter, Engel, 'New Light on the "20. and Odd Negroes" Arriving in Virginia, August 1619', *William and Mary Quarterly* (1997), p. 396; Blassingame, *FDP* 1, pp. 374–5.

6 Sluiter, 'New Light on the "20. and Odd Negroes"', pp. 395–8; Woolley, Benjamin, *Savage Kingdom: Virginia and the Founding of English America* (London: Harper Press, 2007), pp. 353–4, 363–4.

7 Reynolds, David, *America: Empire of Liberty* (London: Penguin, 2010), p. 28.

8 Drescher, Seymour, *Abolition: A History of Slavery and Anti-Slavery* (New York, NY: Cambridge University Press, 2009), pp. 124–5.

9 Davis, David Brion, *Inhuman Bondage: The Rise and Fall of Slavery in the New World* (New York, NY: Oxford University Press, 2006), p. 126.

10 'Resolutions of the Germantown Mennonites', 18 Feb. 1688: www.avalon.law.yale.edu/17th_century/meno1.asp

11 Drescher, *Abolition*, p. 112.

12 Mayer, Henry, *All on Fire: William Lloyd Garrison and the Abolition of Slavery* (New York, NY: St Martin's Griffin, 2000), p. 49.

13 Mayer, *All on Fire*, p. 94.

14 Mayer, *All on Fire*, p. xiii.

Chapter 1: 'The Fugitive's Song'

1 Dickens, Charles, *American Notes* (New York, NY: D. Appleton & Co., 1868), pp. 5–8.

2 For the list of first-class passengers on board the *Cambria*, see *Boston Daily Atlas*, 18 Aug. 1845. John Sturgis Nye's great-great-great-grandfather Benjamin Nye is reputed to have arrived in America on board the *Abigail* in 1635. He was certainly well-established in the colony of Massachusetts a few years later, marrying a Katherine Tupper, some of whose family were related to descendants of those who had sailed on the *Mayflower* in 1620. John Sturgis Nye may have been travelling to Manchester in 1845. He certainly had some connection with the city, his first child, William Munroe Nye, born there in 1852. For more on Nye and his family, see www.nyefamily.org and Nye,

David Fisher (ed.), *A Genealogy of the Nye Family* (Cleveland, OH: The Nye Family of America Association, 1907). Edward Hutchinson Robbins's father, also Edward Hutchinson Robbins, a Speaker of the Massachusetts House of Representatives and Lieutenant Governor of Massachusetts, moved in the same political circles as John Adams. The younger Robbins is mentioned in the diaries of Charles Francis Adams, son of John Quincy Adams and grandson of John Adams: Friedlaender, Marc et al (eds), *Diary of Charles Francis Adams*, 8 vols (Cambridge, MA: The Belknap Press, 1968–1986), 3, p. 36. Revd Henry Hotham and his wife Mary, daughter of a well-known Canadian politician John Hale, may have been travelling to England for a honeymoon or to visit his family, his father, Revd Frederick Hotham, the Prebendary of Rochester, a senior figure in the Anglican Church. For Hotham's marriage in July 1845, see Hall, Roger and Shelton, S. W. (eds), *The Rising Country: The Hale-Amherst Correspondence, 1799–1825* (Toronto, ON: Champlain Society, 2002), p. xv. Edmund A. Grattan was a career diplomat later knighted for his services. His father, Thomas Colley Grattan, British consul to Boston at the time Edmund was made vice-consul, was best known for a collection of travel writings called *Highways and Byways* and for a history of the Netherlands. For more on the French-Canadian missionary priest and prelate Blanchet, including his often remarkable travels in the Pacific Northwest, see Blanchet, F. N., *Historical Sketches of the Catholic Church in Oregon, During the Past Forty Years* (Portland, OR: 1878).

3   For examples of J. C. Burnham's multifarious business interests, including medicines and slave-worked sugar plantations, see Curry-Machado, Jonathan, '"Sin Azúcar No Hay País": The Transnational Counterpoint of Sugar and Nation in Nineteenth-Century Cuba', *Bulletin of Hispanic Studies* (2007), pp. 25–42 together with references to J. C. Burnham & Co. in the online guides to the 'Business Letters Describing the Financial Market in Cuba, 1867–1871' in the George A. Smathers Libraries at the University of Florida and to the papers of the large New York-based wholesale druggists firm of Lanman and Kemp at the Manuscript and Archives Department of the Hagley Museum and Library in Wilmington, Delaware. Barings Bank had been increasingly involved with Cuban businesses from the 1830s and certainly gave substantial loans to J. C. Burnham & Co. from the mid-1840s. For more on these ties, see Curry-Machado, Jonathan, *Cuban Sugar Industry: Transnational Networks and Engineering Migrants in Mid-Nineteenth Century Cuba* (New York, NY: Palgrave Macmillan, 2011), pp. 157–9. Burnham also had links with New Orleans, home to the biggest slave market in America, as shown in references to J.C. Burnham & Co. in the online guide to the William Appleton and Company Records, 1813–1889 at the Baker Library of Harvard Business School.

4 For Dunnell, see *Representative Men and Old Families of Rhode Island: Genealogical Records and Historical Sketches of Prominent and Representative Citizens and of Many of the Old Families* (Chicago, IL: J. H. Beers & Co., 1908), pp. 445–7. For Welch, see Slouth, William L., *Olympians of the Sawdust Circle: A Biographical Dictionary of the Nineteenth Century American Circus* (San Bernardino, CA: The Borgo Press, 1998), p. 320.

5 Buffum has been treated rather condescendingly in many works, labelled an 'enterprising but slow-thinking carpenter whose means permitted him to indulge a taste for abolitionism' and a 'wealthy, if slightly insipid, Garrisonian from Lynn'. This hardly does justice to a man who after being one of the earliest subscribers to the *Liberator* in 1831 was still working to help freed slaves in the 1870s. And besides, most people would look slightly insipid when measured against the intellectually and physically powerful Douglass. See Quarles, Benjamin, *Frederick Douglass* (New York, NY: Atheneum, 1976), p. 38 and Soskis, Benjamin, 'Heroic Exile: The Transatlantic Development of Frederick Douglass, 1845–1847' (Senior honours thesis, Yale University, 1997): www.yale.edu/glc/soskis

6 Douglass, Frederick, *My Bondage and My Freedom* [1855] (London: Penguin Books, 2003), pp. 269–70.

7 Douglass, *Bondage*, p. 294.

8 For Douglass's age and lineage, see Preston, Dickson J., *Young Frederick Douglass: The Maryland Years* (Baltimore, MD: The Johns Hopkins University Press, 1985), pp. 3–10.

9 For Douglass's early years, see Douglass, *Bondage*, pp. 29–40. Written ten years after *Narrative*, Douglass's second autobiography is now widely considered the fuller, more accomplished piece of writing. It certainly contains a great deal more material on his earliest years.

10 Douglass, Frederick, *Narrative of the Life of Frederick Douglass, an American Slave* [1845] (Dublin: A Little Book Company, 2011), p. 31.

11 Douglass, *Bondage*, p. 31.

12 Douglass, *Bondage*, p. 40.

13 Douglass, *Narrative*, p. 33.

14 Douglass, *Narrative*, p. 52.

15 Douglass, *Narrative*, p. 57.

16 Stauffer, John, *Giants: The Parallel Lives of Frederick Douglass and Abraham Lincoln* (New York, NY: Twelve, 2009), pp. 62–4.

17 Douglass, *Bondage*, pp. 120–1.

18 Preston, *Young Frederick Douglass*, pp. 105–17.

19 Douglass, *Narrative*, p. 80.

20 Douglass, *Narrative*, p. 83. Covey's industry, if not his morality, would be rewarded. He became a wealthy gentleman planter and by the time of the American Civil War owned slaves and property worth $2 million in today's money: Stauffer, *Giants*, p. 47.

21 Douglass, *Bondage*, pp. 177–80.

22 Douglass, *Bondage*, p. 181.

23 Preston, *Young Frederick Douglass*, p. 169.

24 Douglass, *Bondage*, p. 196.

25 Douglass, *Bondage*, p. 220.

26 McFeely, William S., *Frederick Douglass* (New York, NY: W. W. Norton, 1995), p. 13.

27 Cockrell, *Excelsior*, p. 317.

28 Warburton, George, *Hochelaga; or, England in the New World*, 2 vols (London: Colburn & Co., 1851), 2, p. 356.

29 Library of Congress, Washington, DC, Frederick Douglass Papers [LCDP], 'Thoughts and Recollections of a Tour in Ireland' (1886), p. 4; Hutchinson, John W., *Story of the Hutchinsons (Tribe of Jesse)*, 2 vols (Boston, MA; Lee and Shepard, 1896), 1, p. 147.

30 Douglass, *Narrative*, pp. 64–5.

31 Douglass, *Bondage*, pp. 107–8.

32 McFeely, *Douglass*, p. 70.

33 Douglass, Frederick, *The Life and Times of Frederick Douglass* [1892] (Mineola, NY: Dover Publications, 2003), p.139.

34 Douglass, *Life and Times*, p. 139.

35 Alexander, J. E., *L'Acadie; or, Seven Years' Explorations in British America*, 2 vols (London: Henry Colburn, 1849), 2, p. 261.

36 Cockrell, *Excelsior*, pp. 318–19. For Mrs Widder's husband, Frederick, the British-born chief commissioner of the Canada Company, formed by royal commission in 1826 to develop vast tracts of land in the Canadian wilderness, see Lee, Robert C., *The Canada Company and the Huron Tract, 1826–1853: Personalities, Profits and Politics* (Toronto, ON: Natural Heritage Books, 2004), pp. 149–204.

37 Blassingame, *FDP* 2, pp. 373–4.

38 Douglass, *Bondage*, p. 263; Mayer, *All on Fire*, p. 306.

39 Douglass, *Bondage*, pp. 264–5.

40 Howe, Daniel Walker, *What Hath God Wrought: The Transformation of America, 1815–1848* (Oxford: Oxford University Press, 2009), p. 649.

41 Foner, Philip S. (ed.), *The Life and Writings of Frederick Douglass*, 5 vols [LWFD] (New York, NY: International Publishers, 1950–75), 1, pp. 48, 52.

42 Jordon, Ryan, 'Quakers, "Comeouters" and the Meaning of Abolitionism in the Antebellum Free States', *Journal of the Early Republic* (2004), pp. 587–608.

43 McFeely, *Douglass*, p. 108.

44 'I believe he wrote with his right hand,' Adrienne Cannon, curator of the Frederick Douglass Papers at the Library of Congress, informed Tom Chaffin, author of *Giant's Causeway: Frederick Douglass's Irish Odyssey and the Making of an American Visionary* (Charlottesville, VA: University of Virginia Press, 2014). 'He could not write for long periods because of the injury to the hand, his handwriting would deteriorate. This explains the visual difference in examples of his handwriting.' See Chaffin, *Giant's Causeway*, p. 229, n. 1.

45 Douglass, *Bondage*, p. 266.

46 Douglass, *Narrative*, pp. 152, 169–71; Foner, *LWFD* 1, p. 60.

47 Nelson, Bruce, *Irish Nationalists and the Making of the Irish Race* (Princeton, NJ: Princeton University Press, 2012), p. 92.

48 Nelson, *Irish Nationalists*, pp. 99–100.

49 Quaker Historical Library, Dublin [QHL], SR/P/23, Nineteenth Century Manuscripts, 'Reminiscences of Alfred Webb from 1837–1905', 2 vols, 1, pp. 67–8; Harrison, Richard S., *Richard Davis Webb: Dublin Quaker Printer, 1805–72* (Cork: Red Barn Publishers, 1993), p. 43.

50 Douglass, *Bondage*, p. 267.

51 Douglass, *Bondage*, p. 270; Hutchinson, *Story of the Hutchinsons* 1, p. 144; *Liberator*, 26 Sept. 1845.

52 For Judkins's actions on board the *Acadia*, see Pettinger, Alasdair, 'Send Back the Money: Douglass and the Free Church of Scotland', in Rice, Alan J. and Crawford, Martin (eds), *Liberating Sojourn: Frederick Douglass and Transatlantic Reform* (Athens, GA: The University of Georgia Press, 1999), pp. 46–7.

53 For the disturbance on board the *Cambria* and its aftermath: Douglass, *Bondage*, pp. 270–1, 281; Hutchinson, *Story of the Hutchinsons* 1, pp. 145–6; Cockrell, *Excelsior*, pp. 320–1; Chaffin, *Giant's Causeway*, pp. 27–31; Warburton, *Hochelaga* 2, pp. 359–62; Alexander, *L'Acadie* 2, pp. 261–2; Soskis, 'Heroic Exile'; *Liberator*, 26 Sept., 3 Oct. and 10 Oct. 1845; *Belfast News-Letter*, 9 Dec. 1845.

Chapter 2: 'A Total Absence of Prejudice'

1 Foner, *LWFD* 1, pp. 119–20.

2 Hart, W. A., 'Africans in Eighteenth-Century Ireland', *Irish Historical Studies* (2002), pp. 19–23.

3 Hart, 'Africans in Eighteenth-Century Ireland', p. 24.

4 Rodgers, Nini, 'Limerick Merchants and the Slave Trade', in Lee, David and Jacobs, Debbie (eds), *Made in Limerick: A History of Trades, Industry and Commerce*, 2 vols (Limerick: Limerick Civic Trust, 2006), 2, p. 77.

5 Rodgers, 'Limerick Merchants', pp. 88–9; Rodgers, Nini, *Ireland, Slavery and Anti-Slavery: 1612–1865* (New York, NY: Palgrave Macmillan, 2007), p. 158.

6 Foner, *LWFD* 1, pp. 115–18.

7 *Freeman's Journal*, 30 Aug. 1845. For more on the popularity of mesmerism and phreno-mesmerism in Victorian Britain and Ireland, see Winter, Alison, *Mesmerised: Powers of Mind in Victorian Britain* (Chicago, IL: University of Chicago Press, 1998).

8 *Freeman's Journal*, 8 Sept. 1845; Geoghegan, Patrick, '"A Consistent Advocate of Nigger Emancipation": Daniel O'Connell and the Campaign Against Slavery', *History Ireland* (2010), p. 23; Ames, Julius Rubens, *Liberty* (Boston, MA: American Anti-Slavery Society, 1837), p. 173.

9 Wigham, Maurice J., *The Irish Quakers: A Short History of the Religious Society of Friends in Ireland* (Dublin: Historical Committee of the Religious Society of Friends in Ireland, 1992), pp. 63, 75.

10 QHL, 'Alfred Webb' 1, p. 67; Andrews, Helen, 'Allen, Richard (1803–86)', *Dictionary of Irish Biography* (Cambridge: Cambridge University Press, 2009).

11 *Freeman's Journal*, 13 Sept. 1845.

12 Boston Public Library, Anti-Slavery Collection [BPL], James Buffum to Maria Weston Chapman, 16 Sept. 1845.

13 McFeely, *Douglass*, p. 100.

14 For Methodism and slavery in America, see Finkelman, Paul (ed.), *Encyclopaedia of African American History, 1619–1895: From the Colonial Period to the Age of Frederick Douglass* (Oxford: Oxford University Press, 2006), pp. 353–5.

15 Foner, *LWFD* 1, p. 119.

16 There were twelve pence (12d) in a shilling and twenty shillings (20s) in a pound (£1) in pre-decimal currency.

17 *Freeman's Journal*, 18 Sept. 1845.

18 *Freeman's Journal*, 24 Sept., 4 Oct. 1845.

19 Ferreira, Patricia J., 'Frederick Douglass in Ireland: The Dublin Edition of His Narrative', *New Hibernia Review* (2001), p. 64.

20 *Pilot*, 1 Oct. 1845; *Boston Pilot*, 25 Oct. 1845. For the impact O'Connell's anti-slavery stance had on support for the Repeal movement in America, see Murphy, Angela F., 'Daniel O'Connell and the "American Eagle" in 1845:

Slavery, Diplomacy, Nativism and the Collapse of America's First Irish Nationalist Movement', *Journal of American Ethnic History* (2007).

21 Fenton, Laurence, *Frederick Douglass in Ireland: 'The Black O'Connell'* (Cork: The Collins Press, 2014), pp. 118–19.

22 *Wexford Independent*, 15 Oct. 1845.

23 Foner, *LWFD* 1, pp. 138–42.

24 BPL, Richard D. Webb to Maria Weston Chapman, 16 May 1846.

25 McFeely, *Douglass*, p. 122; BPL, Richard D. Webb to Maria Weston Chapman, 16 May 1846; BPL, James Haughton to Maria Weston Chapman, 1 Apr. 1847.

26 BPL, Richard D. Webb to Maria Weston Chapman, 16 May 1846; Hutchinson, *Story of the Hutchinsons* 1, p. 164.

27 BPL, Isabel Jennings to Maria Weston Chapman, 15 Oct. 1845; *Southern Reporter*, 11 Oct. 1845.

28 BPL, Isabel Jennings to Maria Weston Chapman, 15 Nov. 1842, 30 Nov. 1845.

29 *Blackwood's Edinburgh Magazine*, 1820, pp. 199–200; *Phrenological Journal*, 1841, p. 339; Murphy, David, 'Dowden, Richard', *Dictionary of Irish Biography* (online edition).

30 BPL, Jane Jennings to Maria Weston Chapman, 26 Nov. 1845.

31 *Cork Examiner*, 15 Oct. 1845; Blassingame, *FDP* 1, pp. 39–45.

32 Harrison, Richard S., 'The Cork Anti-Slavery Society, Its Antecedents and Quaker Background, 1755–1859', *Journal of the Cork Historical and Archaeological Society* (1992), pp. 69–79.

33 Harrison, 'Cork Anti-Slavery Society', p. 75; Blassingame, *FDP* 1, pp. 45–54.

34 Blassingame, *FDP* 1, p. 71; Douglass, *Bondage*, p. 266.

35 LCDP, 'Casey, Daniel', n.d.; BPL, Isabel Jennings to Maria Weston Chapman, 30 Nov. 1845.

36 Fenton, *Douglass in Ireland*, pp. 152–4.

37 Moore, Charlotte, *Hancox: A House and a Family* (London: Viking, 2010), pp. 55–6.

38 Thackeray, W. M., *The Irish Sketchbook of 1842* (Dublin: Nonsuch Publishing, 2005), pp. 132–3.

39 *Limerick Reporter*, 11 Nov. 1845.

40 Blassingame, *FDP* 1, p. 77.

41 *Limerick Reporter*, 11 Nov. 1845.

42 McDaniel, W. Caleb, 'Repealing Unions: American Abolitionists, Irish Repeal, and the Origins of Garrisonian Disunionism', *Journal of the Early Republic* (2008), pp. 243–4. For more on Garrison and O'Connell's complicated and occasionally antagonistic relationship, see Kinealy, Christine, *Daniel*

O'Connell and the Anti-Slavery Movement: *"The Saddest People the Sun Sees"* (London: Pickering & Chatto, 2011).

43 Sweeney, Fionnghuala, '"The Republic of Letters": Frederick Douglass, Ireland and the Irish *Narratives*', in Kenny, Kevin (ed.), *New Directions in Irish-American History* (Madison, WI: The University of Wisconsin Press, 2003), p. 131.

44 Hogan, Liam, '"Oh What a Transition it was to be Changed from the State of a Slave to that of a Free Man!": Frederick Douglass's Journey from Slavery to Limerick'. www.theirishstory.com

45 *Limerick Reporter*, 25 Nov. 1845.

46 LCDP, 'Thoughts and Recollections', pp. 15–16.

47 Foner, *LWFD* 5, pp. 13–14.

48 Blassingame, *FDP* 1, pp. 86–97.

49 Foner, *LWFD* 5, pp. 13–15; Taylor, Clare (ed.), *British and American Abolitionists: An Episode in Transatlantic Understanding* (Edinburgh: Edinburgh University Press, 1974), pp. 97–8.

50 Foner, *LWFD* 5, p. 14.

51 Hutchinson, *Story of the Hutchinsons* 1, p. 171; Taylor, *British and American Abolitionists*, pp. 247–8.

52 Foner, *LWFD* 1, pp. 125–9.

Chapter 3: 'Send Back the Money'

1 BPL, Frederick Douglass to Francis Jackson, 29 Jan. 1846.

2 McCosh, James, *The Scottish Philosophy* (New York, NY: R. Carter, 1875), p. 398; Chalmers, Thomas, *A Few Thoughts on the Abolition of Colonial Slavery* (Glasgow: W. Collins & Co., 1826), p. 5; Smyth, Thomas, *Autobiographical Notes, Letters and Reflections* (Charleston, SC: Walker, Evans & Cogswell Co., 1914), p. 351.

3 McFeely, *Douglass*, p. 129; Blassingame, *FDP* 1, p. 118.

4 Purchased by Sir John Wedderburn, a Perthshire landowner who made a fortune in the West Indian sugar trade, Knight travelled from Jamaica to Scotland with his new master in the late 1760s. Inspired by the famous Somerset case (1772), he initiated a series of legal proceedings that resulted in Courts of Session in Edinburgh determining that slavery could not be recognised by Scots law. His story forms the basis of the Scottish author James Robertson's award-winning 2003 novel *Joseph Knight*.

5 Whyte, Iain, *Scotland and the Abolition of Black Slavery, 1756–1838* (Edinburgh: Edinburgh University Press, 2006), p. 14. With regard to the popularity of young black slaves – male and female – in Scotland, Whyte (p. 16) makes an important observation about the potential for child sexual

abuse in the cases of these 'unprotected minors ... transported thousands of miles and ... daily subjected to the caprices of strange adults who held absolute power over their lives'.

6 Much of the information for this section has been gleaned from Devine, *Recovering Scotland's Slavery Past* and Whyte, *Scotland and the Abolition of Black Slavery*, two of the finest works in the growing body of literature on Scotland's relationship with slavery and the slave trade. Schaw's experiences in Antigua and St Kitts are recounted in her *Journal of a Lady of Quality: Being the Narrative of a Journey from Scotland to the West Indies, North Carolina, and Portugal, in the Years 1774 to 1776* (New Haven, CT: Yale University Press, 1921). For more on Munro, who seems to have made some allowance for the young slave 'Susannah' with whom he fathered three children in his will, see his entry in University College London's 'Legacies of British Slave-Ownership' website: www.ucl.ac.uk/lbs/person/view/2146630877

7 Smith, James McCune, 'John Murray of Glasgow', in Griffiths, Julia (ed.), *Autographs for Freedom* (Boston, MA: John P. Jewett & Co., 1853), p. 64.

8 Douglass, *Bondage*, p. 281. Douglass had his Irish publisher Richard D. Webb deliver copies of his book to Smeal's 161 Gallowgate address, the home located, as was common practice at the time, above the business premises: Foner, *LWFD* 5, p. 42. For more on Paton, identified as a 'commission merchant' in trade directories of the time, with premises at 31 Argyll Street and a home that he shared with his sister Catherine at 16 Richmond Street, see his obituary in the *Glasgow Herald*, 18 Aug. 1884.

9 Douglass, *Bondage*, p. 281.

10 For more on Murray, see Smith, 'John Murray of Glasgow', pp. 62–7.

11 Dumas, Paula E., *Pro-Slavery Britain: Fighting for Slavery in an Era of Abolition* (New York, NY: Palgrave Macmillan, 2016), pp. 65–6.

12 BPL, Catherine Paton to Maria Weston Chapman, 1 Nov. 1841.

13 Smith, 'John Murray of Glasgow', pp. 66–7.

14 Lyell, Sir George, *Travels in North America: With Geological Observations on the United States, Canada and Nova Scotia*, 2 vols (London: John Murray, 1845), 1, p. 169.

15 *Southern Literary Messenger* (September, 1849), p. 639.

16 Blassingame, *FDP* 1, pp. 131–44.

17 Foner, *LWFD* 1, pp. 122–3. Wright, a great friend of Webb, would actually spend months at a time locked away in a room of the latter's Dublin residence, writing pamphlets and books during breaks in his lecture tours. Webb was annoyed by Douglass's refusal to concert efforts with Wright in late 1845, even though he too had severe doubts about the merits of the so-called 'disunion' campaign.

18 Liberator, 27 Feb. 1846.

19 Whyte, Iain, 'Send Back the Money!' The Free Church of Scotland and American Slavery (Cambridge: James Clarke & Co., 2012), p. 72.

20 Blassingame, FDP 1, pp. 144–56.

21 Lewis, George, Impressions of America and the American Churches (Edinburgh: W. P. Kennedy, 1845), pp. 412–19; Dundee Courier, 10 Feb. 1846.

22 Blassingame, FDP 1, pp. 156–64.

23 Whyte, 'Send Back the Money', p. 75.

24 For reaction to speeches, see local newspapers and accounts in Blassingame, FDP 1; for anonymous Dundee writer, see Pettinger, Alasdair, 'The Bloody Gold': www.bulldozia.com

25 These songs and poems, together with an array of other Douglass-related material, can be found on the Scottish writer Alasdair Pettinger's website www.bulldozia.com

26 Blassingame, FDP 1, p. 187.

27 Blassingame, FDP 1, p. 222.

28 Blassingame, FDP 1, pp. 171–82.

29 Foner, LWFD 5, pp. 21–2; Whyte, 'Send Back the Money', pp. 76–9; Fife Herald, 14 May, 1846; for more on the debate about British reparations to Jamaica and other countries, see Guardian, 30 Sept. 2015, 28 Aug. 2017.

30 Dundee Courier, 10 Feb. 1846; Blassingame, FDP 1, pp. 171–82.

31 Miller, Thomas Yule, The Dundee Courier: Historical Narrative of its Vicissitudes and Successive Proprietors – Colville-Hill-Alexander-Park-Thomson – from 1816 to 1887 (1911), p. 8.

32 Taylor, British and American Abolitionists, pp. 251–2.

33 Foner LWFD 5 pp. 33–7; Liberator, 26 June 1846.

34 Foner, LWFD 1, pp. 142–4.

35 Mayer, All on Fire, p. 202.

36 Levine, Robert S., Martin Delany, Frederick Douglass and the Politics of Representative Identity (Chapel Hill, NC: The University of North Carolina Press, 1997), pp. 102–12.

37 Foner LWFD 5, pp. 37–41; Blassingame, FDP 1, p. 174. For more on Burns and Douglass, see the BBC 2 Scotland documentary Burns in the USA (Finestripe Productions), first broadcast in January 2017. Douglass's copy of Burn's Works (Philadelphia, PA: J. Crissy, 1835) is held in the University of Rochester's Rare Book Collection. The note to his son Lewis can be viewed online at http://rbscp.lib.rochester.edu/4646

38 Foner, LWFD 1, pp. 151–3.

39 University of Rochester Frederick Douglass Project (URFDP), Letter 84, Frederick Douglass to Amy Post, 28 Apr. 1846; Blassingame, *FDP* 1, pp. 243–9; Cockrell, *Excelsior*, p. 340.

40 Mayer, *All on Fire*, pp. 264–7.

41 BPL, Jane Wigham to Maria Weston Chapman, 11 Nov. 1844; Whyte, *'Send Back the Money'*, p. 80.

42 Taylor, *British and American Abolitionists*, p. 261.

43 Foner, *LWFD* 1, p. 150; Morris, R. J., 'John Knox House and the Legacies of Slavery': https://lbsatucl.wordpress.com/2015/01/16/john-knox-house-and-the-legacies-of-slavery/#_edn4

44 *Liberator*, 8 May 1846; Douglass, *Bondage*, p. 282; Pettinger, 'Send Back the Money', p. 47.

Chapter 4: 'A Negro Hercules'

1 Foner, *LWFD* 1, pp. 165–73.

2 Douglass, *Life and Times*, pp. 167–9.

3 Foner, *LWFD* 1, pp. 165–73; Olusoga, *Black and British*, p. 22.

4 For more on Barings Bank and Cuba, including the granting of substantial loans to J. C. Burnham & Co., see Curry-Machado, *Cuban Sugar Industry*, pp. 157–9. For famous black Britons in Georgian times, see Olusoga, *Black and British*, pp. 106–12.

5 Richard, Henry, *Memoirs of Joseph Sturge* (London: S. W. Partridge, 1864), p. 585; Taylor, *British and American Abolitionists*, pp. 242, 272.

6 Taylor, *British and American Abolitionists*, pp. 277–8.

7 Blassingame, *FDP* 1, pp. 269–99.

8 Blassingame, *FDP* 1, pp. 261–4; Hutchinson, *Story of the Hutchinsons* 1, p. 179.

9 Foner *LWFD* 1, pp. 165–73.

10 Morgan, Simon, 'The Anti-Corn Law League and British Anti-Slavery in Transatlantic Perspective, 1838–1846', *Historical Journal* (2009), pp. 94–7.

11 Robbins, Keith, *John Bright* (London: Routledge & Kegan Paul, 1979), p. 60.

12 Taylor, *British and American Abolitionists*, p. 275; Huzzey, Richard, *Freedom Burning: Anti-Slavery and Empire in Victorian Britain* (Ithaca, NY: Cornell University Press, 2012), pp. 93–7.

13 Temperley, Howard, *British Anti-Slavery 1833–1870* (London: Longman, 1972), pp. 153–67.

14 Fenton, Laurence, *Palmerston and The Times: Foreign Policy, the Press and Public Opinion in Mid-Victorian Britain* (London: I. B. Tauris, 2012), p. 57.

15 Oldfield, John, 'Palmerston and Anti-Slavery', in Brown, David and Taylor, Miles (eds), *Palmerston Studies II* (Southampton: Hartley Institute, University of Southampton, 2007), p. 24; Taylor, *British and American Abolitionists*, pp. 264–7.

16 Blassingame, *FDP* 1, p. 252.

17 LCDP, Douglass Sprague, R., 'Anna Murray Douglass: My Mother As I Recall Her', p. 13.

18 BPL, Richard D. Webb to Maria Weston Chapman, 31 Oct. 1846.

19 Murray, Hannah-Rose, 'A "Negro Hercules": Frederick Douglass's Celebrity in Britain', *Celebrity Studies* (2016), 267.

20 BPL, Isabel Jennings to Maria Weston Chapman, 2 Aug. 1847; Taylor, *British and American Abolitionists*, p. 305.

21 Howe, *What Hath God Wrought*, pp. 649–50.

22 Rice, Alan, 'Transatlantic Portrayals of Frederick Douglass and his Liberating Sojourn in Music and Visual Arts, 1845–2015', in Bernier, Celeste-Marie, and Lawson, Bill E. (eds), *Pictures and Power: Imaging and Imagining Frederick Douglass, 1818–2018* (Liverpool: Liverpool University Press, 2017).

23 Blassingame, *FDP* 4, p. 181; Taylor, *British and American Abolitionists*, p. 305.

24 Cockrell, *Excelsior*, p. 346; *Manchester Examiner*, 11 July 1846.

25 *Manchester Examiner*, 11 July, 1846; Blassingame, *FDP* 1, pp. 50–1.

26 Maclear, J. F., 'Thomas Smyth, Frederick Douglass and the Belfast Anti-Slavery Campaign', *South Carolina Historical Magazine* (1979), pp. 293–4; Taylor, *British and American Abolitionists*, pp. 272–3.

27 Foner, *LWFD* 5, pp. 45–6.

28 *Liberator*, 11 Dec. 1846; Foner, *LWFD* 1, pp. 181–4; Foner, *LWFD* 5, pp. 47–8.

Chapter 5: 'Friends of Freedom'

1 *Liberator*, 11 Sept. 1846.

2 Stewart, Jules, *Albert* (London: I. B. Tauris. 2012), p. 54.

3 Lehman, Eric. D., *Becoming Tom Thumb: Charles Stratton, P.T. Barnum and the Dawn of American Celebrity* (Middletown, CT: Wesleyan University Press, 2013), p. 60; Bates, Stephen, *Penny Loaves & Butter Cheap: Britain in 1846* (London: Head of Zeus, 2014), pp. 280–3; Cockrell, *Excelsior*, p. 339.

4 Sweeney, Fionnghuala, *Frederick Douglass and the Atlantic World* (Liverpool: Liverpool University Press, 2007), p. 107; *Edinburgh Evening Post*, 23 Dec. 1846.

5 *Limerick Reporter*, 11 Nov. 1845; Blassingame, *FDP* 2, p. 31; Foner, *LWFD* 1, p. 164.

6 *Liberator*, 11 Sept. 1846; Merrill, Walter M. and Ruchames, Louis (eds), *The Letters of William Lloyd Garrison*, 6 vols [WLG] (Cambridge, MA: Harvard University Press, 1971–81), 3, p. 363.

7 Merrill and Ruchames, *WLG* 3, pp. 363–4.

8 Merrill and Ruchames, *WLG* 3, pp. 364–5.

9 Merrill and Ruchames, *WLG* 3, pp. 361–2.

10 Merrill and Ruchames, *WLG* 3, pp. 364, 368.

11 *Proceedings of the World's Temperance Convention, 1846* (London: C. Gilpin, 1846), pp. vii–viii.

12 *World's Temperance Convention*, p. 2.

13 Foner, *LWFD* 1, pp. 189–99. For more on the anti-abolitionist attacks on Cox, see Williams Jr, Donald E., *Prudence Crandall's Legacy: The Fight for Equality in the 1830s, Dred Scott, and Brown v. Board of Education* (Middletown, CT: Wesleyan University Press, 2014), pp. 183–4.

14 Merrill and Ruchames, *WLG* 3, p. 362; *Illustrated London News*, 15 Aug. 1846.

15 *Liberator*, 18 Sept. 1846; Merrill and Ruchames, *WLG* 3, pp. 377–9.

16 *Liberator*, 18 Sept. 1846.

17 Merrill and Ruchames, *WLG* 3, p. 378; *Report of the Proceedings of the Evangelical Alliance, 1846* (London: Partridge and Oakey, 1847), pp. 290–341. For a recent treatment of the Evangelical Alliance, see Ritchie, Daniel, 'Abolitionism and Evangelicalism: Isaac Nelson, the Evangelical Alliance and the Transatlantic Debate over Christian Fellowship with Slaveholders', *Historical Journal* (2014), pp. 421–46. For more on the rise of evangelical ministers in Britain at this time, see Bates, *Penny Loaves & Butter Cheap*, pp. 208–14.

18 Blassingame, *FDP* 1, pp. 407–16; *Liberator*, 16 Oct. 1846.

19 BPL, Andrew Paton to William Lloyd Garrison, 6 Oct. 1846; *Bucks Herald*, 3 Oct. 1846; *Norfolk News*, 3 Oct. 1846. In a letter seeking more information on Clarke, Paton described him as an 'apologist' for American slaveholders – 'many of whom he declares to be good men and exemplary Christians' – who also claimed 'the slaves are well off and very contented with their lot': *Liberator*, 30 Oct. 1846.

20 Howitt, Mary, *An Autobiography* (London: Isbister & Co., 1889), p. 180; Saunders, John (ed.), *People's Journal* (London: People's Journal Office, 1847), vol. 2, pp. 187, 302; Temperley, *British Anti-Slavery*, p. 215.

21 Hutchinson, *Story of the Hutchinsons* 1, pp. 181–9.

22 Douglass, *Life and Times*, p. 170.

23 Taylor, *British and American Abolitionists*, pp. 284–6.

24 Ashurst Venturi, Emile (ed.), *Joseph Mazzini: His Life, Writings and Political Principles* (New York, NY: Hurd and Houghton, 1872), p. viii. Garrison and Mazzini's political and personal relationship has been examined in depth in a number of recent scholarly works, including Del Lago, Enrico, *William Lloyd Garrison and Giuseppe Mazzini: Abolition, Democracy and Radical Reform* (Baton Rouge, LA: Louisiana State University Press, 2013).

25 For more on Agustin Prichard the emergence of anaesthetics, see Powell, John, 'Anaesthesia, Cholera and the Medical Reading Society of Bristol: A Lecture to the Bristol Medico-Historical Society, March 2007': www.johnpowell.net

26 Douglass, *Life and Times*, p. 170.

27 Merrill and Ruchames, *WLG* 3, pp. 369–74; Taylor, *British and American Abolitionists*, p. 287.

28 Merrill and Ruchames, *WLG* 3, pp. 369–74; Stauffer, John *et al.* (eds), *Picturing Frederick Douglass: An Illustrated Biography of the Nineteenth Century's Most Photographed American* (New York, NY: Liveright, 2015), p. 82.

29 For American reaction to Dickens's works, see Wells, Jonathan Daniel, 'Charles Dickens, the American South and the Transatlantic Debate over Slavery', *Slavery & Abolition* (2015), pp. 1–25.

30 Merrill and Ruchames, *WLG* 3, p. 394.

31 Bradbury, Richard, 'Frederick Douglass and the Chartists', in Rice and Crawford, *Liberating Sojourn*, pp. 169–86; Merrill and Ruchames, *WLG* 3, p. 393; Taylor, *British and American Abolitionists*, p. 308; Blassingame, *FDP* 1, p. 365.

32 Foner, *LWFD* 1, pp. 186–8.

33 Douglass, *Life and Times*, p. 171.

Chapter 6: 'The Lion of the Occasion'

1 *London Gazette*, 1 Sept. 1846.

2 Flanders, Judith, *Consuming Passions: Leisure and Pleasure in Victorian Britain* (London: Harper Press, 2006), p. 225.

3 Merrill and Ruchames, *WLG* 3, p. 377.

4 BPL, Mary Estlin to Maria Weston Chapman, 4 Mar. 1846.

5 James, Revd William, *Memoir of John Bishop Estlin* (London: Charles Green, 1855), p. 13; Chaffin, *Giant's Causeway*, pp. 112–13.

6 Taylor, *British and American Abolitionists*, p. 235; Estlin, John B., *A Brief History of American Slavery and the Abolition Movement* (Bristol: H. C. Evans, 1846), p. 2.

Notes

7 BPL, John B. Estlin to Samuel May Jr, 1 Sept. 1846.

8 Blassingame, *FDP* 1, pp. 341–52.

9 *Bristol Mercury*, 29 Aug. 1846; BPL, Mary Carpenter to William Lloyd Garrison, 3 Sept. 1846; Taylor, *British and American Abolitionists*, p. 279.

10 Taylor, *British and American Abolitionists*, pp. 279–80; Merrill and Ruchames, *WLG* 3, pp. 392–5.

11 Taylor, *British and American Abolitionists*, pp. 280–4.

12 For more on the Unitarians and anti-slavery at this time, see Strange, Douglas C., *British Unitarians Against American Slavery, 1833–65* (London: Associated University Presses, 1984), pp. 60–6 and Turley, David, 'British Unitarian Abolitionists, Frederick Douglass and Racial Equality', in Rice and Crawford, *Liberating Sojourn*, pp. 56–70. Caroline Garrison Bishop, meanwhile, would go on to become a leading proponent of kindergarten education in Britain.

13 Blassingame, *FDP* 1, pp. 352–63.

14 Taylor, *British and American Abolitionists*, pp. 280–2; Blassingame, *FDP* 1, pp. 363–71; BPL, Lucy Browne to Maria Weston Chapman, 15 Oct. 1846.

15 Blassingame, *FDP* 1, pp. 371–98; *Worcestershire Chronicle*, 9 Sept. 1846.

16 Taylor, *British and American Abolitionists*, pp. 286–7; Whyte, *'Send Back the Money'*, p. 161; *Birmingham Journal*, 5 Sept. 1846.

17 Taylor, *British and American Abolitionists*, pp. 286–7. Closed in 2008, Hiatt & Co. was controversial to the last, protesters picketing its headquarters in 2005 after it emerged prisoners at the American detention centre Camp X-Ray in Guantánamo Bay, Cuba, were being restrained with their waist chains and handcuffs: *Guardian*, 9 Sept. 2005.

18 Taylor, *British and American Abolitionists*, p. 283; Hutchinson, *Story of the Hutchinsons* 1, pp. 200–9; Webb, R. K., 'Martineau, Harriet (1802–1876)', *Oxford Dictionary of National Biography* (Oxford: Oxford University Press, 2004).

19 Foner, *LWFD* 1, p. 186.

20 Merrill and Ruchames, *WLG* 3, pp. 402–8, 410–17; Garrison, Wendell Phillips and Garrison, Francis Jackson, *William Lloyd Garrison, 1805–1879: The Story of His Life Told by His Children*, 4 vols (New York, NY: The Century Co., 1885–89), 2, p. 395.

21 Merrill and Ruchames, *WLG* 3, pp. 402–8.

22 BPL, John B. Estlin to Samuel May Jr, 15 Apr. 1846; *Sheffield Independent*, 12 Sept. 1846; Merrill and Ruchames, *WLG* 3, pp. 408–10.

23 Merrill and Ruchames, *WLG* 3, pp. 410–17.

24 *Liberator*, 13 Nov. 1846; Merrill and Ruchames, *WLG* 3, pp. 423–5.

25 Bates, *Penny Loaves & Butter Cheap*, pp. 157–81.

26 BPL, Isabel Jennings to Maria Weston Chapman, undated [1847]; *Northern Whig*, 29 Nov. 1845; Bates, *Penny Loaves & Butter Cheap*, p. 172; Barker, Juliet, *The Brontës* (London: Phoenix Press, 1994), p. 449.

27 Merrill and Ruchames, *WLG* 3, pp. 426–7.

28 Merrill and Ruchames, *WLG* 3, pp. 431–5; Foner, *LWFD* 1, pp. 186–8.

29 Merrill and Ruchames, *WLG* 3, pp. 431–5, 437–41.

30 BPL, Richard D. Webb to Maria Weston Chapman, 26 Feb. 1846; Merrill and Ruchames, *WLG* 3, pp. 437–41; Adams, Amanda, *Performing Authorship in the Nineteenth-Century Transatlantic Lecture Tour* (New York, NY: Routledge, 2016), p. 23.

31 Merrill and Ruchames, *WLG* 3, pp. 450–1; Williams, Daniel G., *Black Skin, Blue Books: African Americans and Wales, 1845–1945* (Cardiff: University of Wales Press, 2012), p. 32.

32 For more on Liverpool's links with slavery and the slave trade, see Richardson, David, Schwarz, Suzanne and Tibbles, Anthony (eds), *Liverpool and Transatlantic Slavery* (Liverpool: Liverpool University Press, 2007) and chapter 2 of Sherwood, Marika, *After Abolition: Britain and the Slave Trade Since 1807* (London: I. B. Tauris, 2007).

33 *Liberator*, 11 Dec. 1846; Merrill and Ruchames, *WLG* 3, pp. 443–6.

34 Merrill and Ruchames, *WLG* 3, pp. 441–6.

35 Merrill and Ruchames, *WLG* 3, pp. 450–1.

36 Merrill and Ruchames, *WLG* 3, pp. 451–2; *Manchester Times*, 6 Nov. 1846.

37 BPL, Richard D. Webb to Maria Weston Chapman, 31 Oct. 1846; *Liberator*, 29 Jan. 1847.

38 Foner, *LWFD* 5, pp. 48–9; Taylor, *British and American Abolitionists*, pp. 293–4; now located in the Frederick Douglass Papers at the University of Rochester, Douglass's 19 Aug. 1846 letter to Anna Richardson in Newcastle can be read online at the website of the rare historic documents dealer Seth Kaller, Inc: www.sethkaller.com/item/283-Frederick-Douglass-to-the-Woman-who-was-Negotiating-to-Buy-his-Freedom

39 BPL, Frederick Douglass to William Lloyd Garrison, undated [Oct. 1846].

Chapter 7: 'I Am a Man'

1 Preston, *Young Frederick Douglass*, pp. 174–5.

2 Foner, *LWFD* 1, pp. 179–8; Preston, *Young Frederick Douglass*, pp. 173–4.

3 Chaffin, *Giant's Causeway*, p. 122.

4 Preston, *Young Frederick Douglass*, pp. 174–5.

5 Midgley, Clare, 'Richardson, Anna (1806–1892)', *Oxford Dictionary of National Biography* (Oxford: Oxford University Press, 2004). Although the 'free produce' movement of the 1840s and 1850s never gained the same

level of success as the 'free sugar' movement of the 1790s, the historian Clare Midgley has argued it was significant as an example of a female-led organisation and as a moral protest that kept the issue of American slavery alive among British women: Midgley, *Women Against Slavery: The British Campaigns, 1780–1870* (London: Routledge, 1995), p. 136.

6 LCDP, Pumphrey, Thomas and Pumphrey, Emma R. (eds), *Ellen Richardson and Ann Richardson Foster: In Memoriam* (Newcastle-upon-Tyne, 1896), pp. 5–17.

7 BPL, Mary Welsh to Maria Weston Chapman, 17 Nov. 1846; Taylor, *British and American Abolitionists*, pp. 298–9; *Liberator*, 15 Jan., 19 Mar. 1847.

8 McFeely, *Douglass*, p. 144; *Liberator*, 15, 29 Jan. 1847.

9 *Manchester Times*, 16 Oct. 1846; for more on Manchester's links with slavery, see http://revealinghistories.org.uk/home.html

10 Douglass, *Life and Times*, pp. 166–7.

11 BPL, Rebecca Moore to William Lloyd Garrison, 9 Sept. 1846; for more on Rebecca Moore, see chapter 4 of Charlotte Moore's *Hancox*. It is possible Douglass's lodgings in St Ann's Square were arranged through the linen draper Alexander Morris, who had business premises in the area and who would later be named as one of the people to whom donations for a 'testimonial' for Douglass could be sent.

12 BPL, William Logan to William Lloyd Garrison, 28 Sept. 1846; Blassingame, *FDP* 1, pp. 475–85; Taylor, *British and American Abolitionists*, p. 296; for more on Douglass's speeches in and around Manchester, see the *Manchester Times* and *Manchester Courier* for Nov. and Dec. 1846.

13 Blassingame, *FDP* 1, pp. 475–85; *Manchester Times*, 20 Nov. 1846.

14 *Liberator*, 29 Jan., 5 Feb. 1847.

15 *Liberator*, 29 Jan., 5 Feb. 1847.

16 *Liberator*, 26 Mar. 1847.

17 Taylor, *British and American Abolitionists*, p. 305.

18 BPL, Frederick Douglass to Elizabeth Pease, 3 Mar., 11 Mar. 1847; Douglass, *Bondage*, pp. 286–7; Fought, Leigh, *Women in the World of Frederick Douglass* (New York, NY: Oxford University Press, 2017), pp. 92–3; Levine, Robert S., *The Lives of Frederick Douglass* (Cambridge, MA: Harvard University Press, 2016), p. 107.

19 *Report of Proceedings at the Soirée Given to Frederick Douglass, London Tavern, March 30, 1847* (London: R. Yorke Clarke & Co., 1847), pp. 1–30; Blassingame, *FDP* 2, pp. 19–52.

20 *Liberator*, 30 Apr., 14 May. 1847; Douglass, *Bondage*, p. 287–8; Foner, *LWFD* 1, pp. 233–4; Chaffin, *Giant's Causeway*, pp. 128–31; McFeely, *Douglass*, p. 145.

21 Foner, *LWFD* 1, pp. 278–9.

22 Foner, *LWFD* 1, pp. 138–42.

23 Taylor, *British and American Abolitionists*, pp. 293–4; for more on the Boston Bazaar, see the *Liberator* from Dec. 1846 and Jan. 1847

24 Taylor, *British and American Abolitionists*, pp. 275, 296, 300–1.

25 Brown, Stewart J., 'Chalmers, Thomas (1780–1847)', *Oxford Dictionary of National Biography* (Oxford: Oxford University Press, 2014).

26 BPL, Mary Mannix to Maria Weston Chapman, 29 Oct. 1846; BPL, Richard D. Webb to Maria Weston Chapman, 12 June, 16 Sept. 1847; BPL, Richard D. Webb to Caroline Weston, 2 Feb. 1849; Taylor, *British and American Abolitionists*, pp. 293–4.

27 BPL, Lucy Browne to Maria Weston Chapman, 14 Apr., 1 Nov. 1847.

Chapter 8: 'Cracks in the Anti-Slavery Wall'

1 Douglass, *Life and Times*, pp. 220–32; URFDP, Letter 111, Frederick Douglass to Amy Post, 27 Oct. 1859.

2 Fought, *Women in the World of Frederick Douglass*, pp. 93–4, 108–9; Douglas, J., 'A Cherished Friendship: Julia Griffiths Crofts and Frederick Douglass', *Slavery & Abolition* (2012), pp. 266–7.

3 LCDP, Douglass Sprague, 'Anna Murray Douglass', p. 16; Fought, *Women in the World of Frederick Douglass*, p. 113; Douglas, 'A Cherished Friendship', p. 267;

4 McFeely, *Douglass*, p. 170; Fought, *Women in the World of Frederick Douglass*, pp. 105, 109–12; Douglas, 'A Cherished Friendship', p. 268.

5 LCDP, Douglass Sprague, 'Anna Murray Douglass', pp. 14, 17; Fought, *Women in the World of Frederick Douglass*, p. 124; McFeely, *Douglass*, p. 171.

6 LCDP, Julia Griffiths Crofts to Frederick Douglass, 19 May 1865; LCDP, Douglass Sprague, 'Anna Murray Douglass', p. 18; Fought, *Women in the World of Frederick Douglass*, p. 109.

7 All but dismissed by generations of Douglass biographers, recent work of Leigh Fought and others has put Anna Murray Douglass right at the heart of her husband's story; for 'beloved of my heart', see Frederick Douglass to Anna Richardson, 19 Aug. 1846: www.sethkaller.com/item/283-Frederick-Douglass-to-the-Woman-who-was-Negotiating-to-Buy-his-Freedom

8 Douglas, 'A Cherished Friendship', p. 271.

9 Douglas, 'A Cherished Friendship', p. 271; URFDP, Letter 110, Frederick Douglass to Amy Post (dated 25 May 1860 in catalogue but clearly written in late December 1859); The Gilder Lehrman Institute, Frederick Douglass

to Maria Webb, 30 Nov. 1859: www.gilderlehrman.org/sites/default/files/inline-pdfs/T-08360_30Nov1859_0.pdf

10 Foner, *LWFD* 5, pp. 459–60; The Gilder Lehrman Institute, Frederick Douglass to Maria Webb, 30 Nov. 1859: www.gilderlehrman.org/sites/default/files/inline-pdfs/T-08360_30Nov1859_0.pdf

11 URFDP, Letter 110, Frederick Douglass to Amy Post (dated 25 May 1860 in catalogue but clearly written in late December 1859); University of Rochester, Post Family Papers Project, Amy Post to Frederick Douglass, 13 Feb. 1860: https://rbsc.library.rochester.edu/items/show/1158

12 Douglass, *Life and Times*, p. 232; Foner, *LWFD* 5, pp. 459–60, 465.

13 LCDP, Rosetta Douglass to Frederick Douglass, 6 Dec. 1859; Stauffer, *Giants*, p. 161; Taylor, *British and American Abolitionists*, p. 447; Blassingame, *FDP* 3, p. 315.

14 Blassingame, *FDP* 3, pp. 312–22.

15 Blassingame, *FDP* 3, p. 321; Foner, *LWFD*, 5, p. 460.

16 Weintraub, S., *Victorian Yankees at Queen Victoria's Court: American Encounters with Victoria and Albert* (Newark, NJ: University of Delaware Press, 2011), pp. 60–3; Olusoga, *Black and British*, pp. 260–7.

17 Taylor, *British and American Abolitionists*, p. 437.

18 Blackett, R. J. M., 'Cracks in the Anti-Slavery Wall: Frederick Douglass's Second Visit to England (1859–1860) and the Coming of the Civil War', in Rice and Crawford, *Liberating Sojourn*, pp. 187–206; Taylor, *British and American Abolitionists*, pp. 437–41; BPL, Samuel May Jr to Richard D. Webb, 15 Apr. 1860.

19 Blassingame, *FDP* 3, pp. 276–88, 336.

20 For examples of letters extolling the virtues of the South, see Blackett, 'Cracks in the Anti-Slavery Wall', pp. 196–200.

21 For more on the waning of anti-slavery activity in Britain in the 1850s, see Temperley, *British Anti-Slavery*, pp. 221–47.

22 Blassingame, *FDP* 3, pp. 334–40.

23 Olusoga, *Black and British*, pp. 369–73; Blackett, 'Cracks in the Anti-Slavery Wall', p. 198; for more on the influence of anti-slavery thought in Darwin's life and work, see Desmond, Adrian and Moore, James, *Darwin's Sacred Cause: Race, Slavery and the Quest for Human Origins* (London: Allen Lane, 2009).

24 BPL, Mary Estlin to Anne Warren Weston, 11 Oct. 1851; James, *Estlin*, p. 17.

25 BPL, Mary Estlin to Maria Weston Chapman, 20 Oct. 1859; BPL, Joseph Lupton to Maria Weston Chapman, 9 Dec. 1859; Taylor, *British and American Abolitionists*, p. 441.

26 BPL, Eliza Wigham to Samuel May Jr, 22 Dec. 1859, 10 Feb. 1860.

27 URFDP, Letter 110, Frederick Douglass to Amy Post (dated 25 May 1860 in catalogue but clearly written in late December 1859).
28 BPL, Samuel May Jr to Richard D. Webb, 15 Apr. 1860; *Scottish Banner*, 7 Apr. 1860; Foner, *LWFD* 5, p. 466; McFeely, *Douglass*, pp. 204–7; Blackett, 'Cracks in the Anti-Slavery Wall', pp. 193–4.
29 LCDP, Rosetta Douglass to Frederick Douglass, 6 Dec. 1859; University of Rochester, Post Family Papers Project, Amy Post to Frederick Douglass, 13 Feb. 1860: https://rbsc.library.rochester.edu/items/show/1158; Douglass, *Life and Times*, pp, 232–3; Fought, *Women in the World of Frederick Douglass*, pp. 171–3; McFeely, *Douglass*, p. 207.

Chapter 9: 'Your Second Home'

1 *New York Times*, 17 Oct. 1886; Blassingame, *FDP* 5, p. 285; for more on Helen Pitts Douglass, see Fought, *Women in the World of Frederick Douglass*, pp. 229–63.
2 For more particulars on the *City of Rome* and the journey across the Atlantic, see LCDP, Frederick Douglass Diary (Tour of Europe and Africa), pp. 1–8 and LCDP, Helen Pitts Douglass Diary, 1886, pp. 1–23.
3 Stauffer, *Giants*, p. 162.
4 Douglass, *Life and Times*, pp. 251, 265; Blassingame, *FDP* 4, pp. 74–9.
5 Blassingame, *FDP* 4, p. 434; Blassingame, *FDP* 5, p. 340; Stauffer, *Giants*, p. 311.
6 *Daily News*, 26 Nov. 1862; Brown, David, *Palmerston: A Biography* (New Haven, CT: Yale University Press, 2010), pp. 451–2; Campbell, Duncan Andrew, *Unlikely Allies: Britain, America and the Victorian Origins of the Special Relationship* (London: Hambledon Continuum, 2007), p. 152.
7 Hawkins, Angus and Powell, John (eds), *The Journal of John Wodehouse, first Earl of Kimberley, for 1862–1902* (London: Royal Historical Society, 1997), p. 63; Wells, 'Dickens', p. 15; Campbell, *Unlikely Allies*, p. 147.
8 Goodwin, Doris Kearns, *Team of Rivals: The Political Genius of Abraham Lincoln* (London: Penguin, 2009), p. 397; Chambers, James, *Palmerston: 'The People's Darling'* (London: John Murray, 2005), p. 487.
9 *Manchester Courier*, 3 Jan., 14 Feb. 1863; Cash, Bill, *John Bright: Statesman, Orator, Agitator* (London: I. B. Tauris, 2012) p. 145.
10 LCDP, Mary Carpenter to Frederick Douglass, 24 May 1865, undated (22 Apr. 1867), undated (1872); Douglas, 'A Cherished Friendship', p. 271.
11 Blassingame, *FDP* 5, pp. 192–212.
12 LCDP, Frederick Douglass Diary, pp. 8–12; LCDP, Helen Pitts Douglass Diary, pp. 33–8; Blassingame, *FDP* 5, pp. 1–8; *Bridport News*, 22 Oct. 1886.
13 *Daily News*, 22 Oct. 1886; *Western Daily Press*, 20 Oct. 1886.

14 LCDP, Ethel Leach to Frederick Douglass, 21 Oct. 1886; Leach, Ethel, *Notes of a Three Months' Tour in America* (Great Yarmouth: The *Mercury* Publishing Office, 1883).

15 LCDP, Paul Molyneaux to Frederick Douglass, 3 Nov. 1886.

16 LCDP, Zadel Barnes Gustafson to Frederick Douglass, 16 Nov. 1886; LCDP, Arthur Naish to Frederick Douglass, 9 Dec. 1886; LCDP, Francis J. Garrison to Frederick Douglass, 13 Sept. 1886.

17 LCDP, Eliza Wigham to Frederick Douglass, 9 Oct. 1886 (filed mistakenly under 10 Sept. 1886 in catalogue); Douglass, *Life and Times*, p. 407.

18 McFeely, *Douglass*, p. 327.

19 LCDP, Frederick Douglass Diary, p. 65; LCDP, Helen Bright Clarke to Frederick Douglass, 5 May 1887.

20 LCDP, Frederick Douglass Diary, p. 65; LCDP, Thomas Burt to Frederick Douglass, 27 July 1887.

21 LCDP, Arthur John Naish to Frederick Douglass, 9 June 1887; LCDP, Elizabeth Mawson to Frederick Douglass, 21 July 1887; BPL, John Mawson to William Lloyd Garrison, 15 Oct. 1846.

22 LCDP, Anna Richardson to Frederick Douglass, 19 June 1887; LCDP, Ellen Richardson to Frederick Douglass, 24 June 1887; LCDP, William Jack to Frederick Douglass, 23 June 1887; LCDP, Francis J. Garrison to Frederick Douglass, 13 Sept. 1886; McFeely, *Douglass*, p. 376.

23 Mayer, *All on Fire*, p. 631; *Leeds Mercury*, 11 Oct. 1878; *Illustrated London News*, 12 Oct. 1878.

24 LCDP, Ellen Richardson to Frederick Douglass, 24 June 1887; LCDP, Frederick Douglass to Helen Pitts Douglass, 28 June 1887.

25 LCDP, Frederick Douglass to Lewis Douglass, 1 July 1887; LCDP, Rebecca Moore to Frederick Douglass, 17 June, 2 July 1887.

26 LCDP, Russell Lant Carpenter to Frederick Douglass, 4 July 1887; LCDP, Frederick Douglass to Julia Griffiths Crofts, 9 July 1887; LCDP, Frederick Douglass to Helen Pitts Douglass, 12 July 1887; LCDP, Mary Barlow to Frederick Douglass, 5 July 1887.

27 LCDP, Helen Bright Clarke to Frederick Douglass, 3 July 1887; for more on Catherine Impey, see Bressey, Caroline, *Empire, Race and the Politics of Anti-Caste* (London: Bloomsbury, 2013).

28 LCDP, Helen Pitts Douglass Diary, p. 20; Douglass, *Life and Times*, p. 257.

29 LCDP, Richard D. Webb to Samuel May Jr, 19 July 1862; LCDP, Wilhelmina Webb to Frederick Douglass, 5 Jan. 1885; LCDP, Susanna Webb to Frederick Douglass, 20 July 1888; LCDP, Lydia Shackleton to Frederick Douglass, 10 Nov. 1889; BPL, Richard D. Webb to Maria Weston Chapman, 10 Nov. 1859; QHL, 'Alfred Webb' 2, pp. 330–1.

30 Wigham, Hannah Maria, *A Christian Philanthropist of Dublin: A Memoir of Richard Allen* (London: Hodder and Stoughton, 1886), pp. 212–31.

31 QHL, Allen Family Letters, Frederick Douglass to Richard Allen, 11 Feb., 18 Mar., 18 Apr. 1884; LCDP, Richard Allen to Frederick Douglass, 28 Aug. 1885.

32 QHL, Allen Family Letters, Frederick Douglass to Richard Allen, 19 Oct. 1885; LCDP, Richard Allen to Frederick Douglass, 28 Aug. 1885; LCDP 'Allen, Richard', n.d.

33 LCDP, Wilhelmina Webb to Frederick Douglass, 5 Jan. 1885, 13 May 1886, 5 June 1887, 10 July 1887.

34 LCDP, Wilhelmina Webb to Frederick Douglass, 13 May 1886, 8 Dec. 1887, 11 Mar. 1888, 20 Oct. 1888; LCDP, Deborah Webb to Frederick Douglass, 30 Oct. 1887.

35 LCDP, Frederick Douglass to Anna W. Shackleton, 26 Jan. 1886; LCDP, Hannah M. Wigham to Frederick Douglass, 30 June, 28 July 1887; LCDP, Lydia Shackleton to Frederick Douglass, 11 Mar. 1888.

36 LCDP, Susanna Webb to Frederick Douglass, 20 July 1888.

37 LCDP, Isabel Jennings to Frederick Douglass, 31 July 1887; Wigham, *Richard Allen*, p. 230.

38 LCDP, Thomas Burt to Frederick Douglass, 27 July 1887; LCDP, Ellen Richardson to Frederick Douglass, 23 July 1887; *Driffield Times*, 8 Oct. 1887; *Cornish Telegraph*, 24 Nov. 1887; Blassingame, *FDP* 5, pp. 263–73, 278–306.

39 LCDP, Lady Isabella Somerset to Frederick Douglass, 22 May 1894; LCDP, Charles Aked to Frederick Douglass, 12 Apr. 1894.

40 LCDP, Rebecca Moore to Helen Pitts Douglass, 28 Nov. 1895; Douglas, 'A Cherished Friendship', p. 272.

41 *Daily News*, 22 Feb. 1895; *Banbury Beacon*, 2 Mar. 1895.

42 *Dundee Advertiser*, 22 Feb. 1895; *Norwich Mercury*, 9 Mar. 1895; *South London Press*, 2 Mar. 1895. The quote is from Alfred, Lord Tennyson's *Idylls of the King: Song from the Marriage of Geraint*.

BIBLIOGRAPHY

MANUSCRIPT SOURCES

Boston Public Library (www.archive.org)
Anti-Slavery Collection
Cornell University (http://dlxs.library.cornell.edu/m/mayantislavery/)
Samuel J. May Anti-Slavery Collection
Library of Congress, Washington, DC (www.loc.gov)
Frederick Douglass Papers
Quaker Historical Library, Dublin
Allen Family Papers
'Reminiscences of Alfred Webb from 1837–1905' (2 vols)
University of Rochester (www.library.rochester.edu/rbscp)
Frederick Douglass Project
Post Family Papers Project

NEWSPAPERS, MAGAZINES AND JOURNALS

Banbury Beacon
Belfast News-Letter
Birmingham Journal
Blackwood's Edinburgh Review
Boston Pilot
Bridport News
Bristol Mercury
Bucks Herald

Cork Examiner
Cornish Telegraph
Daily News
Driffield Times
Dundee Advertiser
Dundee Courier
Edinburgh Evening Post
Fife Herald

Freeman's Journal
Glasgow Herald
Guardian
Illustrated London News
Leeds Mercury
Liberator
Limerick Reporter
London Gazette
Manchester Courier
Manchester Examiner
Manchester Times
New York Times
Norfolk News
Norwich Mercury

Northern Whig
People's Journal
Phrenological Journal
Pilot
Scottish Banner
Sheffield Independent
Southern Literary Messenger
Southern Reporter
South London Press
Times
Western Daily Press
Wexford Independent
Worcestershire Chronicle

INTERNET

https://atlanticslaverydebate.stanford.edu/ (Material on the British anti-slavery movement)

http://avalon.law.yale.edu/17th_century/meno1.asp ('Resolutions of the Germantown Mennonites, 18 Feb. 1688')

www.bbc.co.uk/history/british/abolition/ (Short articles on the impact of slavery on towns and cities across Britain)

www.bulldozia.com (Scottish writer Alasdair Pettinger's website containing an array of Frederick Douglass-related material)

www.digitalcommonwealth.org (Material from the Boston Public Library Anti-Slavery Collection and other collections)

http://frederickdouglass.infoset.io/ (Indiana University-Purdue University Indiana Frederick Douglass Papers)

www.frederickdouglassinbritain.com (English academic Hannah-Rose Murray's website containing valuable information on Douglass and other visiting African-American abolitionists)

www.revealinghistories.org.uk (Website with information on Manchester, slavery and anti-slavery)

www.revolutionaryplayers.org.uk (History West Midlands website containing information on anti-slavery activists in the area)

www.ucl.ac.uk/lbs (University College London, Legacies of British Slave-Ownership Database)

www.yale.edu/glc (Gilder Lehrman Centre for the Study of Slavery, Resistance and Abolition)

www.wikipedia.org

Bibliography

BOOKS AND ARTICLES

Adams, Amanda, *Performing Authorship in the Nineteenth-Century Transatlantic Lecture Tour* (New York, NY: Routledge, 2016)

Alexander, J. E., *L'Acadie; or, Seven Years' Explorations in British America*, 2 vols (London: Henry Colburn, 1849)

Ames, Julius Rubens, *Liberty* (Boston, MA: American Anti-Slavery Society, 1837)

Andrews, Helen, 'Allen, Richard (1803–86)', *Dictionary of Irish Biography* (Cambridge: Cambridge University Press, 2009)

Ashurst Venturi, Emile (ed.), *Joseph Mazzini: His Life, Writings and Political Principles* (New York, NY: Hurd & Houghton, 1872)

Barker, Juliet, *The Brontës* (London: Phoenix Press, 1994)

Bates, Stephen, *Penny Loaves & Butter Cheap: Britain in 1846* (London: Head of Zeus, 2014)

Bingham, Caleb (ed.), *The Columbian Orator: Containing a Variety of Original and Selected Pieces, Together with Rules, Calculated to Improve Youth and Others in the Ornamental and Useful Art of Eloquence* (Baltimore: Philip H. Nicklin, 1811)

Blackett, R. J. M., 'Cracks in the Anti-Slavery Wall: Frederick Douglass's Second Visit to England (1859–1860) and the Coming of the Civil War', in Rice, Alan and Crawford, Martin (eds), *Liberating Sojourn: Frederick Douglass and Transatlantic Reform* (Athens, GA: The University of Georgia Press, 1999)

Blanchet, F. N., *Historical Sketches of the Catholic Church in Oregon, During the Past Forty Years* (Portland, OR: 1878)

Blassingame, John W. (ed.), *The Frederick Douglass Papers*, series 1, 5 vols (New Haven, CT: Yale University Press, 1979–92)

Bradbury, Richard, 'Frederick Douglass and the Chartists', in Rice, Alan and Crawford, Martin (eds), *Liberating Sojourn: Frederick Douglass and Transatlantic Reform* (Athens, GA: The University of Georgia Press, 1999)

Bressey, Caroline, *Empire, Race and the Politics of Anti-Caste* (London: Bloomsbury, 2013)

Brown, David, *Palmerston: A Biography* (New Haven, CT: Yale University Press, 2010)

Brown, Stewart J., 'Chalmers, Thomas (1780–1847)', *Oxford Dictionary of National Biography* (Oxford: Oxford University Press, 2004)

Campbell, Duncan Andrew, *Unlikely Allies: Britain, America and the Victorian Origins of the Special Relationship* (London: Hambledon Continuum, 2007)

Cash, Bill, *John Bright: Statesman, Orator, Agitator* (London: I. B. Tauris, 2012)

Chaffin, Tom, *Giant's Causeway: Frederick Douglass's Irish Odyssey and the Making of an American Visionary* (Charlottesville, VA: University of Virginia Press, 2014)

Chalmers, Thomas, *A Few Thoughts on the Abolition of Colonial Slavery* (Glasgow: W. Collins & Co., 1826)

Chambers, James, *Palmerston: 'The People's Darling'* (London: John Murray, 2005)

Cockrell, D. (ed.), *Excelsior: Journals of the Hutchinson Family Singers, 1842–1846* (Stuyvesant, NY: Pendragon Press, 1989)

Curry-Machado, Jonathan, '"Sin Azúcar No Hay País": The Transnational Counterpoint of Sugar and Nation in Nineteenth-Century Cuba', *Bulletin of Hispanic Studies* (2007)

Curry-Machado, Jonathan, *Cuban Sugar Industry: Transnational Networks and Engineering Migrants in Mid-Nineteenth Century Cuba* (New York, NY: Palgrave Macmillan, 2011)

Davis, David Brion, *Inhuman Bondage: The Rise and Fall of Slavery in the New World* (New York, NY: Oxford University Press, 2006)

Del Lago, Enrico, *William Lloyd Garrison and Giuseppe Mazzini: Abolition, Democracy and Radical Reform* (Baton Rouge, LA: Louisiana State University Press, 2013)

Desmond, Adrian and Moore, James, *Darwin's Sacred Cause: Race, Slavery and the Quest for Human Origins* (London: Allen Lane, 2009)

Devine, T. M. (ed.), *Recovering Scotland's Slavery Past: The Caribbean Connection* (Edinburgh: Edinburgh University Press, 2015)

Dickens, Charles, *American Notes* (New York, NY: D. Appleton & Co., 1868)

Douglas, Janet, 'A Cherished Friendship: Julia Griffiths Crofts and Frederick Douglass', *Slavery & Abolition* (2012)

Douglass, Frederick, *Narrative of the Life of Frederick Douglass, an American Slave* [1845] (Dublin: A Little Book Company, 2011)

Douglass, Frederick, *My Bondage and My Freedom* [1855] (London: Penguin Books, 2003)

Douglass, Frederick, *The Life and Times of Frederick Douglass* [1892] (Mineola, NY: Dover Publications, 2003)

Drescher, Seymour, *Abolition: A History of Slavery and Anti-Slavery* (New York, NY: Cambridge University Press, 2009)

Dumas, Paula E., *Pro-Slavery Britain: Fighting for Slavery in an Era of Abolition* (New York, NY: Palgrave Macmillan, 2016)

Estlin, John B., *A Brief History of American Slavery and the Abolition Movement* (Bristol: H. C. Evans, 1846)

Fenton, Laurence, *Palmerston and The Times: Foreign Policy, the Press and Public Opinion in Mid-Victorian Britain* (London: I. B. Tauris, 2012)

Fenton, Laurence, *Frederick Douglass in Ireland: 'The Black O'Connell'* (Cork: The Collins Press, 2014)

Ferreira, Patricia J., 'Frederick Douglass in Ireland: The Dublin Edition of His Narrative', *New Hibernia Review* (2001)

Finkelman, Paul (ed.), *Encyclopaedia of African American History, 1619–1895: From the Colonial Period to the Age of Frederick Douglass* (Oxford: Oxford University Press, 2006)

Flanders, Judith, *Consuming Passions: Leisure and Pleasure in Victorian Britain* (London: Harper Press, 2006)

Foner, Philip S. (ed.), *The Life and Writings of Frederick Douglass*, 5 vols (New York, NY: International Publishers, 1950–75)

Fought, Leigh, *Women in the World of Frederick Douglass* (New York, NY: Oxford University Press, 2017)

Garrison, Wendell Phillips and Garrison, Francis Jackson, *William Lloyd Garrison, 1805–1879: The Story of His Life Told by His Children*, 4 vols (New York, NY: The Century Co., 1885–89)

Geoghegan, Patrick, '"A Consistent Advocate of Nigger Emancipation": Daniel O'Connell and the Campaign Against Slavery', *History Ireland* (2010)

Goodwin, Doris Kearns, *Team of Rivals: The Political Genius of Abraham Lincoln* (London: Penguin, 2009)

Harrison, Richard S., 'The Cork Anti-Slavery Society, Its Antecedents and Quaker Background, 1755–1859', *Journal of the Cork Historical and Archaeological Society* (1992)

Harrison, Richard S., *Richard Davis Webb: Dublin Quaker Printer, 1805–72* (Cork: Red Barn Publishers, 1993)

Hart, W. A., 'Africans in Eighteenth-Century Ireland', *Irish Historical Studies* (2002)

Hawkins, Angus and Powell, John (eds), *The Journal of John Wodehouse, first Earl of Kimberley, for 1862–1902* (London: Royal Historical Society, 1997)

Hogan, Liam, '"Oh What a Transition it was to be Changed from the State of a Slave to that of a Free Man!": Frederick Douglass's Journey from Slavery to Limerick' (www.theirishstory.com)

Howe, Daniel Walker, *What Hath God Wrought: The Transformation of America, 1815–1848* (Oxford: Oxford University Press, 2009)

Howitt, Mary, *An Autobiography* (London: Isbister & Co., 1889)

Hutchinson, John W., *Story of the Hutchinsons (Tribe of Jesse)*, 2 vols (Boston, MA; Lee and Shepard, 1896)

Huzzey, Richard, *Freedom Burning: Anti-Slavery and Empire in Victorian Britain* (Ithaca, NY: Cornell University Press, 2012)

James, Revd William, *Memoir of John Bishop Estlin* (London: Charles Green, 1855)

Jordan, Ryan, 'Quakers, "Comeouters" and the Meaning of Abolitionism in the Antebellum Free States', *Journal of the Early Republic* (2004)

Kinealy, Christine, *Daniel O'Connell and the Anti-Slavery Movement: 'The Saddest People the Sun Sees'* (London: Pickering & Chatto, 2011)

Leach, Ethel, *Notes of a Three Months' Tour in America* (Great Yarmouth: The *Mercury* Publishing Office, 1883)

Lehman, Eric. D., *Becoming Tom Thumb: Charles Stratton, P. T. Barnum and the Dawn of American Celebrity* (Middletown, CT: Wesleyan University Press, 2013)

Levine, Robert S., *Martin Delany, Frederick Douglass and the Politics of Representative Identity* (Chapel Hill, NC: The University of North Carolina Press, 1997)

Levine, Robert S., *The Lives of Frederick Douglass* (Cambridge, MA: Harvard University Press, 2016)

Lewis, George, *Impressions of America and the American Churches* (Edinburgh: W. P. Kennedy, 1845)

Lyell, Sir George, *Travels in North America: With Geological Observations on the United States, Canada and Nova Scotia*, 2 vols (London: John Murray, 1845)

Maclear, J. F., 'Thomas Smyth, Frederick Douglass and the Belfast Anti-Slavery Campaign', *South Carolina Historical Magazine* (1979)

McCosh, James, *The Scottish Philosophy* (New York, NY: R. Carter, 1875)

McDaniel, W. Caleb, 'Repealing Unions: American Abolitionists, Irish Repeal, and the Origins of Garrisonian Disunionism', *Journal of the Early Republic* (2008)

McFeely, William S., *Frederick Douglass* (New York, NY: W. W. Norton, 1995)

Mayer, Henry, *All on Fire: William Lloyd Garrison and the Abolition of Slavery* (New York, NY: St Martin's Griffin, 2000)

Merrill, Walter M. and Ruchames, Louis (eds), *The Letters of William Lloyd Garrison*, 6 vols (Cambridge, MA: Harvard University Press, 1971–81)

Midgley, Clare, *Women Against Slavery: The British Campaigns, 1780–1870* (London: Routledge, 1995)

Midgley, Clare, 'Richardson, Anna (1806–1892)', *Oxford Dictionary of National Biography* (Oxford: Oxford University Press, 2004)

Miller, Thomas Yule, *The Dundee Courier: Historical Narrative of its Vicissitudes and Successive Proprietors – Colville-Hill-Alexander-Park-Thomson – from 1816 to 1887* (1911)

Moore, Charlotte, *Hancox: A House and a Family* (London: Viking, 2010)

Morgan, Simon, 'The Anti-Corn Law League and British Antislavery in Transatlantic Perspective, 1838–1846', *Historical Journal* (2009)

Murphy, Angela F., 'Daniel O'Connell and the "American Eagle" in 1845: Slavery, Diplomacy, Nativism and the Collapse of America's First Irish Nationalist Movement', *Journal of American Ethnic History* (2007)

Murphy, David, 'Dowden, Richard', *Dictionary of Irish Biography* (online edition)

Murray, Hannah-Rose, 'A "Negro Hercules": Frederick Douglass's Celebrity in Britain', *Celebrity Studies* (2016)

Nelson, Bruce, *Irish Nationalists and the Making of the Irish Race* (Princeton, NJ: Princeton University Press, 2012)

Oldfield, John, 'Palmerston and Anti-Slavery', in Brown, David and Taylor, Miles (eds), *Palmerston Studies II* (Southampton: Hartley Institute, University of Southampton, 2007)

Olusoga, David, *Black and British: A Forgotten History* (London: Macmillan, 2016)

Pettinger, Alasdair, 'The Bloody Gold' (www.bulldozia.com)

Pettinger, Alasdair, 'Send Back the Money: Douglass and the Free Church of Scotland', in Rice, Alan and Crawford, Martin (eds), *Liberating Sojourn: Frederick Douglass and Transatlantic Reform* (Athens, GA: The University of Georgia Press, 1999)

Powell, John, 'Anaesthesia, Cholera and the Medical Reading Society of Bristol: A Lecture to the Bristol Medico-Historical Society, March 2007' (www.johnpowell.net)

Preston, Dickson J., *Young Frederick Douglass: The Maryland Years* (Baltimore, MD: The Johns Hopkins University Press, 1985)

Proceedings of the World's Temperance Convention, 1846 (London: C. Gilpin, 1846)

Bibliography

Pumphrey, Thomas and Pumphrey, Emma R. (eds), *Ellen Richardson and Ann Richardson Foster: In Memoriam* (Newcastle-upon-Tyne, 1896)

Quarles, Benjamin, *Frederick Douglass* (New York, NY: Atheneum, 1976)

Report of Proceedings at the Soirée Given to Frederick Douglass, London Tavern, March 30, 1847 (London: R. Yorke Clarke & Co., 1847)

Report of the Proceedings of the Evangelical Alliance, 1846 (London: Partridge and Oakey, 1847)

Reynolds, David, *America: Empire of Liberty* (London: Penguin, 2010)

Rice, Alan, 'Transatlantic Portrayals of Frederick Douglass and his Liberating Sojourn in Music and Visual Arts, 1845–2015', in Bernier, Celeste-Marie and Lawson, Bill E. (eds), *Pictures and Power: Imaging and Imagining Frederick Douglass, 1818–2018* (Liverpool: Liverpool University Press, 2017)

Richard, Henry, *Memoirs of Joseph Sturge* (London: S. W. Partridge, 1864)

Richardson, David, Schwarz, Suzanne and Tibbles, Anthony (eds), *Liverpool and Transatlantic Slavery* (Liverpool: Liverpool University Press, 2007)

Ritchie, Daniel, 'Abolitionism and Evangelicalism: Isaac Nelson, the Evangelical Alliance and the Transatlantic Debate over Christian Fellowship with Slaveholders', *Historical Journal* (2014)

Robbins, Keith, *John Bright* (London: Routledge & Kegan Paul, 1979)

Rodgers, Nini, 'Limerick Merchants and the Slave Trade', in Lee, David and Jacobs, Debbie (eds), *Made in Limerick*, vol. 2: *A History of Trades, Industry and Commerce* (Limerick: Limerick Civic Trust, 2006)

Rodgers, Nini, *Ireland, Slavery and Anti-Slavery: 1612–1865* (New York, NY: Palgrave Macmillan, 2007)

Schaw, Janet, *Journal of a Lady of Quality: Being the Narrative of a Journey from Scotland to the West Indies, North Carolina, and Portugal, in the Years 1774 to 1776* (New Haven, CT: Yale University Press, 1921)

Shelden, Michael, 'Dickens, *The Chimes* and the Anti-Corn Law League', *Victorian Studies* (1982)

Sherwood, Marika, *After Abolition: Britain and the Slave Trade Since 1807* (London: I. B. Tauris, 2007)

Slouth, William L., *Olympians of the Sawdust Circle: A Biographical Dictionary of the Nineteenth Century American Circus* (San Bernardino, CA: The Borgo Press, 1998)

Sluiter, Engel, 'New Light on the "20 and Odd Negroes" Arriving in Virginia, August 1619', *William and Mary Quarterly* (1997)

Smith, James McCune, 'John Murray of Glasgow', in Griffiths, Julia (ed.), *Autographs for Freedom* (Boston, MA: John P. Jewett & Co., 1853)

Smyth, Thomas, *Autobiographical Notes, Letters and Reflections* (Charleston, SC: Walker, Evans & Cogswell, 1914)

Stauffer, John, *Giants: The Parallel Lives of Frederick Douglass and Abraham Lincoln* (New York, NY: Twelve, 2009)

Stauffer, John et al. (eds), *Picturing Frederick Douglass: An Illustrated Biography of the Nineteenth Century's Most Photographed American* (New York, NY: Liveright, 2015)

Stewart, Jules, *Albert* (London: I. B. Tauris, 2012)

Strange, Douglas C., *British Unitarians against American Slavery, 1833–65* (London: Associated University Presses, 1984)

Sweeney, Fionnghuala, '"The Republic of Letters": Frederick Douglass, Ireland and the Irish *Narratives*', in Kenny, Kevin (ed.), *New Directions in Irish-American History* (Madison, WI: The University of Wisconsin Press, 2003)

Sweeney, Fionnghuala, *Frederick Douglass and the Atlantic World* (Liverpool: Liverpool University Press, 2007)

Taylor, Clare (ed.), *British and American Abolitionists: An Episode in Transatlantic Understanding* (Edinburgh: Edinburgh University Press, 1974)

Temperley, Howard, *British Anti-Slavery 1833–1870* (London: Longman, 1972)

Thackeray, W. M., *The Irish Sketchbook of 1842* (Dublin: Nonsuch Publishing, 2005)

Turley, David, 'British Unitarian Abolitionists, Frederick Douglass and Racial Equality', in Rice, Alan and Crawford, Martin (eds.), *Liberating Sojourn: Frederick Douglass and Transatlantic Reform* (Athens, GA: The University of Georgia Press, 1999)

Warburton, George, *Hochelaga; or, England in the New World*, 2 vols (London: Colburn & Co., 1851)

Webb, R. K., 'Martineau, Harriet (1802–1876)', *Oxford Dictionary of National Biography* (Oxford: Oxford University Press, 2004)

Weintraub, Stanley, *Victorian Yankees at Queen Victoria's Court: American Encounters with Victoria and Albert* (Newark, NJ: University of Delaware Press, 2011)

Wells, Jonathan Daniel, 'Charles Dickens, the American South and the Transatlantic Debate over Slavery', *Slavery & Abolition* (2015)

Whyte, Iain, *Scotland and the Abolition of Black Slavery, 1756–1838* (Edinburgh: Edinburgh University Press, 2006)

Whyte, Iain, *'Send Back the Money!' The Free Church of Scotland and American Slavery* (Cambridge: James Clarke & Co., 2012)

Wigham, Hannah Maria, *A Christian Philanthropist of Dublin: A Memoir of Richard Allen* (London: Hodder & Stoughton, 1886)

Wigham, Maurice J., *The Irish Quakers: A Short History of the Religious Society of Friends in Ireland* (Dublin: Historical Committee of the Religious Society of Friends in Ireland, 1992)

Williams, Daniel G., *Black Skin, Blue Books: African Americans and Wales, 1845–1945* (Cardiff: University of Wales Press, 2012)

Williams Jr, Donald E., *Prudence Crandall's Legacy: The Fight for Equality in the 1830s, Dred Scott, and Brown v. Board of Education* (Middletown, CT: Wesleyan University Press, 2014)

Winter, Alison, *Mesmerised: Powers of Mind in Victorian Britain* (Chicago, IL: University of Chicago Press, 1998)

Woolley, Benjamin, *Savage Kingdom: Virginia and the Founding of English America* (London: Harper Press, 2007)

THESES

Jezierski, Rachael A., 'The Glasgow Emancipation Society and the American Anti-Slavery Movement' (PhD thesis, University of Glasgow, 2011)

Soskis, Benjamin, 'Heroic Exile: The Transatlantic Development of Frederick Douglass, 1845–1847' (Senior honours thesis, Yale University, 1997)

ACKNOWLEDGEMENTS

This book would not have been written without the immense investment libraries and educational institutions in the United States have put into making a great wealth of Frederick Douglass- and anti slavery movement-related material freely available online, in particular the Library of Congress, Boston Public Library, the University of Rochester, Stanford University, Cornell University and Yale.

On this side of the Atlantic, I would like to thank the Quaker historian Richard S. Harrison in Cork and Christopher Moriarty of the Quaker Historical Library in Dublin. Thanks, too, to Professor Alan Rice, Director of the Institute for Black Atlantic Research at the University of Central Lancashire, for allowing me to read his recent article on Douglass before it was published and to Shaun Barrington, Matilda Richards and all at Amberley Books.

INDEX

Harris, Henry 28
Harris, John 28
Harrison, Benjamin 237
Haughton, James 51,
  59–60, 167, 191, 234
Hawkins, Sir John 8
Haydon, Benjamin
  Robert 105, 123–4, 233
Hayes, Rutherford B. 217
Hibernian Anti-Slavery
  Society 50, 51, 54, 56
Hilditch, Blanche 162–3,
  165, 189
Hilditch, Sarah 162–3,
  165, 189
Himid, Lubaina 239
Hincks, Revd
  William 138
Hobhouse, John Cam 104
Hood, E. P. 177, 246–7
Howitt, Mary 134–7,
  138, 156, 176, 182,
  197, 227
Howitt, William 134–7,
  138, 182, 183
Hutchinson Family 18,
  30, 34–5, 40–4, 55, 60,
  71, 97, 111, 119–20,
  121, 124–5, 135, 139,
  155, 237

Illustrated London
  News 131, 144, 195
Impey, Catherine 231
Independent Church
  (Congregationalist
  Church) 54, 65, 67,
  68, 70, 100, 106, 134,
  138, 188, 195
Ireland, Alexander 120
Ireland, Mary 71
Isle of Wight 9, 189

Jack, William 228
Jefferson, Thomas 11–12
Jennings, Francis 62
Jennings, Isabel 60–1, 62,
  65, 66, 118, 121, 160,
  165, 167, 189, 196–7,
  232, 236
Jennings, Jane 61–2, 66,
  189

Jennings, Thomas 61
Jerrold, Douglas 138–9, 182
Johnson, Nathan 34
Joseph, John 177–8, 205

Kansas 193, 195, 215
King, Martin Luther 231
Kirk, Revd Edward
  N. 133
Knight, Joseph 74
Ku Klux Klan 217

Lansdowne, Lord 102
Leach, Ethel 223–4
Leeds 156, 177, 199,
  200–1, 210, 211, 228
Lewis, Revd George 84,
  88–9, 100
Liberator 14, 35, 48, 52,
  58, 64, 81, 113, 117,
  121, 127, 132, 136–7,
  139, 140, 142, 161,
  173, 181, 188, 197, 228
Liberty Party 37, 105–6,
  197, 210
Lichfield 8
Limerick 46–7, 65, 66–9,
  125, 175, 235, 236
Lincoln, Abraham 25,
  215–17, 219–20, 223,
  228
Liverpool 7, 9, 15, 17, 44,
  56, 75, 103, 119, 120,
  122, 125, 161, 162,
  163–5, 174, 176, 181,
  183, 184, 190, 194,
  201, 202, 205, 209,
  215, 219, 220–2, 229,
  231, 236
Lloyd V, Col
  Edward 21–3
London 8, 9, 12, 15, 18,
  45, 49, 57, 68, 71, 77,
  92, 97, 98, 100, 101–12,
  116, 119, 123–4, 126,
  128–41, 144, 145, 151,
  154, 155, 158, 159,
  163, 169, 172, 176,
  180, 181–4, 195, 200,
  204–5, 208, 212, 222–3,
  224, 226–7, 229–30,
  239

Longfellow, Henry
  Wadsworth 136
Lucas, Margaret
  Bright 226
Lundy, Benjamin 14
Lupton, Joseph 210
Lyell, Sir Charles 79–80,
  82
Lynn, MA 18, 36, 117,
  141, 185, 198

McCann, Colum 239
McCosh, James 73
McFeely, William S. 38,
  59, 173
McGee, Thomas
  D'Arcy 56
McLaren, Priscilla
  Bright 175
McQueen, James 78
Macaulay, Zachary 77,
  86
Macclesfield 8
Macready, William 123,
  125, 139
Manchester 71, 104, 120,
  121, 163, 174–7, 219,
  230
Mansfield, Lord 9
Martineau, Harriet 155,
  208, 218, 227
Martineau, James 155
Marx, Karl 135
Massachusetts Anti-Slavery
  Society 35–6
Mawson, Elizabeth 227
May, Samuel J. 116, 206
May Jr, Samuel 146–7,
  150, 206, 210
Mazzini, Giuseppe 137,
  138, 208
Melville, Hermann 34,
  221
Mendelssohn, Felix 153–4
Methodist Church 24,
  52–5, 63, 70, 153, 200
Mexican-American War
  (1846–8) 49, 116
Mexico 10, 49, 67, 68,
  80, 110, 116
Miall, Edward 138
Milton, John 38